Inclusive Learning and Educational Equity
Volume 12

Aims and Scope:

This book series reflects on the challenges of inclusive education as a strategy for improving educational equity. The series addresses issues of diversity in support of the UN Sustainable Development Goals (SDGs) which set the global education agenda for 2030 in SDG 4: Ensure inclusive and quality education for all and promote lifelong learning.

Although considered an important aspect of a global human rights agenda ensuring education for all is a complex endeavour that is subject to the forces of globalization, and the exclusionary pressures associated with migration, mobility, language, ethnicity, disability, and intergenerational poverty. Acknowledgement of the reciprocal links between these markers of diversity and educational underachievement has led to an increasing interest in the development of inclusive education as a strategy for improving educational equity.

By addressing these and related diversity issues, this series aims to contribute important advances in knowledge about the enactment of inclusive education. The development of educational processes and pedagogical interventions that respond to the tensions between education policies that promote competition and those designed to promote inclusion at individual, classroom, school, district, national, and international levels are explored by the contributors to this series.

This series:

- Offers a critical perspective on current practice.
- Stimulates and challenges further developments for the field.
- Explores global disparities in educational provision and compares developments.
- Provides a welcome addition to the literature on inclusive education.

Ioana Boghian • Gabriel Mareş
Editors

Gamification and Inclusion

Challenges of 21st-Century Education

Springer

Editors
Ioana Boghian
Teacher Training Department
Vasile Alecsandri University of Bacău
Bacău, Romania

Gabriel Mareş
Physiotherapy and Occupational
Therapy Department
Vasile Alecsandri University of Bacău
Bacău, Romania

ISSN 2512-1499 ISSN 2512-1510 (electronic)
Inclusive Learning and Educational Equity
ISBN 978-3-031-98389-4 ISBN 978-3-031-98390-0 (eBook)
https://doi.org/10.1007/978-3-031-98390-0

This Springer imprint is published by the registered company Springer Nature Switzerland AG
The registered company address is: Gewerbestrasse 11, 6330 Cham, Switzerland

Preface

The theme of our volume, "Gamification and Inclusion: Challenges of 21st-Century Education," was chosen due to the increasing interest in modern approaches to integrating all students in a classroom, whether typical or with special educational needs.

As the need for inclusive education has increased and children with special educational needs are increasingly and more efficiently integrated into mainstream classes, it was only natural that a general interest in how to integrate all students would become a concern for all educators. Among the techniques that have recently been explored and found to be effective for working with students with special educational needs is therefore the game-based approach to the educational process, i.e. the use of serious games, educational games, and digital games as teaching and learning methods. Added to this is gamification as a process through which regular teaching, learning, and assessment techniques can be made more interactive, engaging, supportive, and stimulating by incorporating game elements such as badges, competitions, scoreboards, challenges, surprises, choices, progression, rules, and rewards. Adding game elements to educational activities ensures personalized learning, increases learner engagement, improves collaboration, supports different learning styles, helps build greater confidence, provides immediate feedback, reduces assessment anxiety, promotes 21st-century skills such as communication, collaboration, critical, analytical, and creative skills, makes learning fun, and contributes significantly to an inclusive environment.

The challenges in ensuring an inclusive learning environment for all students and implementing gamification in education are related to inaccurate official specific procedures, funding issues aimed at making academic space and learning materials freely accessible to all students, the absence or lack of staff trained to work with students with special educational needs and/or disabilities, and training opportunities that enable teachers to build an inclusive classroom.

To address the above issues, this book is organized into eleven chapters, divided into two main sections, one predominantly theoretical and the other predominantly illustrative, dealing with the gamification of education and inclusion.

One of the ideas shared by all chapters is the need for teacher training to empower teachers to introduce gamification practices and to build and maintain an inclusive educational environment. Another common denominator is the socio-economic and professional difficulties involved in using gamification and ensuring inclusive education. Other aspects that the authors of this volume have in common relate to the solutions they propose to the problems mentioned above. As the proposed solutions have been formulated by researchers and teachers from different countries—Spain, Romania, Pakistan, Slovenia—and for different levels of education, this volume appeals to teachers, education policy makers, curriculum designers, and developers of teaching materials all over the world.

The first chapter, "An Introduction to Gamification for an Inclusive 21st-century Classroom," defines the key concepts discussed throughout the book, namely gamification and inclusion in education. This introduction provides the theoretical framework for the key concepts discussed throughout the book, namely gamification, higher education, students with special educational needs and/or disabilities, and inclusion, and highlights the challenges and opportunities in today's academic educational context. The chapter also highlights the difficulties that students with special educational needs and their teachers, as well as educational institutions, face when it comes to ensuring access to education for all and proposes gamification as a solution for promoting an inclusive educational environment. The chapter provides a series of recommendations for teachers on how to build and maintain an inclusive learning environment, as well as a series of actions that leaders of educational institutions should implement in this sense.

The second chapter, "The Right to Education for All in the Context of Online Education," addresses the challenges in ensuring the right to education for all in the context of online education. The authors highlight the causes of the difficulties in providing education for all, an issue that has been exacerbated in the context of the COVID-19 pandemic. Online education, which was the immediate solution to continue education in the restrictive context of the pandemic, faced a number of problems that had either not been previously anticipated or inadequately addressed: some of these problems were related to the provision of educational opportunities for students from socially and financially vulnerable groups and for students with special educational needs; other challenges of online education were related to the reluctance of some teachers, students and their families, and heads of institutions toward online education; and still other challenges were closely related to the technological support and know-how needed to deliver quality education in the virtual environment; last but not least, ethical challenges related to online education were also highlighted by the authors. For each of the highlighted categories of online education challenges, the authors propose a number of solutions.

The third chapter, "The Current Status of Gamification Knowledge Among Romanian Teachers: An Exploratory Approach," provides an insightful overview of k-12 teachers' gamification knowledge, gamification principles, and the use of gamification principles in the teaching–learning process. The authors provide a detailed theoretical approach to gamification to highlight the aspects targeted by their research. The mixed-methods approach used in the study is described in detail, which supports the data analysis and interpretation. The findings, although related to the Romanian context, are very valuable as they highlight some aspects related to teachers' knowledge about gamification that may be shared by other teachers abroad and that can be improved. The research methodology is a model for conducting similar research in other countries. The authors also suggest several future research directions related to gamification in the educational context and present the practical implications of the research findings.

In the fourth chapter, "Innovative Inclusion and Gamification Strategies in Higher Education: New Directions Regarding Teacher Training," a number of valuable findings are presented on the current situation regarding the integration of inclusive education and gamification strategies in higher education, inclusive practices based on gamification, the positive impact of gamification on academic curriculum innovation, and teacher training strategies/programs. The authors address the need for training that enables teachers to implement gamification in order to create and promote an inclusive classroom. Teacher training should therefore focus on the dimensions of digital competences to use available open resources and to create further resources, competences related to the implementation of gamification in general and gamification for inclusion in the classroom. This means that national and international teacher training programs should provide teachers with knowledge, skills, and attitudes related to the use of gamification to promote inclusion in the classroom.

The fifth chapter, "Initial Teacher Training for Inclusive Education and Gamification," emphasizes the importance of high-quality initial teacher education that prepares teachers to work with students with special educational needs and/or disabilities and to use gamification to support the learning of all students by fostering an inclusive educational environment. The authors propose a model for initial teacher education that enables teachers to work with students with special educational needs and/or disabilities by implementing gamification practices into the teaching–learning–assessment process. The authors provide a detailed theoretical approach to inclusive education and a description of the competence profile of the inclusive teacher to better clarify how gamification can be used to promote it and on which dimensions teacher training programs should focus. Several transnational projects are also described in which useful open resources on the use of gamification for an inclusive educational environment have been created and to which the authors have contributed. In addition, this chapter presents a number of best practices for the use of gamification in inclusive education and the model for initial teacher training elaborated by the authors, which enables future teachers to work with SEN students and gamification.

The sixth chapter, "Learning Behavior in the Context of Gamification," analyzes the impact of a gamified educational environment on learning behavior, examining the various changes individuals experience when engaged in a gamified environment. Both the positive results and the possible negative effects of using gamification features in the educational process on learning behavior are highlighted. The chapter looks at the differences between learners who play games and those who do not in terms of engagement in learning tasks, motivation to learn, and academic performance. Given the general definition of game as an activity aimed at achieving a goal, the author highlights the fact that gamification contributes to personal and professional growth by modeling the learner's behavior, attitudes, and expectations in terms of work, effort, and progress. The topic is of great importance as it helps teachers, curriculum and instructional materials developers, educational leaders, and policy makers to understand how gamification contributes to improving students' academic performance.

The seventh chapter, "Differentiation and Inclusive Approach in Teaching Activities from Higher Education: Using Gamification in a Constructivist Teaching-learning Context with Gifted Students," discusses effective ways to incorporate the differentiated and inclusive approach in the college curriculum and the relevance of using gamification in differentiating the teaching–learning context for gifted students to improve the efficiency of the development mechanisms of the differentiated and inclusive curriculum at the educational system level. The author conducts a brief analysis of academic curriculum design and highlights the challenges in implementing curriculum changes aimed at the inclusion of students with special educational needs in general and gifted students in particular. The issue of ensuring quality education for gifted students is a welcome one, as they are a category of learners who also require special attention. The author therefore proposes the constructivist approach to curriculum differentiation and combines it with gamification and the use of open educational resources to meet the educational needs of gifted students.

The eighth chapter, "Serious Games in Education for Students with Special Needs," explores the application of the SADDIE method when working with students. The acronym of the SADDIE method developed by the authors stands for the successive phases of the methodology that guides practitioners through the process of conceptualizing, designing, implementing, evaluating, and integrating serious games into the learning environment. It emphasizes the crucial role of participatory and iterative design processes, intuitive user interfaces, adaptive content and multisensory feedback mechanisms, the integration of collaborative elements and advanced technologies such as virtual reality and adaptive artificial intelligence to improve accessibility and effectiveness and thus establish serious games as a crucial component of inclusive education. Serious games as part of the gamified approach to education can help teachers create and maintain an inclusive educational environment that meets the diverse needs of students while aiming to support them in achieving their educational goals. The authors illustrate how serious games can be used to promote inclusion.

The ninth chapter, "Empowering Learners with Autism Spectrum Disorder (ASD) through Gamification," explores the potential of gamification in promoting the development of skills in learners with autism spectrum disorder (ASD) and highlights the challenges that need to be addressed and overcome for successful inclusive education. The author highlights the specificities of learning for students with ASD and how gamification can support them to improve their learning outcomes. Serious games and other dimensions of gamification are presented to illustrate their potential, but also the risks and barriers when applied to teaching students with ASD. The recommendations for implementing gamification in educational settings with students with ASD are aimed at educational policy makers, curriculum developers, school managers and administrators, teachers and parents, and game developers.

The tenth chapter, "The Approach to Inclusion in Literary Education in Spain: A Case Study," presents a collective case study on addressing inclusion in the literature classroom and highlights, among other things, types of activities and literary works that teachers use to work on inclusion in the classroom. The study, based on a semi-structured clinical interview, sheds light on the relationship between literary competence, literature teaching practices, and inclusive practices in primary schools from Spain. The authors emphasize the challenges of teaching literature to students with special educational needs and propose activities to support and promote inclusion in the classroom through gamification of literature classes.

The eleventh chapter, "Using Gamification to Enhance Learning, Reduce Stress, and Promote Inclusion in Academic Online Education," presents the results of a questionnaire-based study on students' perceptions of online education and the potential of using games in education to improve learning, reduce the stress associated with online education, and promote inclusion in the context of and after the COVID-19 pandemic. The study is based on a questionnaire-based survey and involved students from a Romanian college who are also participating in a teacher training module. The results show that online teaching creates a certain level of stress for students and brings a number of additional challenges for students with special educational needs. The solutions proposed by the authors refer to the implementation of gamification practices in online education for all students in order to improve their academic performance and promote their personal development. From this perspective, inclusive education promotes social inclusion for all.

Bacău, Romania Ioana Boghian
Bacău, Romania Gabriel Mareş

Contents

Chapter 1
An Introduction to Gamification for Inclusive Twenty-First-Century Education

Gabriel Mareş and Ioana Boghian

Abstract This chapter aims to define the key concepts that will be discussed throughout the book, namely gamification in higher education in relation to inclusion. In this introduction, the main concepts discussed in this book, namely gamification, higher education, students with special educational needs and/or disabilities, and inclusion, are framed theoretically, highlighting the challenges and opportunities in today's academic educational context.

It addresses the terms game, gamification, disability, and special educational needs and provides arguments for the use of gamification to build an inclusive educational environment in education at all levels, but particularly in higher education. The theoretical approach draws on recent national and international practices and recommendations on the requirements for building an inclusive, supportive educational environment to ensure quality education for all. The proposed recommendations relate to how higher education institutions can overcome the challenges associated with ensuring inclusive education in terms of regulatory procedures, financial issues, and staff training requirements. This introductory chapter promotes inclusive education in the context of the challenges of the twenty-first century.

Keywords Gamification · Inclusion · Special educational needs · Disability · Game

G. Mareş
Physiotherapy and Occupational Therapy Department, Vasile Alecsandri University of Bacău, Bacău, Romania
e-mail: mares.gabriel@ub.ro

I. Boghian (✉)
Teacher Training Department, Vasile Alecsandri University of Bacău, Bacău, Romania
e-mail: boghian.ioana@ub.ro

I. Boghian, G. Mareş (eds.), *Gamification and Inclusion*, Inclusive Learning and Educational Equity 12, https://doi.org/10.1007/978-3-031-98390-0_1

Brief Theoretical Approach to Key Concepts

The unprecedented technology boom, global health crises, social conflicts, and unequal social dynamics have led to rapid changes in the labor market and thus also in education. To adapt to the specificities, versatility, and demands of today's labor market, universities at home and abroad have expanded their course offerings to meet the educational needs of a wide range of new professional requirements. In addition to the fact that technological developments have brought with them a number of specific challenges for education, there is another requirement for the educational context, namely to meet the needs of disadvantaged students. Vulnerable students are learners with special educational needs who face physical, educational, emotional, and social barriers and difficulties from an early age, and as they grow older their educational challenges can broaden and diversify if support systems are not working properly.

The topic of our volume, gamification and inclusion in higher education, was chosen because of the increasing interest in modern approaches to integrating all students in a classroom, whether typical or with special educational needs.

Traditionally, many people assume that play is an activity reserved only for children. They ignore the fact that the need to play and approach even serious activities in a playful way makes them more rewarding and motivating. Therefore, we can assume that play as a human occupation/activity has no age, only a set of age-specific characteristics and adaptations.

From the perspective of educational practice, play is one of the most productive and efficient learning methods, as it provides a reward not only for the end result achieved, but also during the process leading to the learning outcome. The gamification of learning leads not only to the achievement of learning objectives specific to each discipline, but also to the training of a wide range of soft skills that can be used to acquire a life of the highest possible quality (Smiderle et al., 2020; Abbasi et al., 2021).

Developmental psychology has long recognized play as one of the most natural forms of learning, and numerous researchers have argued that play is critical to children's cognitive, physical, social, and emotional development (Homer et al., 2020; Lillard et al., 2013; Ginsburg, 2007; Hirsh-Pasek et al., 2009a, 2009b; Piaget, 1962; Vygotsky, 1966; Flavell et al., 1987). Play is an everyday activity and an excellent experience for children, adolescents, and adults of all ages. Play has been defined as the following: an intensive learning experience in which participants voluntarily invest significant time, energy, and engagement while deriving great pleasure from the overall experience (Rieber et al., 1998); an important facilitator and reinforcer of learning and socialization throughout life (Tsai et al., 2012); an intellectual activity that is pursued for its own sake and is associated with exploratory processes that follow the player's exposure to new stimuli (Fabricatore, 2000); a source of pleasure that people voluntarily choose to engage in that is intense and fully absorbing and promotes the formation of social groupings (Prensky, 2001a). Play is critical for children's cognitive, physical, social, and emotional development (Ginsburg, 2007; Hirsh-Pasek et al., 2009a, 2009b; Lillard et al., 2013).

The concept of game has been studied by many researchers. To understand what a game is, we can refer to some definitions according to which a game is a subset of play and fun and defines it as organized play that provides enjoyment and pleasure (Prensky, 2001a); a set of activities involving one or more players that have goals, constraints, payoffs, and consequences that are in some sense rule-based and artificial and involve some aspect of competition, even if that competition is with oneself (Dempsey et al., 2002); "a system in which players engage in an artificial conflict defined by rules that leads to a quantifiable outcome" (Salen & Zimmerman, 2004). Although approaches to defining games may vary, most game definitions have some characteristics in common, according to which games are rule-based and follow clearly defined rules of play; they are responsive, allow for player actions and provide feedback and responses to the system; they are challenging and often contain an element of chance; progression within a game is usually cumulative and reflects previous actions; and finally, games are inviting and motivate the player to participate; the design elements that make up a game are the game mechanics, incentive structure, visual esthetics, auditory esthetics, and narrative (Dempsey et al., 2002; Plass et al., 2012, 2013, 2015, 2020a, 2020b).

Game-based learning (GBL) has been defined as a learning process that uses digital games. GBL is an environment in which game content and gameplay promote the acquisition of knowledge and skills through game activities such as problem solving and challenges that give players/learners a sense of achievement (Kirriemuir & McFarlane, 2004; Gee, 2003; McFarlane & Sparrowhawk, 2002; Prensky, 2001a, 2001b). In contrast to gamification, which is essentially achieved by adding game elements to usually non-game-based learning environments, GBL involves redesigning learning tasks to make them more engaging, meaningful and therefore more effective for learning than a non-gamified or gamified task. GBL focuses on designing effective learning mechanisms from the ground up, based on discipline-specific theory and ultimately taking the form of a game. GBL has specific learning objectives and measurable outcomes.

Gamification is the application of game elements or game mechanics (e.g., a reward system and narrative structure) with the primary goal of increasing learner enjoyment and engagement in order to increase learner motivation to achieve a seemingly secondary goal of acquiring knowledge, building and developing a range of competencies and skills such as autonomy and self-confidence, communication and collaboration with teachers and peers. In short, gamification is a practical solution to transform a traditional learning task into a more engaging, active, efficient, and socially rewarding task. By adding incentives such as competitions, stars, points, achievements, or leaderboards, gamification encourages the learner to put effort into an otherwise uninteresting or boring task. Although some researchers claim that gamification promotes extrinsic motivation more than intrinsic motivation, there is already an extensive literature on how gamification in education can promote academic achievement by increasing learner motivation and engagement (Plass et al., 2015, 2020a, 2020b; Plass & Homer, 2012; Kirriemuir & McFarlane, 2004; McFarlane & Sparrowhawk, 2002; Prensky, 2001a, 2001b).

Play, game-based learning and gamification have also been studied to highlight their effectiveness in promoting the growth and development of students with special educational needs (Sharma & Kumar, 2024).

A disability is a condition, not a choice, made by the person at birth or at some point in life. Disability is often associated with difficulties, barriers, crises, exclusion, disadvantage, and risk. Of all these barriers, the educational barriers that occur at different stages of development can block access to a higher education institution or cause difficulties throughout academic education. The challenges in higher education that seem insurmountable to students with special educational needs can cause them to give up on their studies, with serious consequences for their overall current and future emotional, physical, financial, and social well-being.

The challenges faced by students with special educational needs in higher education are related to accessibility, adaptation, rules, information, and financial resources, as well as the willingness to create an inclusive environment.

Special education professionals have long sought newer, better, and more efficient ways to work with students with special educational needs. As the need for special education support has increased and children with special educational needs are increasingly and more efficiently integrated into mainstream classes, it was only natural that a general interest in how to integrate all students became a concern for all educators. Among the techniques that have recently been explored and found to be effective for working with students with special educational needs is therefore the game-based approach to the educational process, which involves the use of serious games, educational games and digital games as teaching-learning methods, to which gamification is added as a process, through which regular teaching-learning assessment techniques can be made more interactive, engaging, supportive, and stimulating through the inclusion of game elements such as badges, competitions, scoreboards, challenges, surprises, choices, progression, rules, and rewards (Mohammed et al., 2024; Dicks, 2023; Görgen et al., 2020; Liu et al., 2018; Aslan & Balci, 2015; Rugelj, 2015, 2016, 2018; Deterding et al., 2011).

A number of studies have shown that games can support learners with disabilities to acquire certain skills and abilities to a similar extent as learners without disabilities and that they connect players across time and space (Hatzigiannakoglou & Okalidou, 2019; Sharma & Kumar, 2024).

The Inclusive Classroom in Higher Education: Definition, Challenges, and Difficulties

Special educational needs (SEN) refer to certain characteristics and specificities that manifest themselves in the educational process in certain groups of people and that are the result of cognitive, sensory, psychomotor, physiological, and other disorders or are caused by learning difficulties, behavioral disorders or as a result of particular psycho-affective, socio-economic, or other circumstances that affect a person's psycho-intellectual development. Special educational needs are those educational needs that go beyond the general objectives of school/academic education and require schooling tailored to the individual characteristics and/or features of a learning disability/weakness, as well as specific intervention (Vrăşmaş, 2001: 27).

The OECD (2006) has defined the main categories of people with SEN as follows:

- *People with different types of disabilities (A)*—for these individuals, special educational needs are usually considered to be consecutive or derived from the different deficits/disorders of the structures or functions of the organism.
- *People with specific learning difficulties (B)* (e.g., dyslexia), disorders of neurological development or cognitive functioning (hyperactivity, autism spectrum disorders), communication, behavioral, emotional and relational disorders that are not considered to be associated with factors that allow them to be classified in categories A or C.
- *People from disadvantaged socio-economic, cultural, and/or linguistic backgrounds (C)*—people who, for various existential reasons, may face major adjustment and integration problems in the educational environment.

In more recent literature, a distinction is made between disability and special educational needs. The concept of inclusion helps to differentiate between people with disabilities and people with special educational needs, as it has been shown that not all people with disabilities have special educational needs and that special educational needs are the result of many other situations and circumstances and are not only due to the presence of a disability. Therefore, disability should not be confused with special educational needs. A disability may or may not result in special educational needs, which in turn may be permanent or temporary. The relationship between disability and special educational needs is significantly influenced by the cultural and social reference system. In some countries, for example, the level of accessibility for people with disabilities and the available support systems and equipment can reduce or even eliminate the extent of special educational needs in school and out-of-school education (Gherguț, 2023: 28).

Education for all, as defined at the 199 UNESCO conference in Jomtien, Thailand, aims to ensure access to education for all and quality education for all children/youth through two objectives: (1) Ensuring the conditions for all children/youth to participate in education, regardless of their differences and personal development model that deviates from what society considers normal; (2) Ensuring quality education for all students by identifying, implementing, and improving the dimensions of the educational process, learning content and educational agents that promote open, flexible and efficient education, thus ensuring student success (UNESCO, 1994). The pedagogy of diversity has thus emerged as a branch of general pedagogy to meet the educational needs of students, which may be the result of factors independent of the children's will: disability, ethnic, religious, linguistic or cultural background, psychological, emotional, relational conditions or disorders that may hinder school integration and adaptation, intellectual level and abilities that may differ from those of the majority of the school population (Gherguț, 2023: 30).

The concept of inclusion has emerged as a broader alternative to the concept of integration to cover a wider range of challenges related to the access of children with special educational needs to mainstream education. In short, in addition to children with disabilities, which were the focus of integration, inclusion also encompasses other categories of children with special educational needs who require specific interventions, including school support services, in order to be integrated into everyday school life: children with learning difficulties, emotional and behavioral disorders, children from vulnerable socio-economic, cultural and ethnic groups, and children from foster care (UNICEF, 2017).

From a social perspective, inclusion refers to a "set of measures and actions from various fields aimed at eliminating social exclusion and ensuring the active participation of people in all aspects of economic, social, educational, cultural and political life" (Gherguţ, 2023: 31).

From an educational perspective, inclusion means building and maintaining open, positive interpersonal relationships between students, making curricula more flexible, diversifying pedagogical strategies and ensuring interventions and support for students with special educational needs, promoting equality of rights and responsibilities for all, ensuring equal access to learning opportunities and a functioning partnership between school and family/parents and students, and actively involving the community in school projects and activities (idem.).

Inclusive education enables and supports all students to learn and grow together for the benefit of all. In addition to equality, another similarly relevant concept for understanding inclusive education is equity, the first referring to equal opportunities and rights, the second to meeting the needs of all equally. The OECD recommendations for ensuring equity and inclusion in education focus on developing a policy framework in this regard and embedding it in all areas of education policy; ensuring a flexible and responsive education system that meets the needs of all students; ensuring that the principles of equity and inclusion are respected in the allocation of educational resources and funding; engage all relevant stakeholders in upholding the principles of equity and inclusion in schools and classrooms; train and support teachers and school leaders to build and develop their competencies and skills in equity and inclusion; identify students' needs in order to support them, monitor students' progress and continuously seek to improve and engage support systems (OECD, 2023). Equity means ensuring the right to quality education for all, so that every student has the best opportunity to reach their full potential.

Studies have identified a number of challenges and problems that hinder equal, free access to quality education for all (Roşan, 2015, 2023). In our country, the following barriers were highlighted in 2016 that can limit, hinder, or discourage access to higher education for students with special educational needs (SEN): the lack of procedures in higher education institutions to ensure equal access and educational opportunities for students with SEN; the lack of such procedures forces the student with SEN to negotiate access to study materials, participation in lectures and seminars, and examination matters with the lecturer, which is perceived as discriminatory; physical access to college spaces is usually made difficult and sometimes impossible by architectural barriers, the lack of elevators or adapted toilets, etc. the attitude of teaching staff is generally positive and accepting, even if they consider students with SEN to be unable to meet the demands of the academic education process. However, they are supportive and willing to help such students upon request; the attitude of students towards their peers with SEN is similar to that of faculty, and their help is sometimes crucial to the academic success of the student with SEN; most foreign universities have built a culture of acceptance of SEN students and have created facilities and procedures to support and help these students; there are students with SEN who have successfully graduated from college, but there is still the question of whether their success is due to the facilities provided by the education system and institutions or due to the efforts and support of their families (Manea, 2016).

Based on the above, we can distinguish between two main types of measures to ensure an inclusive classroom in higher education: one type of action includes official procedures, resourced campuses, and accessible study rooms and halls; another type of action includes the concrete attitudes and actions that faculty can demonstrate and implement to promote an inclusive classroom. Nevertheless, material support also remains crucial for the second type of intervention mentioned above, as ensuring accessible learning materials for students with SEN requires, in addition to goodwill, the provision of funds to cover the costs of equipping students with audiobooks, books, and texts in digital format, Relief printing, Braille printing, free speech synthesis, text-to-speech software, access to virtual libraries, screen magnification computers in ordinary libraries, free sign language translation and other specific devices that ensure access to information for students with sensory, motor, etc. disabilities.

Regarding the type of intervention that is the responsibility of teachers to ensure inclusive teaching, there are a number of solutions, of which gamification has been increasingly promoted and studied as it meets the diverse (special) needs of learners (Sharma & Kumar, 2024; Zourmpakis et al., 2023; Kalogiannakis et al., 2021; Dicheva et al., 2015; Prensky, 2001a, 2001b) by ensuring that:

- Personalized learning—tailored learning experiences allow and encourage students to progress at their own pace; game elements such as challenges, rewards, levels built into learning activities provide flexible learning tasks that encourage all students to complete the task.
- Higher engagement—game elements such as points, badges, leaderboards increase student engagement by making the learning activity more fun and engaging, thus also encouraging retention of knowledge.
- Better collaboration—certain game elements require students to work as a team and collaborate; when solving the task as a team, they help each other, share ideas and work and value each other's contribution.
- Support for different learning styles—game elements such as visual aids, sound effects and hands-on activities appeal to visual, auditory, kinaesthetic or combined learning styles.
- Increased confidence—game elements such as the opportunity to retry a failed task create a learning context where trial and error plays a role, helping students to build resilience and confidence.
- Immediate feedback—this type of feedback helps students to become aware of what they know and what they need to know in order to continue with the task and solve it successfully; such feedback increases motivation to persevere with the task until it is solved correctly.

- Inclusion—game elements can be added to make learning activities and tasks accessible to students with SEN and/or disabilities; for example, customizable interfaces and difficulty levels, different devices to ensure that all students can participate in the learning process regardless of their physical or cognitive abilities.
- Reduced anxiety—game elements can be successfully used in assessment methods to reduce the anxiety associated with traditional assessment situations; reducing anxiety can help students perform better during the assessment task.
- Improved critical thinking and problem-solving skills—game elements such as multiple stories and scenarios with different challenges, tasks and outcomes promote analytical, critical and creative thinking and other twenty-first century skills such as communication, problem solving and collaboration.
- Learning activities that are fun—when learning is fun, it is more engaging and rewarding, contributing to a positive attitude towards peers, teachers, learning, and education.

Over time, teachers have found that gamified approaches in teaching and learning activities reduce or even eliminate the perception of people with special needs as disabled, and people with special needs themselves no longer perceive themselves as different. Even though inclusive and participatory approaches are difficult and resource-intensive, require relational systems and openness to understand the life perspective of people with special needs (Sherlaw & Hudebine, 2015), the use of gamification and gamified learning increases both the level of inclusion and the level of participation in academic and social life.

Formal and non-formal academic activities, whether face-to-face or online, when gamified or game-based, enable people to maximize their personal potential and use their individual resources; they positively change the role of the teacher by reinforcing the idea that he or she is a partner in the serious game of professional training and personal development; learning becomes deep, experiential, sustainable and friendly; interpersonal relationships are more dynamic, intense, authentic and connected to the specificities of the learning space (online or face-to-face); they allow creativity to flourish not only in terms of the approach to the content to be learned but also in terms of the use of (sometimes unique) resources; they allow both the physical and social environment to embrace the person with special needs and make them feel an authentic part of it.

Conclusions and Recommendations

A crucial dimension for the success of inclusive education is the attitude of others towards students with disabilities, more specifically, their value bias, either towards a negative, prejudiced perception or a positive one based on a desire for knowledge and understanding, empathy, the offer of help and encouragement. Of equal importance to the success of inclusive education, apart from the nature and severity of the deficit, is the attitude of the person concerned to their disability or, in other words, to their abilities and limitations: this attitude can range from acceptance and courage, hope, determination, and perseverance in the effort to overcome one's limitations and achieve goals, to refusal to accept one's condition and to act positively and proactively. Attitudes manifest themselves as behavior.

The three-dimensional structure of attitudes includes the following components: a cognitive component or belief; affective reactions or the emotional component; behavioral reactions or the conative component (Callo, 2014: 74). Gamification helps students with special educational needs and their teachers to acquire knowledge about the subject but also about the different disabilities, promotes positive emotions and improved emotion management as well as better behavioral manifestations as a result of engagement with gamified teaching-learning-assessment tasks; gamification provides an effective combination of fun, cognitive focus, and emotional engagement that impacts attitudes and behavior to achieve an outcome (Mateus et al., 2024; Smiderle et al., 2020; Arif et al., 2019).

Even if gamification is not specifically designed to promote inclusion, it can be designed to meet the needs of students with disabilities by incorporating accessibility features to ensure the principle of inclusion that everyone, regardless of their abilities and limitations, should have access to education (Salvador-Ullauri et al., 2020). Mateus et al. propose an approach to education to promote inclusion through gamification that includes four dimensions: "theoretical support (Vygotsky's zone of proximal development, scaffolding, collaborative learning, use of tools and cultural resources), digital gamification tool, persuasive narrative, inclusion processes" (Mateus et al., 2024: 9). In this model, persuasive narrative refers to a communication process that involves observing the desired behavior at a character in a game or other players and adopting aspects of the respective behavior either fully or at least partially. Narrative persuasion as part of gamification is effective in supporting the learning of certain desired behaviors and promotes inclusivity as the game provides an equal learning environment for all and combines techniques such as "personalization, transportation, identification, regular feedback, and cooperation" that motivate all learners to engage in the activity regardless of their skills and abilities (idem, p. 7). The authors further argue that gamification helps to overcome stereotypes and prejudices as all learners are encouraged to use their skills and abilities in an emotionally safe environment defined by the rules of the game, which also promotes inclusion. In online education, gamification promotes inclusion by eliminating the visual perception of learners: physical characteristic and especially physical differences are eliminated, which also helps to promote engagement in the gamified learning activity and build a sense of belonging and social cohesion (idem). In a face-to-face learning environment, gamification also promotes social cohesion by encouraging learners to collaborate, cooperate, develop empathy, and show solidarity, although perhaps to a lesser extent than in the virtual environment, due to the theory of visual perception.

Gamification promotes inclusion and acceptance of diversity through a range of techniques that encourage collaboration in decision making and problem solving, planning, and goal setting (Kiryakova et al., 2014).

There are a number of challenges associated with implementing gamification in education to promote inclusion, such as insufficient or inadequate technological resources, teachers' reluctance to change, adapting gamification to learners' individual needs, balancing external rewards and constructive feedback to build intrinsic motivation, and ensuring that the designed gamified activities efficiently enhance students' learning.

To help overcome the challenges mentioned above, and support the design and use of gamification for inclusion, in addition to teaching methods that can improve the educational process of teachers working with SEN students, there are a number of solutions that can be implemented at the management level of all higher education institutions to promote inclusion (Gherguț, 2023: 39):

- Securing funding for equipment to provide students with learning content and related study materials in an accessible format (elevators, audio books, relief printing, Braille printing, text-to-voice software, screen magnifier computers, sign language translation, etc.);
- Establish a department within the higher education institution that advises students with SEN and/or disabilities and solves problems such as accommodation, communication with peers and teachers, scholarships;
- Ensure that there is a teacher in each faculty who is responsible for relations with students with SEN and/or disabilities, guiding them and helping them to navigate all educational areas and curricular and extra-curricular activities;
- Encourage and support initiatives and proposals from students with SEN and/or disabilities that can help create a supportive, collaborative environment that promotes learning and creativity for all;
- Ensure the training of teachers for an inclusive university to strengthen the inclusive skills and competences of teachers and encourage teachers to promote an inclusive academic environment among peers and students;
- Ensure that student unions and organizations include in their initiatives activities where students with SEN and/or disabilities are integrated, supported, and encouraged to contribute to the current/future projects based on their potential.

This book aims to promote inclusive education and an inclusive higher education environment through the use of gamification. By sharing experiences and knowledge from the Romanian and other educational contexts, we can inspire each other with practical ideas for the use of gamification as an effective methodological tool to promote inclusive education.

References

Abbasi, A. Z., Hassan, M., Rehman, U., Hlavacs, H., Ting, D. H., & Shah, M. U. (2021). How engagement with gamified applications impacts quality of life: A conceptual model. In HCI international 2021-late breaking papers: HCI applications in health, transport, and industry:

23rd HCI international conference, HCII 2021, virtual event, July 24–29, 2021 proceedings 23 (pp. 3-10). Springer. https://doi.org/10.1007/978-3-030-90966-6_1.
Arif, F. K. M., Zubir, N. Z., Mohamad, M., & Yunus, M. M. (2019). Benefits and challenges of using game-based formative assessment among undergraduate students. *Humanities & Social Sciences Reviews, 7*(4), 203–213. https://doi.org/10.18510/hssr.2019.7426
Aslan, S., & Balci, O. (2015). GAMED: Digital educational game development methodology. *SIMULATION, 91*(4), 307–319. https://doi.org/10.1177/0037549715572673
Callo, T. (2014). *Pedagogia practică a atitudinilor*. Litera.
Dempsey, J. V., Haynes, L. L., Lucassen, B. A., & Casey, M. S. (2002). Forty simple computer games and what they could mean to educators. *Simulation and Gaming, 33*(2), 157–168.
Deterding, S., Sicart, M., Nacke, L., O'Hara, K., & Dixon, D. (2011). Gamification: Using game-design elements in nongaming contexts. In *Proceedings CHIEA '11* (pp. 2425–2428). ACM Press.
Dicheva, D., Dichev, C., Agre, G., & Angelova, G. (2015). Gamification in education: A systematic mapping. *Educational Technology and Society, 18*(3), 75–88.
Dicks, J. (2023). The impact of digital game-based learning on learning outcomes for students with special education needs. *A Systematic Review*. https://doi.org/10.13140/RG.2.2.25163.98084
Fabricatore, C. (2000). Learning and videogames: An unexploited synergy.
Flavell, J. H., Flavell, E. R., & Green, F. L. (1987). Young children's knowledge about the apparent-real and pretend-real distinctions. *Developmental Psychology, 23*(6), 816–822. https://doi.org/10.1037/0012-1649.23.6.816
Gherguţ, A. (2023). Cerinţe educaţionale speciale în mediul universitar. In M. Rusu (Ed.), *Dizabilitate şi incluziune în mediul universitar* (pp. 25–40). Editura Academiei Române.
Gee, J. P. (2003). *What video games have to teach us about learning and literacy*. Palgrave Macmillan.
Ginsburg, K. R. (2007). The importance of play in promoting healthy child development and maintaining strong parent-child bonds. *Pediatrics, 119*(1), 182–191. https://doi.org/10.1542/peds.2006-2697
Görgen, R., Huemer, S., Schulte-Körne, G., & Moll, K. (2020). Evaluation of a digital game-based reading training for German children with reading disorder. *Computers & Education, 150*, 103834. https://doi.org/10.1016/j.compedu.2020.103834
Hatzigiannakoglou, P. D., & Okalidou, A. (2019). Development of an auditory rehabilitation tool for children with Cochlear implants through a mobile-based VR and AR serious game. *International Journal of Online and Biomedical Engineering (iJOE), 15*(02), 81–90. https://doi.org/10.3991/ijoe.v15i02.9709
Hirsh-Pasek, K., Golinkoff, R. M., Berk, L. E., & Singer, D. G. (2009a). *A mandate for playful learning in preschool: Presenting the evidence*. Oxford University Press.
Hirsh-Pasek, K., Berk, L. E., & Singer, D. (2009b). *A mandate for playful learning in preschool: Applying the scientific evidence*. Oxford University Press.
Homer, B. D., Raffaele, C., & Henderson, H. (2020). Games as playful learning: Implications of developmental theory for game-based learning. In J. L. Plass, R. E. Mayer, & B. D. Homer (Eds.), *Handbook of game-based learning* (pp. 25–52). The MIT Press.
Kalogiannakis, M., Papadakis, S., & Zourmpakis, A.-I. (2021). Gamification in science education. A systematic review of the literature. *Education Sciences, 11*(1), 22. https://doi.org/10.3390/educsci11010022
Kiryakova, G., Angelova, N., & Yordanova, L. (2014) Gamification in education. In: 9th international Balkan education and science conference, Edirne, Turkey.
Kirriemuir, J. W., & McFarlane, A. E. (2004). A literature review on games and learning. Nesta Futurelab Bristol. http://www.nestafuturelab.org. Accessed 27 Nov 2024.
Lillard, A. S., Lerner, M. D., Hopkins, E. J., Dore, R. A., Smith, E. D., & Palmquist, C. M. (2013). The impact of pretend play on children's development: A review of the evidence. *Psychology Bulletin, 139*(1), 1–34. https://doi.org/10.1037/a0029321

Liu, M., Huang, Y., & Zhang, D. (2018). Gamification's impact on manufacturing: Enhancing job motivation, satisfaction and operational performance with smartphone-based gamified job design. *Human Factors and Ergonomics in Manufacturing & Service Industries, 28*(1), 38–51.

Manea, L. (2016). *Accesul la educație al tinerilor cu dizabilități în România, cu focalizare pe învățământul secundar, superior, vocațional*. As. RENINCO.

Mateus, C., Campis, R., Jabba, D., María Erazo, A., & Romero, V. (2024). Gamification as a tool for inclusion. *IntechOpen*. https://doi.org/10.5772/intechopen.113229

McFarlane, A., & Sparrowhawk, Y. (2002). Heald report on the educational use of games TEEM (teachers evaluating educational multimedia). Cambridge.

Mohammed, M., Fatemah, A., & Hassan, L. (2024). Effects of gamification on motivations of elementary school students: An action research field experiment. *Simulation & Gaming, 55*(4), 600–636. https://doi.org/10.1177/10468781241237389

Piaget, J. (1962). *Play, dreams, and imitation in childhood*. Norton.

OECD. (2023). *Equity and inclusion in education: Finding strength through diversity*. OECD Publishing. https://doi.org/10.1787/e9072e21-en. Accessed 27 Nov 2024.

OECD. (2006). *Education policies for students at risk and those with disabilities in southeastern Europe*. OECD Publishing. https://www.oecd.org/content/dam/oecd/en/publications/reports/2006/03/education-policies-for-students-at-risk-and-those-with-disabilities-in-south-eastern-europe_g1gh66b6/9789264036161-en.pdf. Accessed 27 Nov 2024.

Plass, J. L., Mayer, R. E., & Homer, B. D. (Eds.). (2020a). *Handbook of game-based learning*. Mit Press.

Plass, J. L., Homer, B. D., Mayer, R. E., & Kinzer, C. K. (2020b). Theoretical foundations of game-based and playful learning. In J. L. Plass, R. E. Mayer, & B. D. Homer (Eds.), *Handbook of game-based learning* (pp. 3–24). The MIT Press.

Plass, J. L., & Homer, B. D. (2012). Popular game mechanics as inspirations for learning mechanics and assessment mechanics. Paper presented at the Game Developers Conference, San Francisco, CA, March 5–9, 2012.

Plass, J. L., Homer, B. D., Hayward, E. O., Frye, J., Huang, T. T., Biles, M., et al. (2012). The effect of learning mechanics design on learning outcomes in a computer-based geometry game. In *E-Learning and games for training, education, health and sports. Lecture notes in computer science, 7516* (pp. 65–71). Springer. https://doi.org/10.1007/978-3-642-33466-5_7

Plass, J. L., Homer, B. D., Kinzer, C. K., Chang, Y. K., Frye, J., Kaczetow, W., et al. (2013). Metrics in simulations and games for learning. In A. Drachen, M. S. El-Nasr, & A. Canossa (Eds.), *Game analytics* (pp. 697–729). Springer.

Plass, J. L., Homer, B. D., & Kinzer, C. K. (2015). Foundations of game-based Learning. *Educational Psychologist, 50*(4), 258–283. https://doi.org/10.1080/00461520.2015.1122533

Prensky, M. (2001a). Fun, play and games: What makes games engaging. In *Digital game-based learning*. McGraw-Hill.

Prensky, M. (2001b). *Digital game-based learning*. McGraw-Hill.

Rieber, L. P., Smith, L., & Noah, D. (1998). The value of serious play. *Educational Technology, 38*(6), 29–37.

Roşan, A. (2023). Dizabilitatea şi incluziunea în mediul universitar. Modelul The Disability Inclusion Institutional Framework (DIIF). In M. Rusu (Ed.), *Dizabilitate şi incluziune în mediul universitar* (pp. 43–63). Editura Academiei Române.

Roşan, A. (Ed.). (2015). *Psihopedagogie specială. Modele de evaluare şi intervenție*. Polirom.

Rugelj, J. (2018). *Games and learning. Lifelong learning programme*. University of Ljubljana.

Rugelj, J. (2016). Serious computer games design for active learning in teacher education. In C. Vaz de Carvalho et al. (Eds.), *SGAMES 2015, LNICST* (Vol. 161, pp. 1–9).

Rugelj, J. (2015). Serious computer games in computer science education. In *EAI endorsed. Transactions on serious games* (Vol. 2, p. e6) https://www.researchgate.net/publication/283567970_Serious_computer_games_in_computer_science_education. Accessed 27 Nov 2024

Salen, K., & Zimmerman, E. (2004). *Rules of play: Game design fundamentals*. MIT Press.

Sharma, V., & Kumar, V. A. (2024). Gamification: A new era of inclusion in education. https://www.researchgate.net/publication/381124647_GAMIFICATION_A_NEW_ERA_OF_INCLUSION_IN_EDUCATION. Accessed 27 Nov 2024.

Sherlaw, W., & Hudebine, H. (2015). The United Nations Convention on the rights of persons with disabilities: Opportunities and tensions within the social inclusion and participation of persons with disabilities. *Alter, 9*(1), 9–21.

Smiderle, R., Rigo, S. J., Marques, L. B., de Miranda, P., Coelho, J. A., & Jaques, P. A. (2020). The impact of gamification on students' learning, engagement and behavior based on their personality traits. *Smart Learning Environments, 7*(1), 3. https://doi.org/10.1186/s40561-019-0098-x

Tsai, F. H., Kuang-Chao, Y., & Hsiao, H. S. (2012). Exploring the factors influencing learning effectiveness in digital gamebased learning. *Educational Technology & Society, 15*(3), 240–250.

Salvador-Ullauri, L., Acosta-Vargas, P., & Luján-Mora, S. (2020). Web-based serious games and accessibility: A systematic literature review. *Applied Sciences., 10*(21), 7859. https://doi.org/10.3390/app10217859

UNESCO (1994). *The Salamanca Statement and Framework for Action on Special Needs Education*. Paris: UNESCO.

UNICEF. (2017). Inclusive education. Understanding article 24 of the convention on the rights of persons with disabilities. UNICEF. https://www.unicef.org/eca/sites/unicef.org.eca/files/IE_summary_accessible_220917_0.pdf. Accessed 27 Nov 2024.

Vrăşmaş, T. (2001). *Invăţământul integrat şi/sau incluziv*. Aramis.

Vygotsky, L. S. (1966/2016). Play and its role in the mental development of the child. International research in early Childhood Education, 7(2), 3–20. https://files.eric.ed.gov/fulltext/EJ1138861.pdf.

Zourmpakis, A.-I., Kalogiannakis, M., & Papadakis, S. (2023). Adaptive gamification in science education: An analysis of the impact of implementation and adapted game elements on students' motivation. *Computers, 12*(7), 143. https://doi.org/10.3390/computers12070143

Part I
Exploratory Approaches to Teacher Training, Gamification and Inclusion

Chapter 2
The Right to Education for All in the Context of Online Education

Gabriel Mareş and Venera-Mihaela Cojocariu

Abstract The right to education for all children is a legal, social, cultural, and formative acquisition of great value that is earned over time with effort, commitment, and perseverance. Although there are numerous documents that refer to children and their rights, the Convention on the Rights of the Child (1989) is the only document that is exclusively dedicated to children and that expresses a current approach to children and their rights. The challenges of today's world and the new needs arising from economic, social, and environmental changes are leading to a transformation in the way the education and training process is approached. The current global context created by the COVID-19 pandemic and the quasi-automatic generalization of online education has brought to light a series of paradoxical educational realities expressed in antinomic pairs of concepts such as certainty–uncertainty; inclusion–exclusion; face to face–online; visible–invisible; synchronous–asynchronous; urban–rural; wealth–poverty; equity–inequity. The paper aims to identify and analyze the causes of some of the above discrepancies from the perspective of ensuring equal opportunities and the right to education for as many children as possible. Our interrogative approach is based on questions such as the following: Is the right to education still respected for all children? Do the strategies adopted by online education (objectively) take into account the age/individual characteristics or the economic-social context of the child? Are there alternatives? Our analysis focuses on some of the profound consequences (direct, indirect, immediate, long-term) for students at all levels of education (preschool, elementary school, (pre-)adolescents, adults) resulting from the choice of online schooling that affect the respect of the fundamental right to education.

G. Mareş
Physiotherapy and Occupational Therapy Department, Vasile Alecsandri University of Bacău, Bacău, Romania
e-mail: mares.gabriel@ub.ro

V-.M. Cojocariu (✉)
Teacher Training Department, Vasile Alecsandri University of Bacău, Bacău, Romania
e-mail: venera@ub.ro

I. Boghian, G. Mareş (eds.), *Gamification and Inclusion*, Inclusive Learning and Educational Equity 12, https://doi.org/10.1007/978-3-031-98390-0_2

Keywords Education · Right to education · Online education · COVID 19 pandemic

Rethinking the Right to Education in the Online Context

The legal question of the right to education and its guarantee has increasingly become a significant and systematic part of European concerns in the second half of the last century. This was preceded by theories, ideas, proposals, and documents dealing with the general aspect of children's rights. In this sense, a series of declarations on the rights of the child were published in 1924, which were summarized under the name Geneva Declaration of the Rights of the Child (drafted between 1919–1923 as a result of the efforts of Eglantyne Jebb, who drew attention to the need to protect children and ensure all conditions for their growth and education immediately after the First World War) (Salvaţi copiii, 2019).

In 1959, a step forward was taken with the adoption of the Declaration of the Rights of the Child by the United Nations General Assembly. With the content of Principles 1 (equal rights for all children, without discrimination on any grounds), 7 (free and compulsory education at least up to primary school level), and 10 (protection of the child from discriminatory practices), the basis for the rights of the child was made more solid and systematic.

Given the status of these contents, which circulated only as recommendations, as well as the time in which they were first developed, the need arose (at the end of the last century) to revisit and consolidate the issue.

In 1989, a new, expanded, and updated version of the Convention on the Rights of the Child was adopted by the United Nations General Assembly (Salvaţi Copiii, 2019). Through this document, the signatory states "recognize the right of the child to education and each State shall take measures to ensure the exercise of this right progressively and on the basis of equality of opportunity. Every child has the right to education" (Art. 28, p. 16). The Convention was adopted by a number of 196 countries that are members of the United Nations. The basic idea is "the principle of the best interests of the child" (Art. 3). As an expression of the relevance of its content, it was transformed into international law a year later, in 1990, strengthening the coercive and regulatory aspects it sets out. Given the importance and value of this principle, it was immediately incorporated and integrated into Romanian legislation in 1990 by Law no. 18. Later, in 2004, the law was improved in the version of Law no. 272/2004 in order to ensure a higher level of child protection). The existence of conventions and laws is an extremely important dimension when it comes to placing the educational process under the umbrella of respect for the rights of the child, but it does not automatically and necessarily lead to their respect. Phenomena such as the existence of children in poverty-stricken families, a high infant mortality rate, school dropout or truancy, functional illiteracy, and exploitation through child labor have not disappeared either in Romania or in the countries that have signed the Convention. The period that Romania spent after 1990 was characterized by both light and shadow with regard to children's right to education. On the one hand, there were a number of positive phenomena, both in the field of formal and non-formal education, such as the number of compulsory schools has increased; their range has diversified, both in terms of the form of sponsorship (the emergence and functioning of private institutions alongside public ones at all levels of the education system) and in terms of pedagogical alternatives (Montessori, Step by Step, Freinet); their material base has improved significantly; psychological and professional counseling services have been provided in schools; the non-formal education offer has expanded to a higher level; the partnership of the school with the family and community has taken on new forms. On the other hand, a number of non-achievements were highlighted, such as the widening of the educational gap between rural and urban students/schools; the decrease in the rural school population, the need to send the remaining children to more distant schools and the emergence of economic and financial problems, which also led to an increase in the school dropout rate; the impossibility for children from poor and very poor families to enter and complete their studies; the continued manifestation of some negative phenomena such as violence (verbal, behavioral) in the family and sometimes even at school; the exploitation of child labor, the deliberate keeping of children by their families in the status of unskilled labor, the lack of access to audio-video means of communication, the Internet; the perpetuation and manifestation of some prejudices against some categories of children, based on economic, ethnic, and religious criteria, in the microcommunity and school.

In addition to this already problematic and difficult-to-manage context, all the constraints imposed by the COVID-19 pandemic were added, triggering a (new) question: What does the right to education still mean in the context of the online approach? Can it still be respected? And if so, how?

Although in the twenty-first century, known as the century of the information and knowledge boom and the spread of new learning technologies, electronic learning devices (phone, tablet, computer, internet connection) should provide real support that enables the continuation of learning in the online environment and non-discriminatory access to education for all children (by bringing together students and teachers, families and communities), the more than 2 years of the pandemic have shown that in reality they have rather divided us further into rich and poor; those who have learning devices and those who do not; those who do not have access to technology and those who do; those who can continue their education online and those who cannot.

Therefore, the provision of an alternative to traditional, face-to-face classroom teaching by another, which takes place in a virtual environment, does not automatically mean that the right to education is guaranteed for all. Law no. 272/2004, republished in 2014, establishes in Articles 1 and 2 "the best interests of the child," in Article 51 (1) the idea that "the child has the right to an education that enables him to develop his abilities and personality in non-discriminatory conditions," respectively in Article 52 (1) that "the Ministry of National Education, as a specialized body of the central public administration, as well as school inspectorates and educational units, as bodies of local public administration with competences in the field of education, are obliged to take the necessary measures." However, the content of the law was transgressed by the situations that prevailed during the COVID-19 pandemic, when all these measures, although administratively taken in a genuine, educational manner, could not be guaranteed or provided in some places and for some children. Among the most common causes are the inadequate infrastructure of some schools, the lack of Internet connection at school or at home, the lack of online learning tools, the inadequate training of some teachers in this sense, the reluctance or rejection of online teaching by some of the teaching staff and the insufficient involvement of the institution management in ensuring the necessary conditions.

In 2020, immediately after the suspension of face-to-face classes, the Romanian Student Council conducted a survey among students to identify the risks and propose measures to ensure the right to education for all children. 11.958 students took part in the survey. The main risks identified included (Romania's Council of Students, 2020, pp. 3–18):

- The impossibility of participating in the didactic online process for 1/3 of respondents.
- The lack of authentic, high-quality interaction during the didactic process.
- Good performance was achieved online only in some subjects (with very good and good percentages for Romanian language and literature - 74.2%; mathematics - 62.1%; with average percentages for modern language and literature 1st foreign language - 49.4%; history - 44.9%; geography - 41.3%; computer science - 40.8%; biology - 40.1%; but also with poor percentages for Latin - 8.6%; specialized subjects - 7% and very poor percentages for civic education - 4.1%; plastic education - 3.2%).
- The effectiveness of the methods used by the teachers in the online approach was appreciated by only 68.3% of the students, with 15.3% of them not considering them useful and another 16.4% not being able to assess the value of the teaching methods.
- Participation in the online activities was average: 55.1% of the students estimated that all colleagues participated in the classes, 30.2% considered that only a certain part of their colleagues participated in the online classes, 6.9% estimated that only a few students benefited from this type of learning and 7.8% mentioned that no colleague could benefit from the online courses.
- Among the proposed measures that are of general benefit, not only for the time when the study was conducted, we have systematized the following (idem., pp. 18–21).
- The didactic activity must not be interrupted, the evaluations must take place, the semester/school year must be completed.
- The involvement of the competent ministry in monitoring the organization and development of online teaching to ensure compliance with the principle of equal opportunities.
- Significant investment in teacher training to make online teaching a reality and in ensuring the necessary infrastructure so that every child has access to the digitalization of education.

- The main conclusion of the study referred to the need to "ensure "the digitization of education in a participatory, transparent and fair process to meet the needs of all students, regardless of their background" (idem., p. 21).
- A similar study conducted in mid-2020 (June–July) by the organization Save the Children on a group of 4792 children highlighted another set of relevant ideas about online education:
- The issue of poverty affects around a quarter of the school population surveyed, with 24% of children reporting that their family had been affected by at least one of the vulnerability factors, with 1 in 10 children reporting that an adult in the household had lost their job (Save the Children, 2020, p.6).
- The possibility of conducting online classes only partially for 27.2%, with around 6% of them either never or very rarely participating in online classes.
- The lack of necessary tools for online lessons—the cell phone is the only device most children have access to in order to participate in online lessons, 47% of them rely exclusively on it (idem., p.7).
- The occurrence of interruptions in the educational process in 1/3 of students, despite the efforts of teachers, which means that only 1/3 of them are very satisfied with the quality of online interaction with teachers (idem., p. 10–11).
- The need for support was very high—about 12% had not spoken to teachers during this time and 13% felt they needed more support during the online school period or would need it immediately after returning to face-to-face classes. Of the students who did need support, more than half, 58.6%, received no support (idem., pp. 12–16).
- The most common problems during online classes were those related to misunderstandings with parents in connection with internet activities - 32.4% (idem., p. 18).
- The most common online risks are Internet addiction 54.1%; wrong data 39.5%; cyberbullying 25.8% (idem., p. 19).

The presentation of the results of these two surveys alone, conducted half a year after the pandemic and online school, can illustrate the extent to which the spontaneous, forced, and unprepared transfer of formal education to the online environment is reaching the limits of respecting the right to education. At the same time, both parents and students, teachers, and numerous non-governmental organizations working for children's rights have used the available levers to emphasize the need to resume face-to-face schooling. The right to education, the right to health, and the right to work in a safe environment collide with the risk of further pandemics (Maguire & McNamara, 2020), with governments needing to ensure the right to education for all as a top priority.

Current laws specifying the right to education emphasize the need for states to provide students with learning resources that meet their current needs in a changing world. There is no right to education without quality education (Making the Right to Education a reality in Times of Covid-19, 2020). This implies the duty of governments to provide education in diverse and flexible ways and to ensure access to online learning resources (Geith & Vignare, 2008) that enable students to learn from home at a time when the use of technology in education is increasing. From a legal perspective, it follows that the right to education does not necessarily require the student to participate in didactic activities at school (Maguire & McNamara, 2020), but integrates the idea that the outcomes of their learning, wherever they are achieved, must meet the standards of the system.

Challenges of Online Education

The right to education, in the context of the forced transition from traditional education to online education, has been a source of constraints and limitations resulting from a number of challenges:

1. Pedagogical/formative challenges (Poon & Tang, 2024; Labuschagne et al., 2023; Moorhouse & Kohnke, 2022; Dennis & Harrison, 2021; Monteath-van Dok et al., 2021; NO EDUCATION, NO PROTECTION, 2021; The COVID-19 pandemic and the right to education in Portuguese speaking countries: challenges and confrontations in Angola, Brazil, Cabo Verde and Mozambique, 2021; Declaration on COVID-19 and social rights, 2021; Bárcena & Uribe, 2020; Bender, 2020; Botnariuc et al., 2020; Dreesen et al., 2020; Guiding principles on the COVID-19 pandemic, 2020; Human Rights Dimensions of COVID-19 Response, 2020; LEARNING MUST GO ON, 2020; Making the Right to Education a reality in Times of Covid-19, 2020; Maguire & McNamara, 2020; Educational inequalities in Europe and physical school closures during Covid-19, 2020; Lorente et al., 2020; Policy Brief: Education during COVID-19 and beyond, 2020; Rajab et al., 2020; Schleicher, 2020; Strategia privind digitalizarea educației din România [Strategic initiative for the digitalization of education], 2020; UNESCO COVID-19 education response: how many students are at risk of not returning to school? Advocacy paper, 2020; O'Dowd, R., 2018; Cakmak &Yilmaz, 2014; Alvarez et al., 2009):
   (a) Adapting to a new educational communication format that most teachers and students do not know, a format full of limitations, constraints and the need to use technology. The new way of educational communication limits the possibility of feedback and deprives them of the possibility of accessing the elements related to the non-verbal component and greatly dilutes the paraverbal component. Online education significantly reduces access to non-verbal and paraverbal cues, but also to part of the informational content of communication.
   (b) Initial teacher training placed too little emphasis on the use of information and communication technology elements in activities with and for students. Traditionally, teacher training with the component of new learning technologies (ICT) has mainly dealt with the elements related to the use of the computer and some (far too few) applications useful in the creation of teaching material, in its preparation and support, etc. The use of pedagogical applica-

tions and the use of ICT in activities with and for students has been neglected. Too little importance has been given to the use of pedagogical applications and platforms, which is why even after 2 years of continuous/intermittent online teaching, there are still quite a few teachers who are hesitant or not adapted to working with these resources.

(c) Despite the fact that we are (generally) talking about digital natives, Romanian students have been educated and encouraged to use information and communication technology as a tool for education only to a very limited extent. Most of them are limited to creating technically edited texts or ppt presentations. Thus, to the surprise of some teachers, we find that a significant number of children and adolescents participating in various forms of education have difficulties in using educational applications, searching for valuable educational resources in the online environment or even performing simple activities on platforms dedicated to online learning.

(d) Both teachers and students had no experience in adapting and applying didactic methods to the experience of online education. These steps of redesign and adaptation are essential to facilitate the understanding of content, skills training, etc., without the new approach becoming a pressure factor for teachers and students.

(e) Adaptation and contextualization of teaching and learning and formative/summative assessment—Schools have had to cover a process of adaptation and adjustment of the curriculum (so that it meets the new conditions). Some countries have moved to rethink educational objectives to facilitate interdisciplinary approaches, restructuring through modulation, prioritization of content according to the criterion of relevance, topics related to health protection, the development of critical thinking and the ability to identify and manage news have been included in the curriculum, etc.

(f) Training teachers to provide feedback and support to students/learners in the context of online teaching so that they are able to protect students' mental health.

(g) The adaptation and individualization of teaching for students with special educational needs (SEN) would have required the training of teachers who are able to make intensive use of adult learning skills for the specificities of working with students with SEN. This is mainly due to the fact that teachers working with children with SEN inevitably had to rely on the support of their relatives and make them co-educators (partners in the education/therapy of children with SEN).

(h) At the level of the evaluation process, challenges and relocations can be distinguished in relation to the way we conduct formative and summative evaluations. Educational platforms have become challenges, sources of difficulties, but also opportunities for teachers. The shift to individual assessments and the ability to provide feedback, as well as online evaluation methods or tests that can be accessed by a large number of students, have brought about a paradigm shift in this area of education. However, it is worth reflecting on the aspects related to equity: the technical resources/devices and connection available to each student, the problems caused by connection errors that can occur in some assessments, the level of technical skills that prevents the student from focusing on the task for which he/she is being assessed, etc.

2. **Socioeconomic challenges** (exclusion factors) (Chan et al., 2024; Zdravkov, 2024; Malenya & Ohba, 2023; Gaidelys et al., 2022; Garcia, 2022; Monteath-van Dok et al., 2021; Problems with education around the world during Covid-19, 2021; The COVID-19 pandemic and the right to education in Portuguese-speaking countries: challenges and confrontations in Angola, Brazil, Cabo Verde and Mozambique, 2021; Statement on COVID-19 and social rights, 2021; Botnariuc et al., 2020; Crearea unor sisteme de educaţie reziliente în contextul pandemiei de COVID-19 [Building resilient education systems in the context of the COVID-19 pandemic], 2020; Dreesen et al., 2020; Educational inequalities in Europe and physical school closings during Covid-19, 2020; EU neighbors: coping with COVID-19 in education and training, 2020; Human Rights Dimensions of COVID-19 Response, 2020; INEE, 2020; Global Covid-19 Response, 2020; Lorente et al., 2020; Policy Brief: Education during COVID-19 and beyond, 2020; Policy Brief: The Impact of Covid-19 on children, 2020; Protecting and Transforming Education for Shared Futures and Common Humanity, A Joint Statement on the COVID-19 Crisis, 2020; Schleicher, 2020; The Day After Tomorrow: Confronting Systemic Injustices, Advancing Human Rights, 2020; UNESCO COVID-19 education response: how many students are at risk of not returning to school? Advocacy Paper, 2020):

   (a) The presence of significant economic disparities is often the reason for limited or even no access to education. For most students from socioeconomically disadvantaged backgrounds, online education was synonymous with the inability to access the right to education. Access to resources to acquire data services and devices for education is very limited. Local, national or international efforts to limit the consequences of educational gaps have not been and are not sufficient. They should be doubled by efforts to train children and relatives to know how to use these resources, so we are talking about further costs that are difficult to bear.
   (b) Students who come from families where the parents themselves have a low and very low level of education—The greatest difficulty and challenge of online education for these students arises from the reduced opportunities to benefit from the material and educational support of the family. For them, the lack of understanding of certain content taught by the teacher can rarely be compensated for by parental involvement and support to overcome the cognitive setback. Only a set of coherent and well-formulated support programs tailored to individual needs could come to their aid.
   (c) Low economic resources do not allow some families/students to purchase devices that ensure the maintenance of connection to the data transmission networks/Internet (if they want to make these purchases).

(d) There are also some disadvantaged groups among teachers who cannot afford to purchase a laptop or pay for an Internet subscription on an ongoing basis. As with some students, there are also economic difficulties among teachers that have made them people with little experience in using technology or without access to technology. This situation can have serious consequences, at least in the long term, for the quality of education of future graduates.

(e) High and uninsured economic costs of ensuring hygienic/sanitary conditions/tests etc. for schools from disadvantaged socio-economic backgrounds. Although precarious hygienic/sanitary conditions were commonplace for many schools in disadvantaged areas, this has been further highlighted and deepened by the sanitation crisis. For many schools, the cost of ensuring hygiene and sanitation safety has led to spending budgets being far exceeded, resulting in a reduction of funds normally earmarked for other expenditure.

3. **Infrastructure challenges** (Mhlanga, 2024; Sirikasemsuk et al., 2024; Gharti, 2023; Machusky & Herbert-Berger, 2022; Yeh & Tsai, 2022; Problems with education around the world during Covid-19, 2021; The COVID-19 pandemic and the right to education in Portguese speaking countries: challenges and confrontations in Angola, Brazil, Cabo Verde and Mozambique, 2021; Botnariuc et al., 2020; Crearea unor sisteme de educaţie reziliente în contextul pandemiei de COVID-19, 2020; Lorente et al., 2020; The Day After Tomorrow: Confronting Systemic Injustices, Advancing Human Rights, 2020; Cakmak & Yilmaz, 2014):

(a) Infrastructure at the school level—poor or absent infrastructure—is often an insurmountable challenge for some school communities in some situations. This category of challenges has implications for safeguarding children's right to education, as many students have been unable to learn during the pandemic. The challenges related to ensuring infrastructure in educational institutions were related to the challenges of an administrative nature, which we will present later.

(b) The infrastructure at the level of students' and teachers' homes—not only the infrastructure of educational institutions was a challenge, but also that at the level of students' and teachers' homes. Beyond a number of economic conditions, there are situations where the restriction of the right to education is related to the lack of equipment or access to data networks or, in some situations, the inability to provide electricity to power these devices.

(c) The infrastructure of communication service providers—in some cases, the limitations of communication or electricity service providers are determined by the very long distances between homes or by the uneven relief, but also by the local economic context. Whatever the case, the impact on education and training opportunities is strong. The example of states with low population density that have managed to provide an adequate response to this challenge and thus provide access to education for a large percentage of the population is an example worth emulating (tele-school, radio-school are still used) (Maguire & McNamara, 2020).

4. **Management challenges** (Faza et al., 2024; Das, 2023; Keith & Thompson, 2023; Puiu et al., 2023; Asgari et al., 2022; Problems with education worldwide during Covid-19, 2021; Sarchiapone, 2021; The COVID-19 pandemic and the right to education in Portuguese-speaking countries: Challenges and confrontations in Angola, Brazil, Cabo Verde and Mozambique, 2021; Bárcena & Uribe, 2020; Botnariuc et al., 2020; Bult, 2020; Dreesen et al., 2020; Educational inequalities in Europe and physical school closures during Covid-19, 2020; Global Covid-19 Response, 2020; Paudel, 2020; UNESCO COVID-19 education response: how many students are at risk of not returning to school? Advocacy paper, 2020; Roddy et al., 2017):

    (a) The need to ensure general support measures for all students (safe environment in terms of hygiene; teachers trained to provide support before and after COVID-19; provision of internet access in schools; procurement and management of IT infrastructure at school level to ensure the online teaching process in good conditions; the rapid acquisition of a sufficient number of tablets needed for online teaching), but especially for the disadvantaged students (offering differentiated and individualized learning support activities, carrying out revision/reinforcement activities of the essential content covered during the online learning phase, partial, formative assessments, after the return to face-to-face school.

    (b) Closing only the schools for which this measure is necessary and ensuring access to education for the children in these schools through different channels and means, depending on the actual circumstances—radio, television, internet, computers, telephones, and books. The challenge is to take over administrative decisions related to the closure of schools and, implicitly, to direct/reorient some resources to the online transmission of the educational process.

    (c) Ensuring the necessary, specific, organizational, and logistical measures for access to education for children with disabilities. This challenge is very closely linked to the formative challenges. Many schools have been surprised by the shift to online teaching without having strategic intervention plans in place to benefit children with disabilities;

    (d) Identifying financial resources and support for teachers engaging in post-COVID 19 learning supports. In many situations, support measures were seen as additional tasks that put a strain on the school budget and lead to burnout for some teachers.

    (e) Ensuring internet infrastructure and access to platforms and applications for students (devices and internet connection)—is a challenge that not only has an administrative impact on the allocation of resources, but also impacts decision making when purchasing devices with the best value for money and the most appropriate educational platforms and applications. Often, ignorance of the technical specifications and performance of some applications can lead to inappropriate investment in such infrastructure elements.

(f) Managing and maintaining the devices that students and teachers can access from home—Schools have been faced with the need to provide or train staff capable of maintaining the IT infrastructure and applications used for online teaching and managing the accounts of students and teachers registered on educational platforms and applications.

5. **Ethical challenges** (Marín & Tur, 2024; Balida, 2023; De Agostini, 2023; Mehrfar et al., 2023; Skulmowski, 2023; Bajpa, 2022; Education: From disruption to recovery, 2021; Almseidein & Klaif-Mahasneh, 2020; Han, 2020; Maguire & McNamara, 2020; UNESCO COVID-19 education response: how many students are at risk of not returning to school? Advocacy Paper, 2020):

(a) Exacerbating discrepancies and disparities in the adaptation of education to the specific needs of each child—For education systems, the lack of preparation for the personalization and adaptation of education was evident, with the creativity of some teachers being the only resource that generated an experimental response with the task of limiting these discrepancies.
(b) From the perspective of teaching and learning opportunities, the limitation of the right to education is related to whether one has access to the Internet or is deprived of this access. A relevant number—2,899,305—people studying in one form or another were affected by the COVID-19 pandemic at the time recorded on September 21, 2020 (Global Covid-19 Response, 2020).
(c) Access to the internet and connectivity devices, the platforms that are used to conduct online classes, creates ethical dilemmas, as there is a high correlation between the possibility of acquiring these devices and the material resources of some families or educational institutions.
(d) The almost intrusive access to the private space of the child and his/her family (the disclosure of some aspects of the living conditions of those involved in education raises a number of ethical questions).
(e) Related to the previous challenge is cyberbullying, which is exacerbated by the discovery of the technical inabilities of some students or even teachers. Both teachers and students are not yet sufficiently prepared to prevent, manage, or block this phenomenon specific to online life.
(f) Disruptions in the dynamics of educational activities that are inevitable in online teaching that takes place at home (interruptions, interference from family members, harassment or inappropriate encouragement, etc.).
(g) A reduction in the quality of practical training, particularly for those undertaking vocational training, compared to previous generations. We find that there are students who have spent almost two and a half years studying only online and are asking themselves the question: How am I supposed to know how to practice my profession? (e.g., dentists, car technicians, etc.).

Lessons Learned

(a) Even students who live far away from school can take online courses. In this sense, the models of countries with low population density can be a good example.

(b) The reluctance to use ICT can be overcome and the results of the appropriate use of ICT in education can largely compensate for the physical presence of students in school.
(c) Teachers should be trained to adapt the learning content by grading them and transferring their skills to the online system.
(d) A crisis affecting education systems may last much longer than originally anticipated (initially the period for the online transfer of educational activities was estimated to be a few weeks, but eventually it lasted almost 2 years). Therefore, representatives of education systems should assume the most pessimistic scenario and ensure both infrastructure and training to facilitate the online transfer of educational activities in the event of other pandemics.
(e) Even if technological progress allows the adaptation of educational approaches to the online teaching system, there are still some categories of students whose right to education may still be limited due to the lack of infrastructure and resources for this type of education (McFayden et al., 2021).
(f) Educating parents and training their digital skills should be a priority because, for example, for children in small classes or for children with SEN, the role of parents/caregivers should be similar to that of a co-teacher (partner of the teacher in the educational approach) (Liberman et al., 2020).
(g) Teachers can make adaptations to lessons (idem), including for students with limited resources/limited access to communication networks. For example: using handouts sent home, using email, phone, etc. to provide guidance and feedback are alternatives to withdrawing education altogether. In addition, educational resources can be created and used that incorporate principles and methods that favor guided instruction or approaches with a high degree of learner ownership.
(h) The elements related to the promotion of mental health and the management of social relationships in the online environment should become a priority for those responsible for education.
(i) The well-being of students and teachers should be taken into account when allocating resources for continuing education and for the provision of alternative training opportunities to make education systems more resilient in the face of new times of crisis.
(j) The training systems of large companies or the examples of providers of MOOCs (Massive Open Online Courses) can be inspiring examples for the adaptation of online education, especially when drawing on some MOOCs that can be transferred and adapted to individualized training.

Conclusions

In a context where all children have the right to education, the COVID-19 pandemic has had a devastating impact on education, exacerbating a real educational crisis (Guiding principles on the COVID-19 pandemic, 2020) that humanity was already experiencing, especially at the axiological level. The pandemic has exposed and exacerbated existing problems in education worldwide: many children had less or no access to education; some of them were assigned to care for younger siblings, household activities, or work during the pandemic; some girls were abused or became mothers at a young age; students had less support from teachers; they met or communicated less with their peers; they received less or no economic support from schools—a hot meal, scholarships; overall well-being changed (additional worry about learning outcomes and exams, increased anxiety, decreased/decreased motivation to learn, isolation from friends, stress in the family, doubts about the safety of the online environment) (Monteath-van Dok et al., 2021; NO EDUCATION, NO PROTECTION, 2021; Problems with education around the world during Covid-19, 2021; Sarchiapone, 2021; Statement on COVID-19 and social rights, 2021; INEE, 2020; Lorente et al., 2020; Policy Brief: Education during COVID-19 and beyond, 2020; Protecting and Transforming Education for Shared Futures and Common Humanity, A Joint Statement on the COVID-19 Crisis, 2020; Right to education: impact of the COVID-19 crisis on the right to education; concerns, challenges and opportunities, 2020; The Day After Tomorrow: Confronting Systemic Injustices, Advancing Human Rights, 2020; UNESCO COVID-19 education response: how many students are at risk of not returning to school? Advocacy Paper, 2020).

According to some UNICEF studies (Bult, 2020), although the last decades have brought positive results in terms of respect for children's rights in Romania, "40% of our children still live in poverty or are at risk of social exclusion, one of the highest levels in the European Union" (p. 1), with these risks still having a strong impact on poor, rural, Roma, or disabled children. Around 400,000 children have no access to education at all. The school dropout rate was 15.7% in 2019 (idem).

The pandemic has led to unprecedented lockdowns and measures that highlight the lack of resilience and adaptability in education systems around the world, with fragile contexts being the hardest hit. Local and national governments were not prepared for the large-scale disruptions caused by COVID-19 (Monteath-van Dok et al., 2021) and are still in a continuous process of adaptation. In the same vein, a study published in Romania in 2020 (Botnariuc et al., 2020) showed that at the time of the introduction of the online school form, there were at least 3 elements that were not fully in line with the respect of children's right to education: "1. the school system was only partially prepared for this transition, some teachers were not sufficiently trained for the design and implementation of online lessons; 2. the school curriculum only allowed for variable/sequential/revised implementation in online activities; 3. edtech companies were not encouraged to develop interoperable solutions tailored to the needs of the education system" (p. 7).

On the one hand, some studies (Educational inequalities in Europe and physical school closures during Covid-19, 2020) predict that we can expect a significant increase in educational inequalities in the post-COVID-19 period. These will be all the greater as the success of online schooling depends primarily (to ensure students' access to education) on the resources of families entering the process from very different socio-economic backgrounds, as well as the

educational support they provide to students. On the other hand, the experts point out that the measures taken by states to mitigate the severe impact of the pandemic must be proportionate, necessary and non-discriminatory (COVID-19: States should not abuse emergency measures to suppress human rights, 2020).

In this complex, difficult and sometimes contradictory context, concern about "how to ensure continued access to education for all children" remains an element of continuity (Bult, 2020, **p.1).**

Among the main lines of action that could be undertaken in the near future in relation to respecting the right to education through online education can be mentioned:

1. Securing the sources and financial support that could guarantee both the necessary infrastructure for the schools/families and the motivation of the main actors involved: Teachers, students, parents, managers, medical staff (Mhlanga, 2024; Sirikasemsuk et al., 2024; Gharti, 2023; Machusky & Herbert-Berger, 2022; Yeh & Tsai, 2022; Fredman, 2021; Monteath-van Dok et al., 2021; Botnariuc et al., 2020; Bult, 2020; LEARNING MUST GO ON, 2020; Lorente et al., 2020; Terway & Avelar, 2020).
2. Initial teacher education should be clearly focused on the use of new learning technologies (NLT) as a consistent beginning (Hennessy et al., 2022; Botnariuc et al., 2020) through instrumented practices throughout the duration of the training and not only as an element of exoticism or as an optional, sporadic task now and then, among others. It is necessary to acquire the competence to manage a virtual class (planning activities, techniques for creating materials, making tools, integrating them into online teaching, carrying out hybrid approaches, focusing on the "virtual class, online learning platforms, applications and virtual laboratories." (Teo et al., 2021; Botnariuc et al., 2020, p. 21); Monteath-van Dok et al., 2021; NO EDUCATION, NO PROTECTION, 2021; Sarchiapone, 2021; Dreesen et al., 2020; Making the Right to Education a reality in Times of Covid-19, 2020; Policy Brief: Education during COVID-19 and beyond, 2020; EU neighbors: coping with COVID-19 in education and training, 2020). This would include a higher level of digital literacy among teachers (Strategy for the digitalization of education in Romania, 2020).
3. Innovation of didactic activities through the development of specific (face-to-face or online) or hybrid approaches, rethinking the design, teaching and learning, assessment and recognition of skills so that no student is excluded from the opportunity to develop their full potential, regardless of place of residence, gender, ethnicity, faith, and economic status (Making the Right to Education a reality in Times of Covid-19, 2020; Policy Brief: Education during COVID-19 and beyond, 2020; Strategy on the digitization of education in Romania, 2020).
4. In the circumstances that the digital divide brings us, the effective guarantee of the right to education, especially from the perspective of online education, requires the use of multiple ways to reach learning (digital channels in combination with non-digital ones: radio, television, cell phone, or, in the spirit of

UNESCO, the adoption of a variety of high-tech, low-tech and no-tech solutions to ensure the continuity of the educational process) (Uzorka, 2024; Monteath-van Dok et al., 2021; Bender, 2020; Dreesen et al., 2020; Guiding principles on the COVID-19 pandemic, 2020; Human Rights Dimensions of COVID-19 Response, 2020; Lorente et al., 2020; Making the Right to Education a reality in Times of Covid-19, 2020; Right to education: impact of the COVID-19 crisis on the right to education; concerns, challenges and opportunities, 2020; Terway & Avelar, 2020; UNESCO COVID-19 education response: how many students are at risk of not returning to school? Advocacy Paper, 2020).

5. Strengthening support from teachers, parents, and all those who provide support for online learning Access to content is the first step, which is very important but is not enough if cognitive and psycho-emotional and social support for learning efforts at home is lacking (Monteath-van Dok et al., 2021; Dreesen et al., 2020; Lorente et al., 2020).
6. Ensuring permanent feedback on learning and improving process monitoring in quantitative and qualitative terms, rethinking assessment, certification, and validation processes (Turner et al., 2023; Botnariuc et al., 2020; Dreesen et al., 2020; EU neighbors: coping with COVID-19 in education and training, 2020; Policy Brief: Education during COVID-19 and beyond, 2020).
7. Rethinking/restructuring teacher education and training by ensuring the connection of all content with the delivery of lessons in online or hybrid format. In addition, the discipline of computer-based education needs to update its content by focusing on online applications and software in education (Strategy for Digitization of Education in Romania, 2020).
8. Conducting interdisciplinary research aimed at carrying out online activities, creating content in virtual format, the techniques used, the involvement of parents, but also knowing some of the negative effects that occur in order to reduce them or keep them under control (Dreesen et al., 2020).

The period we have been through during and after COVID-19 makes it clear that there is a priority direction for improving education systems—equitable access to quality education (Policy Brief: Education during COVID-19 and beyond, 2020; Lorente et al., 2020; Schleicher, 2020). Interventions must be inclusive and appropriately contextualized (Lorente et al., 2020).

Ensuring the right to education is a public responsibility, and assuming this responsibility requires that schools are encouraged to adapt their processes to the new circumstances (Making the Right to Education a reality in Times of Covid-19, 2020). This cannot be the result of the teacher's singular action, but the product of an interdisciplinary team in which, in addition to the teacher, "the computer scientist, the systems engineer, the school manager" (Botnariuc et al., 2020, p. 46) are also involved.

Collaboration between institutions and states could lead to the realization of strategic partnerships (Botnariuc et al., 2020) at the local/national/global level in education (Terway & Avelar, 2020), which can prepare school institutions to respond to future pandemics, shocks, uncertainty, and other crises, incorporating the ability to easily, safely, and effectively switch from face-to-face to online learning options when needed (Monteath-van Dok et al., 2021; Policy Brief: Education during COVID-19 and beyond, 2020; EU neighbors: coping with COVID-19 in education and training, 2020; Protecting and Transforming Education for Shared Futures and Common Humanity, A Joint Statement on the COVID-19 Crisis, 2020; Right to education: impact of the COVID-19 crisis on the right to education; concerns, challenges and opportunities, 2020; The Day After Tomorrow: Confronting Systemic Injustices, Advancing Human Rights, 2020). In fact, we are talking about bringing together all members of society, the entire community as a whole, in a holistic approach to ensure the right to education (Sarchiapone, 2021).

The literature of recent years on the topic we have studied leads us to a worrying perspective (Sato et al., 2024; Nottingham et al., 2022; Tate & Warschauer, 2022; Sarchiapone, 2021; The COVID-19 Pandemy and the right to education in Portuguese speaking countries: challenges and confrontations in Angola, Brazil, Cabo Verde and Mozambique, 2021; Lorente et al., 2020; Recht auf Bildung: Impact of the COVID-19 crisis on the right to education; concerns, challenges and opportunities, 2020) in terms of respecting the right to education in the context of online education, especially for the most vulnerable children who come from disadvantaged communities (by gender, special needs, socio-economic background). Precisely for this reason, for a global problem such as Covid-19, the solutions for each of its sub-components (medical, social, educational) must be urgent (Sarchiapone, 2021), convergent and simultaneous (Lorente et al., 2020). All these measures imply a fundamental rethinking of the traditional model of education (Sarchiapone, 2021) from the perspective of (current and/or future!) crisis contexts, building resilience and preparing for the future (NO EDUCATION, NO PROTECTION, 2021), including the recognition of the right to internet access as part of the right to education.

We resume our initial questions—What does the right to education still mean in the online approach? Can it still be respected? If so, how?—we can conclude that the COVID crisis has jeopardized the right to education more than ever in the last 75 years. The closing of schools in April 2020 affected almost 91% of the learning population, i.e., 1.5 billion young people (LEARNING MUST GO ON, 2020). Preserving the right to education in an online context requires a double intervention: quantitative (financial, administrative) and qualitative (strategic, paradigmatic, restructuring and reinterpretation of the curriculum and training of teachers, parents, integration of technology in a relevant and meaningful learning process). Acquiring devices and ensuring their connection to the Internet are absolutely necessary steps, as first steps of infrastructure, but without a holistic approach they will not automatically lead to quality education.

All current (and future!) approaches, all adaptive, but above all proactive measures should manage to control inequalities in access to the right to education (Fredman, 2021; NO EDUCATION, NO PROTECTION, 2021; Sarchiapone, 2021; The COVID-19 Pandemic and the right to education in Portuguese speaking countries: challenges and confrontations in Angola, Brazil, Cabo Verde and Mozambique, 2021).

References

Almseidein, T. A., & Klaif-Mahasneh, O. M. (2020). Awareness of ethical issues when using an e-learning system. *International Journal of Advanced Computer Science and Applications, 11*(1), 128–131.

Alvarez, I., Guasch, T., & Espasa, A. (2009). University teacher roles and competencies in online learning environments: A theoretical analysis of teaching and learning practices. *European Journal of Teacher Education, 32*(3), 321–336. https://doi.org/10.1080/02619760802624104

Asgari, H., Gupta, R., Titiloye, I., & Jin, X. (2022). Challenges, perceptions, and future preferences for post-secondary online education given experiences in the COVID-19 outbreak. *Computational Urban Science, 2*, 29. https://doi.org/10.1007/s43762-022-00058-7

Bajpa, N. (2022). Ethical issues of online teaching-learning. *International Journal of Advanced Research in Science, Communication and Technology (IJARSCT), 2*(1). https://doi.org/10.48175/IJARSCT-7744

Balida, D. A. R. (2023). Ethical challenges in online teaching and learning: A case study of a virtual class. *Russian Law Journal, 11*(3). https://doi.org/10.52783/rlj.v11i3.1959

Bárcena A., & Uribe, C. (2020). *Education in the time of COVID-19*, Informe COVID-19 CEPAL-UNESCO, education in the time of COVID-19 (cepal.org). Accessed 16 Mar 2024.

Bender, L. (2020). Key messages and actions for COVID-19 prevention and control in schools, UNICEF, World Health Organization, Key Messages and Actions for COVID-19 Prevention and Control in Schools (unicef.org). Accessed 9 Nov 2024.

Botnariuc, P., Cucoş, C., Glava, C., Iancu, D., Ilie, M., Istrate, O., Labăr, A. V., Pânişoară, I-O., Ştefănescu, D., & Velea, S. (2020). Şcoala online - elemente pentru inovarea educaţiei, *Raport de cercetare evaluativă*, Bucureşti: Editura Universităţii din Bucureşti.

Bult, P. (2020). *Pandemia de COVID-19 aduce la suprafaţă o altă urgenţă naţională*, https://www.unicef.org/romania/ro/pove%C8%99ti/pandemia-de-covid-19-aduce-la-suprafa%C8%9B%C4%83-o-alt%C4%83-urgen%C8%9B%C4%83-na%C8%9Bional%C4%83. Accessed 23 Sept 2024.

Cakmak, E., & Yilmaz, S. M. (2014). E-learning from the perspective of right to education. *Procedia.- Social and Behavioral Sciences 116*:426–430, https://www.sciencedirect.com/science/article/pii/S1877042814002353?via%3Dihub. Accessed 13 May 2024.

Chan, S. M., Chung, G., Chan, Y. H., et al. (2024). Online learning problems, academic worries, social interaction, and psychological well-being among secondary school students in Hong Kong during the COVID-19 pandemic: the socioeconomic and gender differences. *European Journal of Psychology of Education, 39*, 2805–2826. https://doi.org/10.1007/s10212-024-00882-x

Das, U. (2023). Online learning: Challenges and solutions for learners and teachers. *Management and Labour Studies, 48*(2), 210–213. https://doi.org/10.1177/0258042X211069501

De Agostini, G. (2023). Ethics and online education. *IntechOpen*. https://doi.org/10.5772/intechopen.112337. Accessed 10 Oct 2024.

Dennis, M., & Harrison, T. (2021). Unique ethical challenges for the 21st century: Online technology and virtue education. *Journal of Moral Education, 50*(3), 251–266. https://doi.org/10.1080/03057240.2020.1781071

Dreesen, Th., Akseer, S., Brossard, M., Dewan, P., Giraldo, J.-P., Kamei, A., Mizunoya, S., & Ortiz, J. S. (2020). Promising practices for equitable remote learning emerging lessons from COVID-19 education responses in 127 countries, UNICEF, Innocenti Research Briefs, https://www.unicef-irc.org/publications/1090-promising-practices-for-equitable-remote-learning-emerging-lessons-from-covid.html. Accessed 12 Mar 2024.

Faza, A., Santoso, H. B., & Putra, P. O. H. (2024). Navigating online learning challenges and opportunities: Insights from a small group of lecturers during the pandemic. *Procedia Computer Science, 234*, 1164–1174. https://doi.org/10.1016/j.procs.2024.03.112

Fredman, S. (2021). A human rights approach: The right to education in the time of COVID - 19. *Child Development, 92*, e900–e903. https://doi.org/10.1111/cdev.13654. https://srcd.onlinelibrary.wiley.com/doi/epdf/. Accessed 30 July 2024

Gaidelys, V., Čiutienė, R., Cibulskas, G., Miliauskas, S., Jukštaitė, J., & Dumčiuvienė, D. (2022). Assessing the socio-economic consequences of distance learning during the COVID-19 pandemic. *Education Sciences, 12*(10), 685. https://doi.org/10.3390/educsci12100685

Garcia, M. (Ed.). (2022). *Socioeconomic inclusion during an era of online education.* IGI Global.

Geith, C., & Vignare, K. (2008). Access to education with online learning and open educational resources: Can they close the gap? *Journal of Asynchronous Learning Networks, 12*(1) https://olj.onlinelearningconsortium.org/index.php/olj/article/view/1710. Accessed 18 Sept 2024

Gharti, L. (2023). Challenges of online learning in the post Covid-19 era: Lived experiences of Teachers in Remote Nepal. *English Language Teaching Perspectives, VIII*(1–2), 80–96. https://doi.org/10.3126/eltp.v8i1-2.57861

Han, H. J. (2020). As schools close over coronavirus, protect kids privacy in online learning, Human Rights Watch, As Schools Close Over Coronavirus, Protect Kids' Privacy in Online Learning | Human Rights Watch (hrw.org). Accessed 17 June 2024.

Hennessy, S., D'Angelo, S., McIntyre, N., Koomar, S., Kreimeia, A., Cao, L., Brugha, M., & Zubairi, A. (2022). Technology use for teacher professional development in low- and middle-income countries: A systematic review. *Computers and Education Open, 3*, 100080. https://doi.org/10.1016/j.caeo.2022.100080

Inter-agency Network for Education in Emergencies (INEE) & The Alliance for Child Protection in Humanitarian Action. (2020). Weighing up the risks: School closure and reopening under COVID-19—when, why and what impact. New York, NY. https://inee.org/resources/weighing-risks-school-closure-and-reopening-under-covid-19. Accessed 1 July 2024.

Keith, R., & Thompson, B. M. W. (2023). Challenges and instructor strategies for transitioning to online learning during and after the COVID-19 pandemic: A review of literature. *Frontiers in Communication, 8*. https://doi.org/10.3389/fcomm.2023.1260421

Labuschagne, C., Ramaila, S., & Dhurumraj, T. (2023). Investigation of the challenges in online formative assessment faced by grade 10 physical sciences teachers in south African schools. *Research in Business & Social Science (IJRBS), 12*(8). https://doi.org/10.20525/ijrbs.v12i8.2924

Liberman, J., Levin V., & Luna-Bazalduan, D. (2020). Are students still learning during COVID-19? Formative assessment can provide the answer, Worldbank Blogs, https://blogs.worldbank.org/education/are-students-still-learning-during-covid-19-formative-assessment-can-provide-answer. Accessed 15 September 2024.

Lorente, L. M., Arrabal, A. A., & Pulido-Montes, C. (2020). The right to education and ICT during COVID-19: An international perspective. *Sustainability, 12*. https://doi.org/10.3390/su12219091

Machusky, J. A., & Herbert-Berger, K. G. (2022). Understanding online learning infrastructure in U.S. K-12 schools: A review of challenges and emerging trends. *International Journal of Educational Research, 114*. https://doi.org/10.1016/j.ijer.2022.101993

Maguire, A., & McNamara, D. (2020). Human rights and the post-pandemic return to classroom education in Australia. *Alternative Law J ournal, 45*(3), 202–208.

Malenya, F. L., & Ohba, A. (2023). Equity issues in the provision of online learning during the Covid-19 pandemic in Kenya in Kazuhiro Yoshida, K. (ed.), International Cooperation in Education at the New Stage, *Journal of International Cooperation in Education, 25*(1):96–107. Emerald Publishing Limited. https://doi.org/10.1108/JICE-12-2022-0047.

Marín, V. I., & Tur, G. (2024). Ethical issues in the use of technologies in educational contexts: An overview review. *Education in the Knowledge Society (EKS), 25*, e31301. https://doi.org/10.14201/eks.31301

McFayden, T. C., Breaux, R., Bertollo, J. R., Cummings, K., & Ollendick, T. H. (2021). COVID-19 remote learning experiences of youth with neurodevelopmental disorders in rural Appalachia. *Journal of Rural Mental Health, 45*(2), 72–85. https://psycnet.apa.org/fulltext/2021-39068-002.html. Accessed 15 Aug 2024

Mehrfar, A., Zolfaghari, Z., Hejazi, Y., & Zarifsanaiey, N. (2023). Ethical principles in E-learning; investigating key issues in instructional design and teaching methods: A narrative review. *Interdisciplinary Journal in Virtual Learning in Medical Sciences, 14*(4), 251–262. https://doi.org/10.30476/ijvlms.2023.100458.1261

Mhlanga, D. (2024). Digital transformation of education, the limitations and prospects of introducing the fourth industrial revolution asynchronous online learning in emerging markets. *Discover. Education, 3*, article number 32. https://doi.org/10.1007/s44217-024-00115-9

Monteath-van Dok, A., Davis, A., & Frost, N. (2021). *Education in Crisis: Covid-19 and Adolescents' Education in fragile Contexts*, https://plan-uk.org/file/plan-girls-education-covid-reportpdf/download?token=4_Fb3ZY1. Accessed 12 July 2024.

Moorhouse, B. L., & Kohnke, L. (2022). Conducting formative assessment during synchronous online lessons: University teachers' challenges and pedagogical strategies. *Pedagogies: An International Journal, 18*(3), 431–449. https://doi.org/10.1080/1554480X.2022.2065993

Nottingham, E., Stockman, C., & Burke, M. (2022). Education in a datafied world: Balancing children's rights and school's responsibilities in the age of Covid 19. *Computer Law & Security Review, 45*, 105664. https://doi.org/10.1016/j.clsr.2022.105664

O'Dowd, R. (2018). Innovations and challenges in using online communication technologies in CLIL. *Theory Into Practice, 57*(3), 232240. https://doi.org/10.1080/00405841.2018.1484039

Paudel, P. (2020). Online education: Benefits, challenges and strategies during and after COVID-19 in higher education *in* International Journal on Studies in Education. https://api.semanticscholar.org/CorpusID:224815161. Accessed 30 Aug 2024.

Poon, P. L., & Tang, S. F. (2024). An effective teaching pedagogy involving an online learning platform under a multi-campus teaching model. *Tech Know Learn*. https://doi.org/10.1007/s10758-024-09761-2

Puiu, S., Idowu, S. O., Meghisan-Toma, G.-M., Bădîrcea, R. M., Doran, N. M., & Manta, A. G. (2023). Online education management: A multivariate analysis of students' perspectives and challenges during online classes. *Electronics, 12*, 454. https://doi.org/10.3390/electronics12020454

Roddy, C., Amiet, D.L., Chung, J., Holt, Ch., Shaw, L., McKenzie, St., Garivaldis, F., Lodge, J. M., & Mundy M. E. (2017). Applying best practice online learning, teaching, and support to intensive online environments: An integrative review. *Frontiers in Education* 2(59):1–10, https://www.frontiersin.org https://doi.org/10.3389/feduc.2017.00059/full. Accessed 16 July 2024.

Rajab, M. H., Gazal, A. M., & Alkattan, K. (2020). Challenges to online medical education during the COVID-19 pandemic. *Cureus, 12*(7), e8966. https://doi.org/10.7759/cureus.8966

Sarchiapone, F. (2021). *Rethinking the right to education*, https://www.universal-rights.org/blog/rethinking-the-right-to-education/. Accessed 31 May 2024.

Sato, S. N., Condes Moreno, E., Rubio-Zarapuz, A., Dalamitros, A. A., Yañez-Sepulveda, R., Tornero-Aguilera, J. F., & Clemente-Suárez, V. J. (2024). Navigating the new normal: adapting online and distance learning in the post-pandemic era. *Education Sciences, 14*, 19. https://doi.org/10.3390/educsci14010019

Schleicher, A. (2020). *How can teachers and school systems respond to the COVID-19 pandemic?* Some lessons from TALIS, https://oecdedutoday.com/how-teachers-school-systems-respond-coronavirus-talis/. Accessed 16 May 2024.

Sirikasemsuk, K., Leerojanaprapa, K., & Kankanit, K. (2024). Navigating online learning challenges and educational infrastructure in times of crisis: Insights and solutions among Thai engineering students utilizing a mixed-methods analysis. *Journal of Infrastructure, Policy and Development, 8*(8), 5941. https://doi.org/10.24294/jipd.v8i8.5941

Skulmowski, A. (2023). Ethical issues of educational virtual reality. *Computers & Education: X Reality, 2*. https://doi.org/10.1016/j.cexr.2023.100023

Tate, T., & Warschauer, M. (2022). Equity in online learning. *Educational Psychologist, 57*(3), 192–206. https://doi.org/10.1080/00461520.2022.2062597

Teo, T., Unwin, S., Scherer, R., & Gardiner, V. (2021). Initial teacher training for twenty-first-century skills in the fourth industrial revolution (IR 4.0): A scoping review. *Computers & Education, 170*, 104223. https://doi.org/10.1016/j.compedu.2021.104223

Terway, A., & Avelar, M. (2020). COVID-19 education disruption and the response by the global education community, Network for International Policies and Cooperation in Education and Training, https://www.norrag.org/covid-19-education-disruption-and-the-response-by-the-global-education-community-by-arushi-terway-and-marina-avelar/. Accessed 12 Sept 2024.

Turner, R., Webb, O., & Pritchard, C. (2023). ‘A freedom of students to choose’: Student and staff perspectives on the future role of online learning in higher education. *Innovations in Education and Teaching International, 61*(26), 1164–1183. https://doi.org/10.1080/14703297.2023.2292074

Uzorka, A. (2024). Perspectives on online education in higher education. *International Journal of Technology in Education and Science (IJTES), 8*(1), 111–120. https://doi.org/10.46328/ijtes.523

Yeh, C.-Y., & Tsai, C.-C. (2022). Massive distance education: Barriers and challenges in shifting to a complete online learning environment. *Frontiers in Psychology, 13.* https://doi.org/10.3389/fpsyg.2022.928717

Zdravkov, S. (2024). Exploring socio-economic disparities in E-learning: A study of Bulgarian students' online educational experiences. *Open Journal of Social Sciences, 12*, 380–396. https://doi.org/10.4236/jss.2024.124026

Further Reading

XXX (2021a). *Education: From disruption to recovery*, UNESCO, ttps://en.unesco.org/covid19/educationresponse. (accessed 1 July 2024).

XXX (2021b). NO EDUCATION, NO PROTECTION. What school closures under COVID-19 mean for children and young people in crisis-affected contexts, inter-agency Network for education in emergencies, The Alliance for Child Protection in Humanitarian Action, https://inee.org/system/files/resources/CPHA-EiE%20Evidence%20Paper%20-%20No%20Education%20No%20Protection%20v1.1%20LowRes.pdf. (accessed 12 August 2024).

XXX (2021c). *Problems with education around the world during Covid-19*, Human Rights Watch, https://www.hrw.org/sites/default/files/media_2021/05/global_covideducation0521_ETR.pdf. (accessed 26 July 2024).

XXX (2021d). *Statement on COVID-19 and social rights*, European Committee of Social Rights, https://rm.coe.int/statement-of-the-ecsr-on-covid-19-and-social-rights/1680a230ca. (accessed 10 July 2024).

XXX (2020a). *COVID-19: States should not abuse emergency measures to suppress human rights*, United Nations Human Rights, https://ohchr.org/EN/NewsEvents/Pages/Display News.aspx?NewsID=25722&LangID=E. (accessed 27 August 2024).

XXX (2020b). Crearea unor sisteme de educaţie reziliente în contextul pandemiei de COVID-19: Considerente pentru factorii de decizie de la nivel naţional, local şi de unitate şcolară, UNICEF, Biroul Regional UNICEF pentru Europa şi Asia Centrală, Geneva, Elveţia.

XXX (2020c). *Educational inequalities in Europe and physical school closures during Covid-19*, Fairness Policy Brief Series: 04/2020, https://ec.europa.eu/jrc/sites/default/files/fairness_pb2020_wave04_covid_education_jrc_i1_19jun2020.pdf. (accessed 25 May 2024).

XXX (2020d). *EU neighbours: coping with COVID-19 in education and training*, Europian Training Foundation, https://www.etf.europa.eu/en/news-and-events/news/eu-neighbours-coping-covid-19-education-and-training. (accessed 15 May 2024).

XXX (2020e). *Global Covid-19 Response*, Situation Report No. 6, Save the children, https://resourcecentre.savethechildren.net/pdf/save_the_children_global_covid-19_situation_report_6.pdf. (accessed 2 September 2024).

XXX (2020f). *Guiding principles on the COVID-19 pandemic*, Education International, https://www.ei-ie.org/en/item/23276:guiding-principles-on-the-covid-19-pandemic. (accessed 12 September 2024)..

XXX (2020g). *Human Rights Dimensions of COVID-19 Response*, Human Rights Watch, https://www.hrw.org/news/2020/03/19/human-rights-dimensions-covid-19-response. (accessed 16 July 2024).

XXX Save the Children (2020). *LEARNING MUST GO ON: Recommendations for keeping children safe and learning, during and after the COVID-19 crisis*, Save the Children, UNICEF, INEE, Plan International, Learning must go on, COVID-19 advocacy brief_v20200409.pdf (inee.org). (accessed 18 August 2024).

XXX (2020h). *Making the Right to Education a Reality in Times of Covid-19*, A Roadmap for Action on the Council of Europe education response to COVID-19, Council of Europe, https://rm.coe.int/making-the-right-to-education-a-reality-in-times-of-covid-19-a-roadmap/16809fee7b. (accessed 14 July 2024).

XXX (2020i). *Policy Brief: Education during COVID-19 and beyond*, United Nations, https://www.un.org/development/desa/dspd/wp-content/uploads/sites/22/2020/08/sg_policy_brief_covid-19_and_education_august_2020.pdf. (accessed 12 September 2024).

XXX (2020j). Policy brief: The impact of Covid-19 on children, United Nations, https://unsdg.un.org/sites/default/files/2020-04/160420CovidChildrenPolicyBrief.pdf. (accessed 5 May 2024).

XXX Romania's Council of Students (2020). *Raport privind accesul elevilor la educatie în mediul online*, https://consiliulelevilor.ro/wp-content/uploads/2020/04/Raport-privind-accesul-elevilor-la-educa%C8%9Bie-%C3%AEn-mediul-online.pdf. (accessed 2 May 2024).

XXX (2020k). Opinia elevilor cu privire la educația on-line și efectele perioadei de izolare, Salvați copiii, București, https://www.salvaticopiii.ro/sci-ro/files/d3/d376f652-4ed3-43cc-8947-347265fe6e7e.pdf. (accessed 8 July 2024).

XXX (2020l). ***Protecting and Transforming Education for Shared Futures and Common Humanity, A Joint Statement on the COVID-19 Crisis*, International Commission on the Futures of Education,** A Joint Statement on the COVID-19 Crisis . (accessed 9 September 2024).

XXX (2020m). *Right to education: impact of the COVID-19 crisis on the right to education; concerns, challenges and opportunities*, Human Rights Council, https://www.ohchr.org/EN/Issues/Education/SREducation/Pages/COVID19.aspx. (accessed 29 September 2024).

XXX (2020n). *Strategia privind digitalizarea educației din România [Strategy on the digitization of education in Romania]*, Ministerul Educației și Cercetării, https://www.edu.ro/strategia-de-digitalizare-educa%C8%9Biei-din-rom%C3%A2nia-2021-2027-smart-edu-lansat%C4%83-%C3%AEn-consultare-public%C4%83. (accessed 18 September 2024).

XXX (2020o). The day after tomorrow: Confronting systemic injustices, Advancing Human Rights, ESCR-Net Global, https://www.escr-net.org/news/2020/escr-net-global-call-action-response-covid-19. (accessed 9 October 2024).

XXX (2020p). UNESCO COVID-19 education response: How many students are at risk of not returning to school? *Advocacy paper*, UNESCO, UNESCO COVID-19 education response: How many students are at risk of not returning to school? Advocacy paper - UNESCO Digital Library. (accessed 8 September 2024).

XXX Save the Children Romania (2019). *Convenția cu privire la Drepturile copilului*, București, https://www.salvaticopiii.ro/ce-facem/drepturile-copilului/conventia-onu-cu-privire-la-drepturile-copilului. (accessed 1 October 2024).

XXX (2004). *Legea nr. 272/2004* privind protecția și promovarea drepturilor copilului, http://www.mmuncii.ro/j33/images/Documente/Legislatie/L272-2004-R.pdf. (accessed 26 October 2024).

XXX (1990/2001). *Convenția cu privire la drepturile copilului, Legea nr. 18/1990*, publicată în Monitorul Oficial al României, partea I, nr. 109 din 28 septembrie 1990 și republicată în Monitorul Oficial al României, partea I, nr. 314 din 13 iunie 2001, https://anitp.mai.gov.ro/ro/docs/legislatie/18_1990.pdf. (accessed 28 September 2024).

XXX (1959). Convenția Națiunilor Unite cu privire la Drepturile Copilului, UNICEF.

XXX (n.d.). *Declarația drepturilor copilului*, Salvați copiii, https://www.salvaticopiii.ro/sci-ro/files/32/327ef3da-c4d0-4fff-9f76-8cbcd20fa8c1.pdf. (accessed 2 October 2024).

Chapter 3
The Current Status of Gamification Knowledge Among Romanian Teachers: An Exploratory Approach

Alina Ionescu-Corbu, Andreea Ursu, and Gabriel Cramariuc

Abstract Gamification is viewed as an educational approach that could lead to an increased academic performance through applying game-like elements in a learning context in order to promote the acquisition of knowledge, skills, and attitudes. Despite the growing interest related to gamification, there are still considerable inconsistencies related to this concept. This chapter extends the gamification research area by offering an overview of teachers' gamification knowledge, gamification principles, and usage of gamification principles in the teaching-learning process. Two hundred and seven k-12 school teachers (91% women), aged between 18 and 61 years old, with a mean of teaching experience of 8.68 ($SD = 9.52$, range from a few months of experience to 42 years of experience) defined gamification, described the principles of gamification and answered to scales measuring gamification knowledge, the representativity of some principles in gamification approaches, and the usage of gamification principles during their teaching in the past 2 years. The results of the deductive qualitative analyses showed that gamification was defined by using five themes and the data provided by participants were coded in seven gamification principles. Related to the quantitative approach, no significant differences were found in terms of gamification knowledge level, representativity of some educational principles to gamification, and principles' gamification usage depending on various teachers' socio-demographic characteristics. Finally, we concluded by highlighting the current status of gamification among k-12 school teachers, suggested several future research directions concerning gamification in educational contexts and presented the practical implications of these results.

A. Ionescu-Corbu · A. Ursu (✉) · G. Cramariuc
Gamification Lab, Faculty of Psychology and Sciences of Education, Ştefan cel Mare University of Suceava, Suceava, Romania
e-mail: andreea.ursu@usm.ro

I. Boghian, G. Mareş (eds.), *Gamification and Inclusion*, Inclusive Learning and Educational Equity 12, https://doi.org/10.1007/978-3-031-98390-0_3

Introduction

Incorporating new instructional strategies in the teaching process has become a priority in the last years, especially since technology advances occupy an important role not only in everyday life, but also in education. Given the impact technology may have on pupils' and teachers' experiences throughout their education cycle and the investigated benefits of such practices on learning outcomes, over the last few years, technology oriented instructional strategies have become more and more valuable. Gamification is one of these educational approaches. On a general level, gamification consists of using gaming principles, game mechanics, and game characteristics in non-gaming domains (Deterding et al., 2011; Robson et al., 2015). Despite the growing interest in how gamification can be used in education, which are the predictors of gamification usage, and which are the effects on teachers' and students' outcomes, there are still inconsistencies related to this concept. For instance, a less focused area is represented by investigating and understanding teachers' knowledge about gamification and its principles. Thus, this chapter aims to extend the gamification research area by offering an overview of teachers' gamification knowledge, gamification principles, and usage of gamification principles in the teaching-learning process.

The introduction section is organized in four sections. Firstly, we will give a brief overview of the technology, digitalization, and their effects on educational outcomes. In the second section we will present the current understanding of gamification and a specific approach previously used "Technological Pedagogical Content Knowledge" (TPCK) (Mishra & Koehler, 2006). In the third section we will summarize the principles proposed to be applied in order to make gamification more efficient, the guidelines to use when designing gamified classes. Additionally, we will also highlight the most used game elements in education. Finally, in the last section of introduction, we will present the rational of this study and its objectives.

Technology and Digitalization in Educational Contexts

Digitalization itself led to a series of changed perceptions about how the learning process should be adapted. For example, most students accommodated computerized learning by themselves by using their personal computers, smartphones, and tablets in the learning process. Some authors view this process of linking technology resources with learning as *connected learning* (Figg & Jaipal-Jamani, 2018). Moreover, since the number of internet young users is increasing around the globe and gaming is the most popular activity for this age category (Clement, 2023), it is possible that their expectations regarding learning is also changing, making gamification a helpful tool in teaching contexts. For instance, a recent study showed that gamer students had better performances in computer-based assessments for reading compared to non-gamers, while their outcomes for printed reading tasks were lower (Borgonovi, 2016). In addition, Recabarren and colleagues (2021) found that gamification has positive outcomes in both gamer and non-gamer students in terms of motivation and performance, but non-gamer students might report less satisfaction with gamification over time. These observations led to an increased interest in investigating the benefits of gamification in educational contexts. In one of the most recent meta-analysis, Bai et al. (2020) showed that introducing gamification in the learning process contributes to better academic performances, but these results had various effect sizes depending on the sample size and the duration of the intervention, shorter periods resulting in higher effect sizes. With regard to the teachers' behavioral and intentional use of gamification in the classroom, some studies showed that this is mediated by attitudes towards gamification, on one hand, and having enough information on the topic on the other hand (Sajinčič et al., 2022). Additionally, other studies on Romanian teachers showed that technology proficiency and perceived usefulness of gamification partially mediated the link between Romanian k-12 inservice teachers' self-efficacy and their behavioral intention to use gamification (Cramariuc et al., 2023).

Identifying the level of knowledge about gamification might lead to better teacher training and contribute to promoting the use of more diverse approaches in the teaching-learning process. Some authors also argue that in order to use gamification more efficiently in the classroom, teachers need to gain a more profound understanding of the term with regard to knowledge on and principles of gamification (Mishra & Koehler, 2006). Thus, in this chapter we guided our investigation on the current definitions of gamification in an attempt to better understand the level of knowledge teachers in Romania have on the definition and principles of this concept.

Defining Gamification

Despite the increased interest in gamified approaches in the literature, there is still confusion on what teachers understand by using game designs in the teaching process. There are different ways in which academics refer to gamification. A comprehensive framework of gamification, "Technological Pedagogical Content Knowledge" (TPCK), is presented by Mishra and Koehler (2006) and it poses three main components—content, technology use, and pedagogical elements—that lead to the development of skills and attitudes related to learning in various teaching subjects. In spite of the existing model, definitions of gamification in the literature are rather heterogenous. Previous research papers present gameful approaches in education as gamification, game-based learning, and digital game-based learning (Bacsa-Károlyi & Fehérvári, 2024). In game-based learning, teachers use games to promote learning (Bálint-Svella, 2021) without making the game a central part of the teaching process. Similarly to game-based learning, digital game-based learning refers to introducing a digital game in the teaching process (Leonardou et al., 2021), while, in their well-known definition, Deterding et al. (2011) refer to gamification as engaging individuals in a game-like design and mechanics in a non-game situation. More specifically, in the educational context, teachers use the game elements and mechanics to design one or more teaching activities (Dicheva et al., 2015), which would lead to increased motivation in students (Sailer et al., 2017).

Features and Principles of Gamification

In designing any gamified activity, the literature proposes a set of principles that may be applied in order to make it more efficient. Previous studies suggested that badges, challenges, ranks, levels, storyline, points, progress bar, and teams are the most used game elements and principles in education (Asiri, 2019; Giannetto et al., 2013; Huang & Hew, 2018; Richter et al., 2015; Robson et al., 2015; Sailer et al., 2017). In a summarized manner, Zichermann and Cunningham (2011) propose six guidelines that could be followed when designing such an activity, defining the prize and what it means for a specific learning context, promoting the development of intrinsic motivation through the development of autonomy in the learning process, boosting the emotional engagement in the activity, developing of scalable and meaningful rewards, using platforms, and promoting learning through entertainment. Similarly, in one of the most recent papers, Aminovna (2024) describes some features that gamification may have in the educational context such as (a) gaining knowledge in a more accessible way through consulting online resources; (b) improving transferable skills like communication, public speaking, teamwork, creativity cooperation, and competitivity; and (c) developing positive attitudes towards learning such as active learning and critical thinking.

Based on previous mentioned principles, we proposed the following principles to be used in our qualitative analysis.

(a) Feedback is offered by gamified systems when a player fails to gain the required points and has to repeat a particular function without fear of failure.
(b) Gamification allows players to adopt different roles (leader, wizzard, nurse, warrior, healer).
(c) Gamification allows players reward each other with virtual currency or points.
(d) Gamification allows students to monitor each other's performance on a leaderboard.
(e) Gamification has a positive impact on students' motivation and offers individualized and meaningful feedback on errors.
(f) Gamification encourages students' participation in classroom activities.

Rational for the Current Study Objectives

Previous qualitative research on Education Sciences students (teachers to be) stated that over 50% of the participants correctly defined gamification after being exposed to information on this topic before completing the knowledge scales (Bálint-Svella, 2021). Moreover, Nate and colleagues (2022) found that the interest in participating in continuous professional development, especially trainings regarding the use of technology, decreased with age and experience. This could lead to a gap in their knowledge and abilities about modern teaching approaches in the classroom. In order to better assess the level of knowledge about and promote the use of gamification by teachers in their classrooms, it is necessary to investigate and understand what is the information they possess on gamification. Thus, while there is data on what students know about this approach, less is known about the representation of gamification from the Romanian teachers' perspective. In order to cover this gap, we proposed the following main research questions:

1. What is the current status of gamification knowledge among Romanian k12-school teachers?
   (a) Do k-12 school teachers know how to define gamification?
   (b) Do k-12 school teachers know which are the gamification' principles?
   (c) Descriptive analyses on teachers' responses for gamification knowledge level
2. Are there any differences related to the level of gamification knowledge, representativity of some educational principles to gamification and principles' gamification usage depending on various socio-demographic characteristics?
   (a) The socio-demographic characteristics taken into account are teaching experience, school level of teaching (with four possible answers: kindergarten, primary school, secondary and high school) and the area where the school is located (with two possible answers: rural and urban area)

Method

Participants

A part of participants and procedure are the same as described in Cramariuc et al. (2023). The relevant information is repeated here. Participants consisted of two hundred seven k-12 school teachers (91% women), aged between 18 and 61 years old (M = 35.13, SD = 9.76), with a mean of teaching experience of 8.68 (SD = 9.52, range from a few months of experience to 42 years of experience). Forty-six percent of teachers were teaching in schools located in rural areas. Sixty-five percent of participants were teaching at kindergarten and primary levels.

Procedure

K-12 school teachers were invited to participate in a larger study aiming to investigate the current status of gamification. All participants voluntarily participated in this study. All scales were filled out online. The protocol of the study was approved by the Ethical Committee of Ştefan cel Mare, University of Suceava (86/08.09.2022).

Measures

All scales were developed by the authors of the present chapter based on the current understanding of gamification, its characteristics, and principles. The scales investigated participants` initial knowledge of and use of gamification and the respective principles through open questions. We also adapted the scales to investigate the most representative gamification principles and characteristics by integrating the present understanding of gamification (Asiri, 2019; Dicheva et al., 2015; Çeker & Özdaml, 2017; Robson et al., 2015). For the gamification principles section of the questionnaire, we asked participants to evaluate the extent to which six principles are representative for the use of the gamified approaches in education on a 7-point Likert scale. Examples of items are "Gamification allows students to adopt different roles (leader, wizzard, nurse, warrior, healer); Gamification allows students to monitor each other's performance on a leader board." The Cronbach's alpha of the scale in this study was 0.85. For the characteristics section we used true, false and I don't know choices and we invited k-12 school teachers to evaluate six items. Example of items "Gamification gives students the opportunity to collaborate with their classmates while performing their assigned task; Gamification is a modern teaching-learning method." The Cronbach's alpha of the scale in this study was 0.63. We also assessed teachers` gamification principles usage in the classroom in the past 2 years on a Likert scale from 0 (Never) to 6 (Always— almost every day) by adapting the principles of gamification scale. This scale consists of six items. Examples of items are "I provided quick feedback to students during the teaching activity (without grading) in order to help them to acquire knowledge without fear of failure", "I created game situations where students were able to monitor each other's performance on a leaderboard in real time." The Cronbach's alpha of the scale in this study was 0.94.

Approach for Data Analysis

In order to analyze the content of participants responses for the two open-ended questions which assessed the teachers' knowledge related to the definition of gamification and its principles, deductive analysis (McKibben et al., 2020) was used.

Various theoretical approaches were used to define gamification. For instance, Deterding et al. (2011) defined gamification as the usage of gaming principles and game mechanics in non-game domains. Later on, Su and Cheng (2015) extended this definition by adding the aim, which consists of engaging people and solving current problems. In educational contexts, gamification was conceptualized as including feature and game-experiences into the teaching and learning process in any study domain. Besides promoting and facilitating learning, it also aims to help students to acquire transversal soft-skills and positive attitude towards education and society in general (Caponettol et al., 2014; Dicheva et al., 2015; Zichermann & Cunningham, 2011). Based on these definitions, the first and the second author proposed five categories (see Table 3.1). Additionally, we also provided definitions for these categories and we identified examples. This set of categories with its related definitions and examples was discussed with all authors. The resulting coding schema was then employed by two coders (first and second author, native Romanians, Psychology university teachers) to independently categorize the open-ended data. The inter-rater reliability, Cohen's kappa was 0.83. According to Cohen (1960), the inter-rater agreement is almost perfect.

Related to gamification principles, six categories were proposed (see Table 3.3) based on previously mentioned game elements and principles in the literature. The same procedure was employed for coding the data collected related to gamification principles. The inter-rater reliability, Cohen's kappa was 0.92. According to Cohen (1960) the inter-rater agreement is almost perfect.

Results and Discussions

Qualitative Data

Firstly, we will present the coding schema for each open-ended question (definition and principles), separately. This general overview of the identified themes for defining gamification and the identification of its principles, including responses coded as "I don't know," "other," or "no answer" revealed to us if the themes were sufficiently comprehensive to capture participants knowledge related to gamification. Secondly, we will focus on the content of the responses within each theme.

Definition of Gamification Provided by K-12 School Teachers

Validity of Coding Schema The open-data items assessing k-12 school teachers knowledge related to the definition of gamification were coded in 5 categories. Over 69% of responses were codable into one of these categories displayed in Table 3.1. The rest, 22% of data was coded as follows: 18% of responses were coded in "*other*"

Table 3.1 Coding schema of definitions of gamification: category definitions and examples extracted from previous theories, examples provided by teachers and frequencies and percentages

Theme definition/e.g.	Examples from teachers	Frequency and percentages
Features and game-like experiences into the learning process Mentioning any type of game elements or mechanics E.g.: *game elements*	"Prezența caracteristicilor jocului în activități care nu sunt considerate în mod tradițional și implică în prealabil jocurile pe calculator și realizări online care se pot aplica în procesul de predare-învățare." "Proiectarea situațiilor de învățare intr-un mod asemănător unui joc." ("The presence of game-like characteristics in activities that are not traditionally considered and involve prior computer games and online achievements that can be applied in the teaching-learning process." "Design learning situations in a game-like way.)	14 (7%)
Learning context Linking the learning context with games E.g.: *learning through games, using games to promote learning*	"Jocul în procesul de învățare, predare și evaluare" "Învățare prin joc" "Introducerea jocului în activitatea de învățare" "Folosirea jocurilor video ca strategii didactice" ("Game used in learning, teaching and assessment process" "Learning using game (by playing)" "Using game in learning process" "Using videogames as didactic strategies")	92 (45%)
Knowledge Mentioning any type of knowledge as an outcome E.g.: *Promoting knowledge*	"Modalitate de dobândire a cunoștințelor prin joc," "Introducerea jocurilor video ca metode de transmitere/ consolidare/dobandire a informatiilor, respectiv abilitatilor". "Acquiring knowledge through play", "Introducing video games as a way of transmitting/consolidating/teaching information and skills".	11 (5%)
Transversal soft-skills Mentioning any type of skill as an outcome E.g.: *Promoting team-work*	"Creativitatea și eficacitatea jocului în procesul de predare/ învățare/ evaluare," "Extindere, flexibilitate" "Creativity and effectiveness of play in teaching learning/ assessment", "Expansion, flexibility"	13 (6%)
Attitudes Mentioning any type of attitude as an outcome E.g.: *Promoting positive attitudes towards learning*	"Inovator," "Muncă și distracție," "Atractivizarea procesului de învățare prin joc" "Innovating", "Work and fun", "Making learning through play engaging"	13 (6%)
Almost good enough Answers that partially fall under the construct of gamification E.g.: *game*	"Joc" "Utilizarea jocurilor" "Jocuri folosing tehnologia" "Game", "Using games", "Game using technology"	19 (9%)

theme. Responses such as "I don't know, what is that" represented 3% of responses and were coded in "*I don't know*" theme. Spaces or lines were coded in "*no answer*" and represented 1% of data. We found another interesting category, "*almost good enough.*" In this theme, we coded all the answers mentioning the word "game" and 9% of data was grouped here.

Quantitative and Qualitative Analysis: Percentages and Content

As presented in Table 3.1, the most frequent theme is "*learning contexts,*" 45 percent of data being coded here. In this theme, answers such as mentioning game and learning, game and education, using game for enhancing students' learning, using game in the learning process, teaching and assessment process, using videogames as didactic strategies were coded. These results may be interpreted as k-12 school teachers think that gamification and game-based learning is the same. However, we do not think this. According to Al-Azawi et al. (2016) gamification supposes that the whole learning process is organized as a game, while game-based learning consists of using games during the teaching-learning process. Thus, we believe that k-12 school teachers are more aware of this component of gamification' definition.

Related to the other components of gamification definition, (a) using features and game like-experiences during the learning-teaching process, (b) using gamification to facilitate knowledge, (c) to develop transversal soft-skills and (d) to promote positive attitudes towards learning, the percents were quite similar ranging from 5% to 7% each. For instance, answers such as game-like characteristics in activities that are not traditionally considered and involve prior computer games and online achievements that can be applied in the teaching-learning process, designing learning situations in a game-like way, or using ranks, badges or different roles in teaching process were coded in the theme "*features and game like-experiences*" during the learning-teaching process and it consists of seven percent.

Based on previous theoretical approaches, "*learning contexts*" and "*features and game like-experiences*" are the most important components of gamification definitions (Caponettol et al., 2014; Dicheva et al., 2015) and were also the most frequent themes presented by k-12 school teachers from Romania. Thus, it is worthy to mention that k-12 school teachers identified in a high percent these two fundamental elements of gamification definition. Furthermore, these results are similar to the results of another study conducted in Romania with primary teachers with Hungarian ethnic background as participants where it was showed that gamification was understood as using activities in which teams of students collect points during the class, using different scoring systems in order to determine the final grade of students or leisure activities with specific rules explained to students and rewards offered to students (Hari & Zsoldos-Marchis, 2020).

In the third theme, named "*knowledge,*" answers such as acquiring knowledge through play, introducing video games as a way of transmitting/ consolidating/ teaching information and skills were coded. All these answers consist of five percent. Similar results were provided by the study conducted by Hari and Zsoldos-Marchis (2020) also with Romanian teachers with Hungarian ethnic background where it was showed that gamification can be used in order to acquire new knowledge.

Furthermore, answers such as creativity and effectiveness of play in teaching, learning or assessment, being imaginative and flexible in teaching and learning in order to develop transversal skills to students such as being creative, flexible, and imaginative skills were coded "*transversal soft-skills.*" These answers consisted of six percent. Finally, answers such as innovator, engaging, realizing tasks, and enjoying the time were coded in the last theme named "*attitudes.*" It was already suggesting that gamification besides promoting and facilitating learning, it also aims to help students to acquire transversal soft-skills and positive attitude towards education and society in general (Caponettol et al., 2014; Dicheva et al., 2015; Martí-Parreño et al., 2021). Thus, although these answers and the themes associated with them have been reported at a low percent, they still suggest that k-12 school teachers are aware of the potential offered by the use of gamification in education.

Additionally, in order to have a more standardized measure for the knowledge section on gamification, teachers were asked to answer to seven items regarding this topic on a three-option response set with the following options: *True, False,* and *I don't know.* For data analysis all *False* and *I don't know* answers were treated as *false* and rated with 0, while all *True* answers were treated as correct and rated with 1. Table 3.2 summarizes the percentages of correct answers for each item for the gamification knowledge scale.

As shown in Table 3.2, more than half of the teachers correctly rated each of the seven items on gamification knowledge. The results show that most teachers know that gamification has a game-like component incorporated in the teaching process (88.4%); most teachers agree on the innovative feature of gamification (86.5%); teachers correctly recognized the collaborative feature of gamification (84.5%), while also allowing students to take care of their tasks (83.1%) and maintaining a high level of autonomy in the learning process (73.9%). On the other hand, only slightly over half of participants used gamification related applications in the

Table 3.2 Percentage of correct answers per Gamification Knowledge item

Item	N	% of correct answers/item
1. Gamification provides the opportunity for learners to engage with their classmates while executing their assigned task.	210	83.1
2. Gamification provides the opportunity for learners to collaborate with their classmates while executing their assigned task.	210	84.5
3. Have you ever used teaching website as Kahoot, Menti?	210	55.6
4. Gamification offers autonomy to students.	210	73.9
5. Gamification is an innovative method used in the teaching-learning process.	210	86.5
6. Gamification uses game elements and game designs.	210	56.0
7. Gamification refers to the transfer of a usual learning context in a game-like situation.	210	88.4

classroom (55.6%) and a similar percent of participants correctly recognized the main characteristics of gamification, namely that it uses game elements and designs (56.0).

Qualitative Analysis

Gamification Principles Provided by K-12 School Teachers

Validity of Coding Schema The open-data items assessing k-12 school teachers knowledge related to gamification principles were coded in 6 initial categories. However, both coders independently thought that the same new theme related to objectives and rules should be added. Firstly, they coded the data using the initial six themes. However, after they met and discussed the differences they decided to code one more time the data, using the seventh proposed themes. Over 41% of responses were codable into one of the categories displayed in Table 3.3. The theme with the highest frequency was the "*irrelevant,*" with a percent of 44, were answers related to how gamification is defined were coded. Responses such as "I don't know" represented 8% of responses and were coded in "*I don't know*" theme. Spaces or lines were coded in "*no answer*" and represented 7% of data. These percents may suggest that Romanian k-12 school teachers are aware that they may not know the specific principles of gamification. However, as it can be seen, a medium percent of data (41%) was relevant for the question being asked related to the gamification principle.

Quantitative and Qualitative Analysis: Percentages and Content The theme with the higher percent, 17%, was the one related to the fact that using gamification motivates students to engage more in teaching activities. This principle was previously mentioned as "*Gamification encourages students' participation in classroom activities.*" Answers related to the students' actively involving in activities during the teaching-learning process, motivation challenge principles, collaboration, and cooperation, maintaining students' attention and focus during classes were coded in this theme. A similar pattern of results was suggested by Hari and Zsoldos-Marchis (2020), where Romanian teachers with Hungarian ethnic background reported that gamification maintains or increase students' involvement and motivation for learning.

The following most frequent theme was the one named "*Gamification supposes rules and aims specific to games*" and nine percent of data were coded here. Teachers' answers related to the fact that gamification supposes rules and aims such as "respecting rules," "proposing objective rules," "all games have rules," and "tasks well-structured and formulated" were coded in this theme. In the third most frequent theme, named "*Gamification allows players reward each other with virtual currency or points,*" eight percent of data was coded. Answers related to rewards, rewards principles, surprised discovering, surprised rewards, learning by using rewards and points of badges were coded in this theme. Similar results were reported by Gibson et al. (2015) suggesting using digital badges in education encourages students to have positive behaviors at during classes and in breaks.

Table 3.3 Coding schema of gamification principles: category definitions and examples extracted from previous theories, examples provided by teachers, frequencies and percentages

Principle of gamification	Examples from teachers	Frequency and percentages
Feedback is offered by gamified systems when a player fails to gain the required points and has to repeat a particular function without fear of failure.	"Feedback după fiecare sarcină, elemente de distracție," "feedback imediat," "Oferirea de feedback imediat după fiecare sarcină" "Feedback after every task, fun elements", "immediate feedback", "Giving feedback immediately after each task"	7 (3%)
Gamification allows players to adopt different roles (leader, wizzard, nurse, warrior, healer).	"Rol," "Joc de rol" "Role," "role-play"	2 (1%)
Gamification allows players reward each other with virtual currency or points.	"Principiul recompensei," "recompensă," "recompensă neaşteptată" "The reward principle," "reward," "unexpected reward"	15 (8%)
Gamification allows students to monitor each other's performance on a leaderboard.	"Puncte, clasament," "Principiul din spatele gamificării este de a utiliza dinamica şi mecanica jocului: puncte de acumulat, nivele de atins" "Points, ranking", "The principle behind gamification is to use game dynamics and mechanics: points to accumulate, levels to reach"	7(3%)
Gamification has a positive impact on students' motivation and offers individualized and meaningful feedback on errors.		0 (0%)
Gamification encourages students' participation in classroom activities.	"Motivarea învățării," "Asigurarea unei dinamici care sa mărească implicarea elevilor," "Participarea elevilor activ la toate activitatile" "Motivating learning", "Providing a dynamic to increase student involvement", "Active student participation in all activities"	34 (17%)
Gamification supposes rules and aims specific to games.	"Respectarea unor reguli," "Stabilirea de obiective," "Ghidarea elevilor spre anumite obiective," "Comunicarea corectă şi concretă a regulilor" "Following certain rules", "Setting objectives", "Guiding students towards specific goals", "Correct and concrete communication of the rules"	18 (9%)

Based on "*Gamification allows students to monitor each other's performance on a leaderboard*" principle and on "*Feedback is offered by gamified systems when a player fails to gain the required points and has to repeat a particular function without fear of failure*" principle, we proposed the fourth and the fifth theme to code k-12 school teachers responses. Six percent of data, three percent for each theme, was coded. Specifically, responses related to performance, ranking, ranks, levels to be reached were coded in "*Gamification allows students to monitor each other's performance on a leaderboard.*" Additionally, responses related to feedback after each task, immediate feedback, offering feedback were coded in "*Gamification allows students to monitor each other's performance on a leaderboard*" theme. Two more themes were used in the schema coding, "*Gamification allows players to adopt different roles (leader, wizzard, nurse, warrior, healer)*" and "*Gamification has a positive impact on students' motivation and offers individualized and meaningful feedback on errors.*" We coded one percent of data in the theme related to possible roles that students can have when teachers use gamification during teaching-learning process. Finally, no data was coded in the last theme.

One of the aims of the study conducted with Romanian primary school teachers with Hungarian ethnic background was to identify the positive aspects of gamification. These positive aspects are very similar to the principles previously identified by us. For instance, increasing students' intrinsic motivation, activating learners, instant feedback, and continuous rewards are the positive aspects related to gamification reported to have the higher means (Hari & Zsoldos-Marchis, 2020). Moreover, in the same study, teachers were asked when they use successfully gamification. The majority of them, 55%, reported that they use gamification for a specific given task during teaching a lesson. The rest, 21% and 19% of primary teachers, reported that they use gamification during the whole educational process for facilitating the acquisition of new knowledge.

Main Quantitative Analyses

We also aimed to investigate whether there will be differences related to the level of gamification knowledge, representativity of various educational principles to gamification and principles' gamification usage depending on some socio-demographic characteristics such as teaching experience, school level of teaching (with four possible answers: kindergarten, primary school, secondary and high school), and the area where the school is located (with two possible answers: rural and urban area). For teaching experience, we created a new variable with 3 categories: debutant teachers (with 1 year experience), teachers with teaching experience between 2 and 9 years ($M = 8.67$, $SD = 9.54$), and experienced teachers (teachers who had taught for more than 9 years).

In order to test these hypotheses, one-way ANOVA and t test for independent samples were used. The descriptive statistics for the variables used for these analyses are presented in Table 3.4.

Table 3.4 Means and standard deviation for one-way ANOVA and independent *t* test

	Teaching experience						School level of teaching								School area location			
	Debutant teachers		Average experience teachers		Experienced teachers		Kindergarten		Primary school		Secondary school		High school		Rural		Urban	
	M	*SD*	*M*	*SD*	*M*	*SD*	*M*	*SD*	*M*	*SD*	*M*	*SD*	*M*	*SD*	*M*	*SD*	*M*	*SD*
Gamification knowledge	0.72	0.22	0.75	0.24	0.71	0.27	0.70	0.27	0.75	0.23	0.75	0.24	0.69	0.27	0.73	0.24	0.72	0.26
Representativity of various educational principles to gamification	5.93	0.85	5.94	1.02	5.94	0.98	5.67	1.09	6.09	0.84	6.00	1.06	6.24	0.56	5.94	0.99	5.93	0.99
Principles' gamification usage	3.74	1.52	3.85	1.55	3.58	1.47	3.85	1.60	4.00	1.47	3.43	1.48	3.24	1.52	3.60	1.56	3.86	1.48

The results of one-way ANOVA show no differences in terms of gamification knowledge (F(2, 204) = 0.641, $p = 0.52$); representativity of various educational principles to gamification (F(2, 204) = 0.003, $p = 0.99$); gamification principles usage (F(2, 204) = 607, $p = 0.54$) depending on teachers' experience (as all $p > 0.05$).

A significant p was found between school level of teaching for gamification principles, (F(3, 203) = 2.877, p = 0.03), while no other significant differences were found between teachers based on the school level where they teach for gamification knowledge (F(3, 203) = 0.783, p = 0.50) and principles' gamification usage (F(3, 203) = 2.114, p = 0.10). However, the results of Bonferroni Post Hoc Tests indicate that there are no significant differences between school level of teaching as all $p > 0.05$ ($p = 0.08$, $p = 0.39$, $p = 0.19$) for gamification principles. Furthermore, no differences were found in terms of gamification knowledge ($t(205) = 1.81, p = 0.85$), representativity of various educational principles to gamification ($t(205) = 0.090$, $p = 0.92$) and principles' gamification usage ($t(205) = -1.23, p = 0.21$) based on the area were schools are located ($p > 0.05$).

Conclusions

The primary aims of this chapter were (a) to revise the current status of gamification knowledge among Romanian k12-school teachers and (b) to analyze whether there any differences related to the level of gamification knowledge, representativity of some educational principles to gamification and principles' gamification usage depending on various socio-demographic characteristics. In order to achieve these aims, we used a mixed approach. Firstly, we used a deductive thematic approach for identifying, analyzing, and reporting themes based on k-12 school teachers' knowledge about gamification definitions and gamification principles. Secondly, we analyzed the quantitative data related to gamification aspects. More precisely, we aimed to investigate whether there will be differences related to the level of gamification knowledge, representativity of some educational principles to gamification and principles' gamification usage depending on some socio-demographic characteristics such as teaching experience, school level of teaching (with four possible answers: kindergarten, primary school, secondary and high school), and the area where the school is located (with two possible answers: rural and urban area). In the following, we will present some conclusions on the qualitative analysis.

Gamification Definition The results depicted in Table 3.1 showed that over 69% of data was coded into one of the five themes identified based on previously literature of gamification definition. Based on previous definitions, we proposed the following two main components of definition: *learning contexts* and *features and game like-experiences* (Caponettol et al., 2014; Deterding et al., 2011; Dicheva et al., 2015). Our findings suggest that these two themes are the most frequent ones among the answers of Romanian k-12 school teachers. However, it is worth to mention that the difference in terms of percentage is moderate, more precisely from 45% for learning contexts and 7% for features and game like-experiences. This may suggest that Romanian k-12 school teachers are more aware of the component related to learning contexts. These patterns of results are similar with previous research from Romania and other educational contexts. For instance, Romanian primary school teachers with Hungarian ethnic background defined gamification as using activities in which teams of students collect points during the class, using different scoring systems in order to determine the final grade of students or leisure activities with specific rules explained to students and rewards offered to students (Hari & Zsoldos-Marchis, 2020).

The following themes part of the coding schema are knowledge, transversal soft-skills and attitudes. We can suggest that these themes reflect the results of using gamification during the teaching-learning process, as it also facilitates acquiring knowledge, developing transversal soft-skills and promoting positive attitudes. Similar results were provided by the study conducted by Hari and Zsoldos-Marchis (2020) also with Romanian teachers with Hungarian ethnic background where it was showed that gamification can be used in order to acquire new knowledge. Furthermore, to the best of our knowledge, there is another study measuring the components and characteristics of gamification. This study was conducted with business university teachers from the USA and Canada and found a moderate level of knowledge related to applying basic elements of game design to educational activities (Fisher et al., 2014). The results of a recent meta-analyses showed that gamification has medium positive effect on students' academic performance (Bai et al., 2020). Additionally, other previous studies also suggested that gamification increases students' motivation for learning, promote a positive climate among the students, improve student collaboration skills (Caponettol et al., 2014; Dicheva et al., 2015; Moseikina et al., 2022; Pektaş & Kepceoğlu, 2019) and develop critical thinking and problem-solving skills (Kabilan et al., 2023). Thus, the results of the present chapter bring additional knowledge related to how k-12 school teachers define gamification.

In conclusion, based on previous definitions and Romanian k-12 school teachers' responses, we proposed five themes and we structured the gamification definition as follows: gamification consists of *features and game like-experiences applied* to *learning contexts* with the aim to facilitate acquiring specific *knowledge* to the taught domain, developing *transversal soft-skills* for using them in other classes or contexts and promoting positive *attitudes* towards learning, school and society.

Gamification Principles Six initial categories were proposed for coding k-12 school teachers' responses. However, after coding all the data, both coders independently decided to propose one more category. Thus, when they meet for discussing the differences, they decided to code one more time all data, taking into account all seven categories. The results depicted in Table 3.3 showed that over 41% of data was coded in one of the seven proposed categories. Interesting, the theme with the highest frequency (44%) was the one named "*irrelevant*" where we coded all participants' responses related to the definition of gamification. This may suggest that

Romanian k-12 school teachers have more knowledge about the definition of gamification. However, a medium percent of data (41%) was codable in one of the seven themes. The most frequent theme was "*Gamification encourages students' participation in classroom activities,*" with 17% of data coded. These results are consistent with previous results on guidelines proposed for using gamification in educational contexts where promoting the development of intrinsic motivation through the development of autonomy in the learning process was an important guideline. Moreover, another study with Romanian teachers with Hungarian ethnic background reported that gamification maintains or increase students' involvement and motivation for learning (Hari & Zsoldos-Marchis, 2020). These results suggest that Romanian k-12 school teachers are aware of the gamification's potential in promoting higher levels of student engagement during the teaching-learning process. The following most frequent themes are "*Gamification supposes rules and aims specific to games*" and "*Gamification allows players reward each other with virtual currency or points*" where 17% of data was coded, (9% for the rules and aims, and 8% for rewards). These results showed that teachers are more familiar with the principles related to proposing objective rules, well-structured and formulated tasks as these are the pedagogical principles that they use in general when they formulate the learning objectives for their classes. The results concerning the theme related to rewards are consistent with previous results where it was showed that one of the most important elements of gamification is represented by digital badges or points as encourages students to have positive behaviors at during classes and in breaks (Gibson et al., 2015) and also lead to better academic performance (Bai et al., 2020; Recabarren et al., 2021).

Seven percent of data was coded into the last three themes (*Gamification allows students to monitor each other's performance on a leaderboard.*; *Feedback is offered by gamified systems when a player fails to gain the required points and has to repeat a particular function without fear of failure.*; *Gamification allows players to adopt different roles (leader, wizzard, nurse, warrior, healer),* three percent each for the fourth and fifth theme and one percent for the sixth theme. These low percents may suggest that k-12 school teachers are not familiar with the principles related to the implementation of one gamified approach within their classes because it may need more technical knowledge such as game mechanic and game features. These results are also consistent with the relatively low percentage (7%) for features and game like-experiences, the second most important theme for the gamification definition.

In conclusion, k-12 Romanian school teachers are more aware of principles related to the potential of gamification in promoting students' active participation during classes and gamification principles related to proposing objective rules, well-structured and formulated tasks as these are similar to the pedagogical principles that they use when teaching.

Differences The second principal aim was to assess whether there were differences in terms of the level of gamification knowledge, representativity of various educational principles to gamification and principles' gamification usage based on various socio-demographic characteristics such as teaching experience, school level of teaching (with four possible answers: kindergarten, primary school, secondary and high school) and the area where the school is located (with two possible answers: rural and urban area). No significant differences were found in terms of the level of gamification knowledge, representativity of various educational principles to gamification and principles' gamification usage based on the previous mentioned socio-demographic characteristics. These results suggest that teachers with different characteristics such as debutant teachers, teachers with an average teaching experience of 9 years and experienced teachers and teachers teaching at different school level such as kindergarten, primary school, secondary, and high school have similar moderate levels of gamification knowledge. Additionally, they reported similar moderate levels of representativity of various gamification educational principles. Moreover, they also reported that similar level of using those gamification principles during their classes. The same pattern of results was found when testing differences based on school area location. Similar levels of knowledge, representativity of various gamification principles and their usage were reported by teachers from rural and urban areas. These results add new knowledge in the area of gamification research as no other previous study focused on differences in terms of the level of gamification knowledge, representativity of various educational principles to gamification and principles' gamification usage. To the best of our knowledge, there is a scoping review aiming to investigate differences, but in terms of teachers' gameful practices. Moreover, the results of this review also suggested that there were no differences in teachers' gameful practices based on demographic characteristics such as age, gender, previous teachers' education, and teachers' experiences and practice (Bacsa-Károlyi & Fehérvári, 2024).

Contributions and Limitations

These findings contribute to the gamification literature in several ways. One of the main strengths of this study is that we used a mixed approach, by using both qualitative and quantitative methods. Firstly, we qualitatively analyze the data on two fundamental areas of gamification: its definitions and its principles. We used a deductive approach which enabled us to compare k-12 Romanian school teachers' knowledge about gamification with the previously definitions and theoretical approaches proposed. We found a good level of gamification knowledge among k-12 Romanian school teachers as 69% of data was coded in one of the five proposed themes. Moreover, based on previous definitions and on data reported by the participants of this study, we were able to propose a more comprehensive definition for gamification organized in two levels: components and results on learning. More precisely, in the view of the presented results, **gamification** consists of *features and game like-experiences applied* to *learning contexts* with the aim to facilitate acquiring specific *knowledge* to the taught domain, developing *transversal soft-skills* for using them in other classes or contexts and promoting positive *attitudes* towards learning, school, and society.

Furthermore, not only based on available gamification principles and game elements, but also on participants' answers, we were able to propose seven gamification principles and we found a moderate level of knowledge about them among k-12 Romanian school teachers, as 41% of data was coded in one of these themes. In addition, another strength is represented by the fact that we assessed knowledge. Finally, we also tested whether there were differences in terms of the level of gamification knowledge, representativity of various educational principles to gamification and principles' gamification usage based on various socio-demographic teachers' characteristics. We found no significant differences, which suggest similar level of gamification knowledge, representativity of various educational principles to gamification and principles' gamification usage among teachers with various characteristics. Another important strength is that we had participants from Romania, a country less focused on when it came to applying gamification in educational contexts.

In addition to these strengths, the data presented in this chapter has some limitations that are worth mentioning. Convenience sample, sample characteristics, cross-sectional design and using self-report scales were the most important limitations. Thus, we recommend caution in generalizing this study' results. Moreover, previously it was suggested that teachers' personal characteristics such as competence (gameful learning, technology use), personality traits such as independence, openness, innovativeness or self-efficacy leaded to difference in using gamification and game-based learning during teaching-learning process (Bacsa-Károlyi & Fehérvári, 2024). It will be interesting to see if these personal characteristics could also lead to differences in gamification knowledge. Another limitation of this study is related to the lack of data concerning teachers' attitudes towards using gamification as a tool to promote inclusion in the classroom. Future studies should include information on inclusive gamified practices in Romania in order to better understand the needs teachers have regarding this topic specifically.

Practical Implications

The results of the current study have some practical implications. One of the most important implications is related to the fact that Romanian k-12 school teachers need more training on how to use and implement gamified activities during the learning-teaching process, as they provided 69% of reliable data for gamification definition and 41% of gamification principles. Moreover, themes from both, gamification definition and principles, had a very low percent of data coded and one principle had no data coded in that theme (see theme 5 from Table 3.3). These low percents may suggest a relatively low level of gamification knowledge on specific themes of gamification definition and on specific gamification principles. Previous studies suggested that a high level of gamification knowledge might promote better attitudes towards gamification use (Martí-Parreño et al., 2016) and the use of gamification by teachers in classes (Alabbasi, 2018). Thus, we believe that improving the level of teachers' knowledge about gamification will lead to meet the expectations of the digital native learners (Bennet et al., 2008) and to create a more appropriate educational environment for the present learners' generation in a more inclusive manner.

Recommendations for Inclusion and Gamification Based on Romanian Teachers' Perspectives

Despite of the lack of previous studies on teachers' attitudes towards using gamification as a tool to promote inclusion in the classroom, this chapter may shed light on some of the most relevant gaps in education when it comes to using gamified approaches in the classroom in order to encourage the development of inclusive practices. Considering Tomé Klock (2024) revealed that gamification was mainly used to promote inclusion in the *knowledge* promoting area and that our k-12 teachers registered best results on this domain, it could mean that they would be more open to tackle inclusion practices by providing knowledge-targeted activities in a more equitable manner through gamification. Following the trends observed by Tomé Klock (2024) in the inclusive gamified approaches throughout the literature, Romanian teachers might feel more comfortable to start with *mathematics, technology, and language* classes, and with training even engage in more specific inclusive practices such as diversity related activities or promoting mental health through such approaches. Moreover, more specific inclusion practices might be affected by the lack of understanding gamification principles, thus teachers might feel less confident in using these approaches in the classroom, and perceive less control over inclusive activities taught through gamification. For example, our study showed a lack of awareness regarding the individualized feedback gamification may include in class activities. No teacher in our group recognized *Gamification has a positive impact on students' motivation and offers individualized and meaningful feedback on errors* as a principle for gamification. This could have relevant implications on how teachers perceive feedback in gamified approaches and more, on how this feedback could contribute to more inclusive practices in their teaching activities. This gap addresses the need for more targeted training opportunities in which teachers learn about and apply, not only domain specific gamified activities in the classroom, but also more inclusion related activities. Based on our results, teachers training in Romania might rely on teachers' most represented principles of gamification, such as the promotion of a better participation in the classroom (principle 6) in order to motivate them to use more inclusive gamified approaches. In addition, such trainings could start form teachers' knowledge regarding gamification features related to applying rules and aims specific to games, another better represented gamification principle in our study. This could lead to more inclusive practices in contexts with limited access to technological resources especially by providing teachers with accessible tools to promote inclusivity in the classroom for the less developed regions in Romania.

In conclusion, this study (a) summarized and proposed on more comprehensive definition for gamification, (b) summarized gamification principles, and (c) provided preliminary evidence for similar levels of gamification knowledge, representativity of various educational principles to gamification and principles' gamification usage among teachers with various socio-demographic characteristics.

References

Alabbasi, D. (2018). Exploring teachers' perspectives towards using gamification techniques in online learning. *Turkish Online Journal of Educational Technology-TOJET, 17*(2), 34–45.

Al-Azawi, R., Al-Faliti, F., & Al-Blushi, M. (2016). Educational gamification vs. Game based learning: Comparative study. *International Journal of Innovation, Management and Technology, 7*(4), 132–136. https://doi.org/10.18178/ijimt.2016.7.4.659

Aminovna, K. M. (2024). Features of gamification implementation in the educational sphere. *Web of Medicine: Journal of Medicine, Practice and Nursing, 2*(3), 101–103.

Asiri, M. J. (2019). Do teachers' attitudes, perception of usefulness, and perceived social influences predict their behavioral intentions to use gamification in EFL classrooms? Evidence from the Middle East. *International Journal of Education and Practice, 7*(3), 112–122. https://doi.org/10.18488/journal.61.2019.73.112.122

Bacsa-Károlyi, B., & Fehérvári, A. (2024). Teachers' views on gameful practices–a scoping review. *Teaching and Teacher Education, 150*(104730), 1–12. https://doi.org/10.1016/j.tate.2024.104730

Bai, S., Hew, K. F., & Huang, B. (2020). Does gamification improve student learning outcome? Evidence from a meta-analysis and synthesis of qualitative data in educational contexts. *Educational Research Review, 30*(100322), 1–20. https://doi.org/10.1016/j.edurev.2020.100322

Bálint-Svella, É. (2021). Prospective preschool and primary school teachers' knowledge and opinion about gamification. *Acta Didactica Napocensia, 14*(1), 104–114. https://doi.org/10.24193/adn.14.1.8

Bennett, S., Maton, K., & Kervin, L. (2008). The "digital natives" debate: A critical review of the evidence. *British Journal of Educational Technology, 39*(5), 775–786. https://doi.org/10.1111/j.1467-8535.2007.00793.x

Borgonovi, F. (2016). Video gaming and gender differences in digital and printed reading performance among 15-year-olds students in 26 countries. *Journal of adolescence, 48*, 45–61. https://doi.org/10.1016/j.adolescence.2016.01.004

Caponetto, I., Earp, J., & Ott, M. (2014, October). Gamification and education: A literature review. In *European conference on games based learning* (Vol. 1, p. 50). Academic Conferences International Limited.

Çeker, E., & Özdaml, F. (2017). What Gamification Is and What It's Not. *European Journal of Contemporary Education, 6*(2), 221–228. https://doi.org/10.13187/ejced.2017.2.221

Cohen, J. (1960). A coefficient of agreement for nominal scales. *Educational and Psychological Measurement, 20*(1), 37–46. https://doi.org/10.1177/001316446002000104

Clement, J. (2023. Global gaming penetration 2023, by age and gender. Statista. https://www.statista.com/statistics/326420/console-gamersgender/ (accessed on 22nd November 2024, 16:30).

Cramariuc, G., Ursu, A., & Ionescu-Corbu, A. (2023). What endorses teachers to use gamified approaches in their classrooms: Self-efficacy technology proficiency, and perceived usefulness. *International Journal of Social and Educational Innovation (IJSEIro)*, 261–271.

Deterding, S., Dixon, D., Khaled, R., & Nacke, L. (2011). From game design elements to gamefulness: Defining "gamification". In *Proceedings of the 15th international academic MindTrek conference: Envisioning future media environments* (pp. 9–15).

Dicheva, D., Dichev, C., Agree, G., & Angelova, G. (2015). Gamification in education: A systematic mapping study. *Educational Technology and Society, 18*(3), 75–88.

Figg, C., & Jaipal-Jamani, K. (2018). Developing teacher knowledge about gamification as an instructional strategy. In *Teacher training and professional development: Concepts, methodologies, tools, and applications* (pp. 1215–1243). IGI Global. https://doi.org/10.4018/978-1-5225-5631-2.ch056

Fisher, D. J., Beedle, J., & Rouse, S. E. (2014). Gamification: A study of business teacher educators' knowledge of, attitudes toward, and experiences with the gamification of activities in the classroom. *Journal of Research in Business Education, 56*(1), 1–16.

Giannetto, D., Chao, J., & Fontana, A. (2013). Gamification in a social learning environment. *Issues in Informing Science and Information Technology, 10*, 195–207. https://doi.org/10.28945/1806

Gibson, D., Ostashewski, N., Flintoff, K., Grant, S., & Knight, E. (2015). Digital badges in education. *Education and Information Technologies*, 403–410. https://doi.org/10.1007/s10639-013-9291-7

Hari, T. H., & Zsoldos-Marchis, I. (2020). Primary school teachers' knowledge and opinion about gamification. In *ICERI2020 proceedings* (pp. 9281–9287). IATED.

Huang, B., & Hew, K. F. (2018). Implementing a theory-driven gamification model in higher education flipped courses: Effects on out-of-class activity completion and quality of artifacts. *Computers & Education, 125*, 254–272. https://doi.org/10.1016/j.compedu.2018.06.018

Kabilan, M. K., Annamalai, N., & Chuah, K. M. (2023). Practices, purposes and challenges in integrating gamification using technology: A mixed-methods study on university academics. *Education and Information Technologies*. https://doi.org/10.1007/s10639-023-11723-7

Leonardou, A., Rigou, M., Panagiotarou, A., & Garofalakis, J. (2021). The case of a multiplication skills game: Teachers' viewpoint on MG's dashboard and OSLM features. *Computers, 10*(5), 1–21. https://doi.org/10.3390/computers10050065

Martí-Parreño, J., Seguí-Mas, D., & Seguí-Mas, E. (2016). Teachers' attitude towards and actual use of gamification. *Procedia-Social and Behavioral Sciences, 228*, 682–688.

Martí-Parreño, J., Galbis-Córdova, A., & Currás-Pérez, R. (2021). Teachers' beliefs about gamification and competencies development: A concept mapping approach. *Innovations in Education and Teaching International, 58*(1), 84–94. https://doi.org/10.1080/14703297.2019.1683464

Mishra, P., & Koehler, M. J. (2006). Technological pedagogical content knowledge: A framework for integrating technology in teachers' knowledge. *Teachers College Record, 108*(6), 1017–1054. https://doi.org/10.1111/j.1467-9620.2006.00684.x

Moseikina, M., Toktamysov, S., & Danshina, S. (2022). Modern technologies and gamification in historical education. *Simulation & Gaming, 53*(2), 135–156. https://doi.org/10.1177/10468781221075965

McKibben, W. B., Cade, R., Purgason, L. L., & Wahesh, E. (2020). How to conduct a deductive content analysis in counseling research. *Counseling Outcome Research and Evaluation, 13*(2), 156–168. https://doi.org/10.1080/21501378.2020.1846992

Nate, S., Mara, D., Croitoru, A., Morândau, F., Stavytskyy, A., & Kharlamova, G. (2022). The Interest Level Assessment in Attending Training Programs among Romanian Teachers: Econometric Approach. *Sustainability, 14*(24), 16335. https://doi.org/10.3390/su142416335

Pektaş, M., & Kepceoğlu, İ. (2019). What do prospective teachers think about educational gamification? *Science Education International, 30*(1), 65–74.
Recabarren, M., Corvalán, B., & Villegas, M. (2021). Exploring the differences between gamer and non-gamer students in the effects of gamification on their motivation and learning. Interactive Learning Environments, 31(6), 3529–3542. https://doi.org/10.1080/10494820.2021.1933543
Richter, G., Raban, D. R., & Rafaeli, S. (2015). Studying gamification: The effect of rewards and incentives on motivation. In T. Reiners & L. C. Wood (Eds.), *Gamification in education and business* (pp. 21–46). Springer.
Robson, K., Plangger, K., Kietzmann, J. H., McCarthy, I., & Pitt, L. (2015). Is it all a game? Understanding the principles of gamification. *Business Horizons, 58*(4), 411–420. https://doi.org/10.1016/j.bushor.2015.03.006
Sailer, M., Hense, J. U., Mayr, S. K., & Mandl, H. (2017). How gamification motivates: An experimental study of the effects of specific game design elements on psychological need satisfaction. *Computers in Human Behavior, 69*, 371–380. https://doi.org/10.1016/j.chb.2016.12.033
Sajinčič, N., Sandak, A., & Istenič, A. (2022). Pre-service and in-service teachers' views on gamification. *International Journal of Emerging Technologies in Learning (iJET), 17*(3), 83–103.
Su, C. H., & Cheng, C. H. (2015). A mobile gamification learning system for improving the learning motivation and achievements. *Journal of Computer Assisted Learning, 31*(3), 268–286. https://doi.org/10.1111/jcal.12088
Tomé Klock, A. C., Palomino, P. T., Rodrigues, L. A. L., Toda, A. M., Simanke, S., Spors, V., Santana, B. S., & Hamari, J. (2024). Gamification towards and alongside equity, diversity and inclusion: Looking back to move forward. *New Media & Society*. https://doi.org/10.1177/14614448241254028
Zichermann, G., & Cunningham. (2011). *Gamification by design: Implementing game mechanics in web and mobile apps*. O'Reilly.

Chapter 4
Innovative Inclusion and Gamification Strategies in Higher Education: New Directions Regarding Teacher Training

Nicoleta Rogoz and Elena Seghedin

Abstract The development of inclusion at higher education level enables a holistic and ethical approach to innovative teaching and learning practices. The realization of a comprehensive framework at the teacher education policy level causes the introduction of changes in curriculum design, both in terms of content, objectives, and teaching-assessment strategies (Stentiford & Koutsouris, 2022; OECD, 2025). Adapting the content of the pre-service and in-service teacher professional development curriculum to the new trends in European policies involves not only taking into account the special needs of students in at-risk situations (migrants, members of ethnic groups, people with disabilities or gifted) (OECD, 2025) but also the call for new technologies and gamification strategies to facilitate learning and understanding. The chapter aims to present identified answers to some research questions for further argumentative debates: What is the current situation regarding the integration of inclusive education and gamification strategies in higher education? What practices of inclusion can include gamification strategies, to highlight the idea that the use of gamification strategies can have a positive impact on academic curriculum innovation and teacher education strategies/programs? We believe that the results of our analysis and some debates they trigger (which we will introduce as later openings of applied research) can be crucial for the effectiveness of inclusion and gamification dimensions in the formal education system.

N. Rogoz · E. Seghedin (✉)
Alexandru Ioan Cuza University, Iasi, Romania
e-mail: nicoleta.rogoz@uaic.ro; elena.seghedin@uaic.ro

I. Boghian, G. Mareş (eds.), *Gamification and Inclusion*, Inclusive Learning and Educational Equity 12, https://doi.org/10.1007/978-3-031-98390-0_4

Introduction

We do not need to find arguments for the idea that education is the core system of any society. Even if we take into account the challenges of the new millennium, higher education (HE) remains the main component of an education system responsible for the initial training of teachers. After the COVID-19 pandemic, when we ask new technologies to help us achieve our educational goals, at all ages and school types, "we find that the relationship between education and technology is in some respects out of balance." Gamification and all kinds of games are nowadays a crucial aspect of human individual development and have become an important part of human culture and society, promoting motivation and engagement (Bozkurt & Durak, 2018). National and international education policy makers are responsible for the quality and currency of teacher education programs, and their strategies must preserve the role of teachers as facilitators of learning around the world. Innovative directions at the higher education institution (HEI) level are supported by the existing changes in inclusive educational practices as well as the introduction of new technologies into the approach of the academic curriculum. Analysis of the literature highlights that "there is now a well-established tradition and a rich body of work on the use of gamification and games in education, including higher education and continuing professional development" (Bado, 2022; Bell, 2018; Bamford & Moschini, 2024; Kim et al., 2018; Plass et al., 2020). Thus, we find that there are obvious effects of learning and professional development based on digital games, especially in terms of motivational aspects (Prensky, 2001, 2006). Thus, the use of digital games, serious games, and game-based learning has been found to increase motivation to participate by creating experiences in an inclusive context and facilitating the identification of students' interests. Internationally, the discourse on inclusive education is being prioritized, while innovative approaches to integrating gamification into teaching-learning-assessment activities are also being considered.

Taking into account the respect for the individual (as the oldest educational principle), in this chapter we present an analysis of ideas, starting from a literature review and the results of some projects implemented within the concept of inclusive higher education, which promotes the development of a unique personality. By using serious games as stimulating materials or gamification teaching and learning strategies, higher education teachers try to reduce the risk situations in higher education and promote the reduction of all kinds of differences among student teachers—age, gender, nationality, religion—which are important issues in a concrete society, culture and development. However, there are many challenges in the implementation of inclusive education that target "social and cultural barriers, lack of teacher training and inadequate resources" (Dewi, 2024; Ngui, 2019; Ohiri et al., 2024).

Current Status of Using Gamification and Inclusion in Higher Education. Theoretical Framework

Academic Curriculum Innovation: Technology-Related Innovation

In the current context, education for innovation is a priority as understanding curriculum change requires expertise in this area. The training of innovators would determine, at the level of the educational process and system, the possibility of integrating new approaches to teaching, learning and assessment into the academic curriculum. If we refer to higher education, we can argue that innovative teaching can address challenges in other areas of life by adapting strategies to the specificities of both formal and non-formal curricula. Therefore, it is very important to identify what competences are important for innovation and how they can be best taught; how we can use changes in the college curriculum to achieve learning outcomes that are in line with what students can use in their personal or professional lives; and what teaching methods should be used and how educational content could be organized to motivate students to learn. In this context, we recognize that innovative teaching is primarily based on the use of technology and digital resources and takes into account the priority of developing digital competences in students. At the same time, for teachers this means developing teaching skills in the e-learning system. It thus becomes necessary to train teachers in what it means to familiarize themselves with the new curriculum changes and the existing trends in curriculum design. Therefore, any curriculum change must be implemented through the benefits of experimentation at the institutional level and at the level of teaching the subjects included in the curriculum.

The use of different terms to evaluate change represents a major responsibility for decision-makers in education. Precisely for this reason, we consider it necessary to take into account some semantic differentiations that force the practitioner, the actor involved, to align with new points of view when analyzing the applied higher education curriculum: not only that of an actor present in the implementation phase, but also that of a designer who develops or evaluates the curriculum. Connecting educational policy makers with new roles takes them to another level of professional qualification that enables them to adapt to contexts of curriculum innovation. The resources they need become more diverse and their creative imagination allows them to propose new curriculum experiences. At the same time, the development of skills useful for this curriculum change will be an ongoing concern. Among the skills that need to be developed within the academic curriculum, we propose as useful those analyzed by recognized authors in the field of innovation analysis from a pedagogical perspective: "critical thinking and problem-solving skills; networking and influencing; flexibility and adaptability; d) initiative and entrepreneurship; access to and analysis of information; effective oral and written communication; curiosity and imagination" (Wagner, 2014, p.35).

These skills, activated in the context of changes in higher education, lead to engaging in a process of actualization by referring to existing international trends. These changes are always questioned, in the sense of a constant examination of the impact they have at national, regional/local or institutional level. Therefore, "there is even talk of maintaining the reforms in the context of rapid social, economic and especially technological change" (Ministry of Education, Institute of Education Sciences, 2020).

Curriculum innovation means bringing about change in the curriculum through the training of creative thinking skills, professional expertise, and a dedicated commitment to implementation and assessment. Therefore, it is necessary to design the curriculum based on the key competencies and use innovative approaches to organize the content. These include those that focus on analyzing current trends in content organization and adapting them to the application of the college curriculum: interdisciplinarity, digitization - digital transformation, inclusion through differentiation and content personalization, integration, modularization, etc. Thus, a redefinition of design is necessary, which can be considered as "the process of meaningful construction and interconnection of the components of a curriculum to address fundamental questions such as what needs to be learned, how and why, what resources are necessary, and how learning will be evaluated" (UNESCO, IBE, 2013, p. 17). In this context, gamification strategies used for inclusion at the classroom level become extremely important.

Innovation at the level of the academic curriculum is linked to the development of key competences and implicitly to the two European recommendations on digital literacy (The Council of the European Union, Council Recommendation of December 18, 2006 on key competences for lifelong learning 2006/962/EC; Council Recommendation on key competences for lifelong learning, 2018/C 189/01). Therefore, it is necessary to reflect on the changes in the curriculum, e.g., on the following aspects: Addressing the use of digital technologies in terms of both opportunities and risks; Developing a reflective and critical attitude towards digital technologies, also considering future possibilities for their development; Using digital technologies as a medium to support active citizenship, social inclusion and the achievement of personal, social or commercial goals; Identifying effective ways to manage and protect digital content as well as digital identity; Analyzing the potential of private open educational resources as digital content, in terms of specific features: use, access, filtering, rating, creation, programming and sharing; raising awareness of the ethical and legal principles involved in the use of ICT/digital technologies; critically addressing the validity, security, and impact of information.

Using Gamification for Inclusive Education

Inclusive education addresses contemporary challenges by introducing gamification resources, which is defined as "the application of game design elements and game principles in non-game contexts" (Deterding et al., 2011a, 2011b). Gamification combines the playful elements and motivational strategies of games with specific content aimed at achieving educational outcomes. (Majuri et al., 2018; Subhash & Cudney, 2018). The gamified aspects of learning experiences "are often based on the use of points or badges, leaderboards, challenges and missions, and an immediate and interactive feedback system. Gamification in higher education can be applied to the design of courses and programs as well as to a broader range of learning experiences to improve participation and engagement" (Adare-Tasiwoopaápi & Silva, 2023; Costello, 2020). In this way, teachers become more receptive to the design of courses and materials in digital format, implicitly increasing the potential for inclusion at the level of school groups. In Romania today, there are several platforms where teachers are encouraged to develop content within the framework of game-based learning. The Romanian educational strategy emphasizes the integration of Open Educational Resources and gamification in the formal educational processes (ex. https://www. jigsawplanet.com/...; https://wordwall.net/resources, etc.).

The key benefits of gamified learning lie in creating a highly motivating environment and increasing engagement. Gamified learning initiatives can increase intrinsic motivation by providing highly satisfying experiences based on students' interests. They "rely on compelling and relevant narratives as well as extrinsic motivational strategies by rewarding the student with recognizable external incentives such as performance indicators (badges, points, levels) and feedback systems" (Costello, 2020; Huang et al., 2020).

Computerized content organization is one of the content implementation methods that is becoming increasingly useful for adapting to online teaching. This method allows the realization of inclusive teaching and can be effective if it brings the following types of changes: The introduction of information courses—training in computer science and ICT, with the status of an independent subject in the curriculum, with the adaptation of content to new themes of educational digitization (artificial intelligence, open educational resources, gamification, game-based learning, etc.); The didactic valorization of educational platforms, virtual spaces, computers and other electronic devices by teachers; The use of the computer as a teaching tool, as a design strategy, software creation, and e-learning.

At the level of academic curriculum design, there is a shift from the use of the computer as a teaching tool to its use as a resource and implicitly as a learning system (in the form of new information and communication technologies) (NTIC). This transition has led to the emergence of national strategies involving interdisciplinary groups of experts from universities, IT companies, and civil society organizations. The analysis of priorities at the level of the higher education system shows that the pillars on which the academic curriculum should be built can be a) the reference to a set of digital competences relevant to the digital transformation; b) the creation of an efficient digital education and training ecosystem; c) changes at the level of the organization of educational content in higher education by proposing a college curriculum focused on emerging professions; d) the development of an infrastructure and digital technological resources by strengthening the capacity of stakeholders to design and promote open educational resources (OER) and open educational practices (OEP); e) the application of cybersecurity standards, online safety, data protection and IT ethics; f) diversifying the roles of teachers and learners in relation to open educational resources (designers, implementers/developers, evaluators); g) reshaping the mentoring relationship by introducing inclusion and gamification practices; h) fostering a creative mindset that supports digital education throughout life; i) the development of supportive strategies related to open education at the institutional level; j) the promotion of inclusion and gamification practices through the sustainability of open education; and k) the facilitation of international collaboration (Atenas et al., 2019; Caniglia et al. 2018; Downes, 2007; Moreno-Guerrero et al., 2020; Nascimbeni et al. 2020; UNESCO, 2019; Zhang et al., 2020). New pedagogical approaches are needed "to maintain student motivation and engagement during this long period of online learning, especially since dropout rates are generally higher in distance learning than in face-to-face learning" (Huang et al., 2020).

The future of education in the twenty-first century is linked to the quality and diversity of educational opportunities. The organization and support of teaching and learning requires imagination, creativity, and innovation. The most suitable teaching, learning, and research materials are Open Educational Resources (OER), as they are considered to have several advantages: Digital learning resources can be used in an educational setting—digital format; The digital format allows for reuse, sharing, adaptation, and redistribution for an educational setting other than the original one (OECD, 2015). Changes and new approaches to the curriculum are about improving or adapting it to new circumstances or priorities (UNESCO, IBE, 2013). The use of innovative approaches to content design is related to modernization to ensure curriculum currency and relevance, new societal developments and the appropriate preparation of learners for life, an innovation that brings new approaches and solutions, a large-scale system-level reform that completely transforms the existing curriculum.

Gamification and Learning

The application of innovative approaches in the organization of content redefines the role of the teacher in the transformation of education, because the most important key is the quality of the learning process and "the core of progress in education is stimulation to learning" (Robinson, Aronica, 2015, p.155). The role of the teacher increases when it comes to nurturing students' passions and strengths, adapting to students' different learning spaces and making assessments that support personal progress and professional success. This allows for a necessary individualization and psychologization of learning, which is achieved through the use of digital resources in inclusive contexts. Therefore, maker education becomes necessary, which requires an excellent team of teachers. Currently, most teachers involved in maker education are information technology teachers. They can apply advanced technologies more easily and "provide students with professional guidance in terms of software and hardware technology, advanced programming, electronic devices, etc.;

however, this support is far from sufficient" (Du et al., 2021; Garces & O'Dowd, 2021; Zhang et al., 2021). Maker space-type spaces offer universities the opportunity to turn teachers and students into creators and promote "hands-on learning, experimentation, and collaboration between parents and other communities." Based on this idea, we will present some findings from some exemplary projects and programs in the empirical sections of the chapter.

Under these conditions, "conventional education in colleges and universities is often a one-sided teaching model, and the weaknesses of this teaching model are obvious" (Liu, 2023). Students are regarded as those who only passively handle knowledge throughout the learning process, and teachers ignore or even suppress their initiative to learn. This model is contradictory to the demands of talent development in modern society because it emphasizes ideas of experiential education, project-based learning methods, innovative education, and the "do it yourself" concept. Students are seen as "creators or contributors of knowledge, not just consumers, when they engage with and explore creative solutions to real-world problems" (Liu, 2023). Therefore, the use of open educational resources (OER) and open educational practices (OEP) is necessary, leading to a diversification of learning activities and increasing student and teacher participation. The author U.D. Ehlers (2011) defined OEP as "practices that support the (re)use and production of OER through institutional policies, promote innovative pedagogical models, and respect and empower learners as co-producers on their lifelong learning journey." At the same time, these practices include references to "open pedagogy, open collaboration and open assessment" (Huang et al., 2020). To develop these practices, new types and strategies of learning are needed that reflect innovative pedagogical approaches such as Flipped Classroom, Project-Based Learning, Cooperative Learning, Gamification, Case-based Learning (CBL), Problem-based learning (PBL), Scenario-based Learning (SBL), Design Thinking, and Thinking-Based Learning. The use of these learning strategy types would lead to the introduction of game elements, game mechanics (points, levels, leaderboards, badges, challenges), and serious games that can be used to increase student motivation and engagement in online learning.

The development of correlated activities leads to explicit learning outcomes and at a theoretical level through reference to Motivation Theory (Deci & Ryan, 2000; Sailer et al., 2017; Taylor et al., 2014), Self-determination Theory (Adams et al., 2017; Deci & Ryan, 2008), Achievement Goal Theory (Dweck & Leggett, 1988; Elliott & Dweck, 1988); Goal-Setting Theory (Huang & Hew, 2018; Landers et al., 2015); Social Learning Theory (SLT) (Bandura, 1977), Situated Learning Theory (Lave, 1988, 1991), Cognitive Load Theory (Sweller, 2003, 2004). In this context, the role of teachers should aim to build open communities, e.g., by "using social networks to help students work in teams on specific learning tasks (e.g. editing a blog, creating a Wikipedia page) and sharing ideas and discussions related to these specific learning tasks" (Kim et al., 2018). These types of initiatives can also involve other teachers and stakeholders to facilitate discussions and provide additional support to students. The premises for open evaluation, where teachers should allow students to evaluate each other (peer evaluation) and use reflective practices to improve their learning outcomes. In this way, the key benefits of gamification and inclusion at the academic curriculum level are highlighted: "active engagement (students can find pleasure through the story, dynamics, and mechanics of games and actively engage in courses; the learning effect (gamified learning and education can help students remember what they have learned more thoroughly and for an extended period of time); personalized experience (students can create their own experiences by completing predetermined missions and earning rewards such as points, levels, or badges)" (Kim et al., 2018).

Gamification and Teaching. Gamification and Teacher Training

This chapter is a critical approach to the important elements of GBL and gamification in relation to inclusion in education, particularly in higher education and teacher education. We have already presented some theoretical foundations on these useful technological forms of teaching and learning, based on the primary studies mentioned in the reviews on gamification, serious games and game-based learning. In the last section, we have described some good practices presented in two case studies on gamification strategies in higher education and in two other teacher training projects we have been involved in, and we have tried to find realistic answers to the following questions: What makes professional development effective? What instructional design and strategies are best suited for updated pre-service teacher education?

Gamification is not effective per se (Sailer et al., 2017)—because it is difficult to design effective gamified interventions (which include serious games and game-based learning), and teaching with these types of games requires theoretical and practical knowledge to develop critical and effective teaching and learning. All authors emphasized in their papers the fact that Gamification can be described as an innovative strategy to improve learning and knowledge application in university study programs and at the same time it is a good set of teaching techniques that achieve not only cognitive knowledge and skills, but also pedagogical levels of learning (i.e., individualization of learning processes, also in terms of personality qualities or character improvement and development).

In teacher education (pre-service and in-service professional development), we need to consider professional standards and the components of professionalism as a starting point for good instructional design. Learning intentions must allow for a focus on individualization of teaching-learning and assessment steps for effective teacher education courses. The higher education teacher's perspective on incorporating gamification and GBL (to individualize learning) is more akin to McGonigal's words, "Increasing learner satisfaction through immediate feedback and individually achievable goals is another reason for gamification" (see McGonigal, 2011).

However, integrating GBL in a way that meets these expectations is a challenge for teachers (Hayak & Avidov-Ungar, 2020). It requires skills and knowledge that may not be part of their teaching repertoire, such as the ability to determine which games are appropriate and/or can be easily adapted to their objectives; introducing the game activity to students and supporting students' learning while they play; and paying attention to whether learners connect the game to the learning content and objectives (Bado, 2022; Nousiainen et al., 2018). According to Palha et al. (2024)—several researchers from the field of education (such as Foster & Shah, 2020; Bado, 2022; Dickey, 2007; McGonigal, 2011) have pointed out the need for the development of teacher training programs that introduce practicing and future teachers to the methods and knowledge required for GBL. The inclusion of a specific teaching typology to support certain types of learning (Inquiry-based learning, Critical thinking development, Game-based Learning, experiential learning and gamification) in academic teachers' activities is no accident. The results of numerous empirical studies (Palha et al., 2024; Siemon & Linda, 2017) show how teachers benefit from digital technology to implement pedagogical strategies, facilitate student learning and support student competence development. We have to admit that digitalization and gamification bring the challenge of keeping up with changes in working life and education and providing students with relevant vocational digital content and learning technologies. Theoretical contributions and empirical studies have increased the knowledge about GBL, gamification, and digitalization in education. Digital games enhance students' learning experience by making learning more fun, interesting and motivating by engaging students in active learning or involving them in new learning methods (Barz et al., 2024; Luarn et al., 2023).

Any educational policy at national level consists of respecting the main commonalities in the profiles of teachers' professional competences identified in the reports of international academic organizations and educational research, as well as in the reports of the European Commission's specific studies for the European countries. For a brief outlook, but important for the understanding of our chapter on development, we propose some recommendations that policy makers in the field of teacher training must take into account in their strategic proposals, if we are aware of the need for innovation and useful updates in this particular policy. The proposal of a professional development course based on the theory of gamification, defined as the use of game design elements in non-game contexts (Deterding et al., 2011a, 2011b; Luarn et al., 2023), is imperative to address the fundamental elements of curriculum design.

Following this view, C. Cretu and N. Rogoz (2014), in an article on the expectations for the quality of professional development programs offered by universities (programs for teacher education and training are developed in most universities worldwide), propose a set of recommendations for academic policies that can become a reference plan for the continuous professional development of teaching staff (including young doctoral students, teaching assistants, and junior lecturers from the college's own faculty). From the perspective of gamification of teacher training, we can select the following:

- "The implementation of coherent medium- to long-term management strategies in relation to professional development programs
- The development of a curriculum that meets the criteria of efficiency and effectiveness (e.g. cross-curricular skills, consistent content aligned to both the practi-

cal application of research methodology and educational teaching practice, teaching-learning evaluation methods in the form of mentoring, tutoring, supervision and monitoring that encourage critical thinking, lateral thinking, creativity, transformative learning, constructive learning or collaborative learning, intrinsic motivation and the desire to immediately apply the knowledge acquired)
- The continuous improvement of programs offered by universities based on the application of research findings; this could also be linked to international recognition
- The increase in training programs in which the target group is made up of trainers and mentors. Mentoring offers a highly individualized approach to professional development. Mentors are trained in working with adult learners so that gamification is applied by both parties and becomes part of a productive relationship
- The formation of teams of trainers who could benefit from professional mobility to receive their training in an appropriate socio-cultural and physical context (not only in lecture halls); escape room content could also take better advantage of a multicultural learning context
- The use of innovative training practices developed within specific adult education programs" (Crețu & Rogoz, 2014)

According to the authors, this analysis offers academic decision-makers an opportunity for reflection and could be considered as a set of prerequisites for a comprehensive framework for the implementation of new professional development strategies in the educational programs offered by universities.

To summarize, all four areas of digital pedagogical competence presented in the major works on teacher professionalism under today's challenges (see, e.g., McGarr & McDonagh, 2019): a. technical knowledge and skills for the use of digital and gamification strategies; b. pedagogical knowledge and skills related to these new teaching strategies; c. ethical aspects that represent a set of beliefs and values related to the best ways of teaching-learning-assessing; d. an attitudinal part that includes positive thoughts, reflective thinking, and open-minded characteristics of a teacher profile.

Case Studies and Best Practices for the Use of Gamification and Inclusion Strategies in Academic Curriculum Development and Teacher Training

According to J.H. Klabbers, there is a lack of clear definitions for gamification and GBL, so that we are dealing with a "terminological ambiguity" (Klabbers, 2009). The development of gamification and inclusion practices through the introduction of strategies in the design of the academic curriculum was based on the analysis of internationally connected needs with regard to the digital transformation of college spaces. At the same time, it was necessary to redesign the academic curriculum to promote the development of digital competencies, ensure cybersecurity measures and safety in the online environment, and also train teachers in e-learning teaching skills.

Based on the challenges identified by education experts in China and the authors of relevant studies in this field, "a few recommendations are presented to improve the future adoption and application of OER and OEP in China and other contexts" (Huang et al., 2020). In particular, alternative tools and technologies have been developed to facilitate learning in both Chinese and international contexts. For example, these readers can use Twitter or Facebook instead of Sina Weibo (a Chinese social network). Efforts have been made to launch institutional initiatives to support the adoption of OER. In 2012, for example, the Open University of China launched the five-minute courses initiative, which aims to develop 30,000 five-minute courses on 100 topics from various fields. This enables not only a context of internationalization, but above all a context of co-creation of open educational resources through the involvement of transdisciplinary teams of professors. Another initiative is "XuetangX, launched in 2013 by Tsinghua University and MOOCCN Information Technology, which provides access to over 1000 free courses from Tsinghua, Fudan, MITx, HarvardX and other universities" (Huang et al., 2020). It is a fact that Chinese universities are constantly striving for the development of OER and OEP. Regarding the efficiency of OER, the initiators of some research projects classify them into three categories, some of which do not fulfill all OER conditions according to the UNESCO definition of OER (Tlili et al., 2019), namely resources that are made available to the public by Chinese universities and libraries free of charge but without open licenses; resources that are under open licenses or protected by Chinese copyright laws that allow free use and/or reuse; and resources that are not under open licenses and are not in the public domain but are made available to the public free of charge through government action (Huang et al., 2020).

Another model of best practice is The Comprehensive Solution for CTE Programs, developed by iCEV. iCEV has been working with educators for over 35 years and has developed all-in-one solutions to meet current tasks and needs (available online: https://www.icevonline.com/learning-center). These solutions are made available through a learning center that provides assistance in identifying resources such as tutorials, guides, virtual events, case studies, white papers, infographics, posters and certified leases (which validate knowledge and skills while promoting professional development and facilitating employability and productivity in the workplace).

We are also witnessing the continuous development and progress of science and technology, which draws the attention of universities to the management of clouds, cloud applications, and other methods that are constantly updated and expanded. Therefore, collaboration initiatives between higher education institutions and IT companies can facilitate the construction of collaborative digital service platforms. Such public cloud service platforms "combine other resources and standard products to develop a unified processing and service engine for digital products, form a standard library of digital products with resource content, and provide personal and institutional users with standard digital products and customized services" (Gao et al., 2023).

GamEducation in University is another example of a project presented by Dominik Siemon and Linda Eckardt in the 11th chapter of a book dedicated to Gamification for higher education (see for details, Siemon & Linda, 2017).

GamEducation was successfully implemented twice over a period of 2 years in a Master's program at the Technical University of Braunschweig, Germany. The GamEducation project was implemented twice over 2 years and evaluated before, during and after the semester. After the first implementation in the Master's program "Cooperation in e-business" in 2012, there were some administrative improvements for the next academic year. In the traditional lecture, the basics of strategic design options for all important areas of e-business are explained and illustrated with practical examples, but for this project the reading material was divided into parts—lecture in four sessions. In addition, a background story is created as a basis for some challenges. In this background story, a fictitious company is presented that is looking for a new business area to be developed within the framework of the challenges. The challenges were created in close coordination with the lecture material and were part of the group work. Each lecture was followed by a challenge; each challenge was presented 1 week after the corresponding lecture. Four additional ad hoc challenges were designed to provide the opportunity to earn individual points. In addition to the lectures, students were provided with a blog system that allowed them to earn additional points (Each student could post lecture-related content and discuss various topics on this blog. The blog also included an up-to-date leaderboard for the groups and each member). Each student was invited to rate each presentation of the challenge, except their own. During the first round of the project, teachers experienced a large increase in supervision and support work—and this became the biggest negative aspect (greatly increased workload for both students and teachers) of this GamEducation gamification project. The evaluations showed that GamEducation can improve the efficiency, motivation, and enjoyment of teaching and can lead to more intensive participation and a better understanding of the lecture material.

In recent years, with digitalization and gamification of teaching and learning playing an important role in higher education, several articles have been published addressing specific studies. The main premise of these studies revolves around the exploration and detailed investigation of a gamification proposal based on the dynamics of escape rooms and aimed at enhancing the learning experience in educational institutions. By immersing students in challenges that require the application of theoretical concepts and problem-solving skills, this approach aims to go beyond traditional teaching methods. The components of gamification are described in detail in the study by M. Sailer et al. (2017). They describe gamification as a unit that typically includes important situational components: a goal to be achieved, rules that define how this goal can be achieved, a feedback system that provides information about progress towards the goal, and the feature that participation is voluntary.

A. G. Moreno (2024) in the chapter, "Enhancing the Learning and Application of Knowledge in University Students: An Escape Room Proposal," describes that the escape room has to do with a list of challenges where students have to apply academic concepts and theories to solve problems and escape from the confined space within a limited time. Durán, A. G. (2024), even presents a specific content proposal for an escape room in the paper (*Gamification in the Art World: An Escape Room to Immerse Yourself in the History and Local Artists of the City*), the research highlights the effectiveness of this strategy in improving students' knowledge retention and motivation to learn. It also highlights the importance of collaboration and communication between participants as key elements for active and participatory learning. It is worth highlighting how the proposal of an educational escape room proves to be an effective strategy to engage college students in their learning process and promote the practical application of their knowledge, which improves their understanding of academic content and strengthens their key competencies.

This methodology, which enables educators to engage and motivate students more effectively (Weitl-Harms et al., 2023 apud Durán, 2024), introduces a critical component to education by changing students' attitudes towards learning, using fun as a tool for change (see Alsawaier, 2018, apud Moreno, 2024). Previous studies have shown that gamification has great appeal not only in primary or secondary education, but also in higher education, providing very effective results when gamification is used as a tool to teach complex concepts.

Zachary et al. (2011) had an interesting proposal in which they explored the use of game performance in a mobile application designed to help new college students. Their article describes the basics of a design framework used to incorporate game elements into a mobile app called Orientation Passport. The system is explained using the design framework and the results of a pilot study with 26 new students are presented. This study contributes to the foundations of a design framework for the general design of gamified achievements, particularly because we believe the authors highlight the potential drawbacks of insufficient understanding and application of the levels. Care should also be taken when enforcing stricter game rules, as usability may be compromised.

An interesting article (Palha et al., 2024) presents us with a brief description of another concrete exercise for implementing GBL at universities. In the Faculty of Education at the Amsterdam University of Applied Sciences, a fully gamified one-semester course on game-based pedagogy was designed for the master's program in teacher education in spring 2023 to introduce teachers to the pedagogical use of games. This course built on a previous math teacher training series on GBP, the design of which was informed by the guiding principles of Palha et al. (2024) and the competence framework of Nousiainen et al. (2018), which was used to guide and assess competency development. The aim of the course application in the fall semester of 2023 was to understand how this GBL challenge impacted participants' competencies in teaching with games. All 16 participants—in-service teachers from different secondary school subject areas—highlighted two aspects in some interview questions: the challenges in designing elements of the gamified course and, on the other hand, the interaction with the course instructors who cared about their competence development in GBL. For both points, the analysis of the answers leads the authors to conclusions about good practices. The authors (Palha et al., 2024) are very precise in their descriptions and emphasize the importance of starting with a good design of a gamified course for teachers. They introduce the skill tree, a collection of gamified paths that integrate educational objectives and content and are organized in a playful way (Backlund et al., 2021). The skill tree offers multiple options to progress from start to finish, giving players the freedom to pursue their interests and promoting agency (Backlund, 2021 apud Palha et al., 2024). In the course, the tasks in the skill tree were linked to points, levels, and scores to enhance the gamified experience. On the platform of the Amsterdam University of Applied Sciences we can find the full skill tree (in Dutch) at https://edu.nl/jrwya. The participants in this study were 13 in-service teachers participating in a master course on GBP and three course leaders. All participants had lessons every 15 days and were asked to work in cross-curricular teams of four on the design and development of their own games in the weeks without lessons. The skill tree was used as a guide for both classroom and independent group work. The final assessment consisted of the developed game and an individual reflection (the full article, which takes up the entire study to discover the details that became important for designing a professional development program for teachers in GBL training).

There have been several projects in which gamification has been used in the initial and continuing professional development of teachers. They involved students and teachers from the Faculty of Psychology and Educational Sciences and the Department of Professional Development of Teachers, both from the "Alexandru Ioan Cuza" University in Iasi, Romania.

Before the Covid pandemic, the project RePlay—Gaming Technology Platform for Social Reintegration of Marginalized Youth (2008–2010), an FP7-ICT project, was developed as an international research partnership. The main objective was to develop a gaming technology platform that provides children with a learning environment for moral values education. Furthermore, the studies show that "the RePlay project proves that the concept of interactive games can be used to improve learning skills, moral awareness and behavior in general" (Ibanez et al., 2010, apud C. Crețu et al., 2012). At the same time, the main goal of our university was to develop the pedagogical framework for the guide for teachers and school counselors (replayproject.eu).

As a result of the way participants engage with the content of the game, changes were observed in relevant behavioral indicators: greater involvement and engagement in solving game tasks, concern for acquiring and expanding knowledge, development of cognitive and procedural skills, and a change in attitude towards peer learning (with a focus on collaborative learning in the online environment). It is a model of best practice that facilitates the inclusion of students with behavior problems in a counseling and educational therapy context, while achieving understanding and adaptation to norms and rules through play. The game content appears in the form of moral dilemmas that allow participants to reflect on their learning and the (socially acceptable) solutions to be chosen.

The Replay project is also a model of good practice for the design and development of an innovative strategy to support educational psychologists in assessing the choices that young people with antisocial behavior (ASB) make in certain situations. Replay also provides an attractive tool for facilitating interactive psycho-educational counseling sessions. The end result is a fully functional 3D game platform that integrates the following tools and technologies: a) 3D video game with multimedia content/scenarios psychologically related to ASB; this content is organized into six main educational activities that vary from game session to game session; b. Interactive and wireless balance board for game control; c. A set of interactive systems for the game sessions (wireless trackball, joystick, keyboard); d. A user recognition system developed to improve the user's interaction with the system and increase engagement; e) Questionnaires and observation sheets for counselors/psychologists (Crețu et al., 2011).

These tools facilitate inclusion through the use of gamification in the school environment. At the same time, their application requires the existence of an interdisciplinary team dedicated to the continuous expansion of game content, the optimization of the technological platform used, and the improvement of tools that enable reflection on teaching and learning.

The Reflect Lab project was a strategic partnership in the field of higher education. Five institutions from five countries are working together to develop an innovative course structure that promotes self-directed learning in higher education (developed at five universities simultaneously). It uses a solid theoretical framework developed as an intellectual output of a European Erasmus + KA 2 project - Reflect Lab. Supporting lecturers in applying inquiry-based learning, 2016-1- DE01-KA203-002891, is a 30-month European project co-funded by the Erasmus+ program (November 2016–April 2019). Erasmus+ supports transnational partnerships between education, training, and youth organizations to foster cooperation and build a bridge between the world of education and the world of work to address the skills gaps we face in Europe. The idea of GBL combined with inquiry-based learning was the starting point for the development of a professional development program for young college teachers. The gamification of traditional teaching strategies and the materials used for the learning content underlay the issues raised by the authors previously associated with this teaching design (Vandercruysse et al., 2012) and was related with teachers reflectivity (Seghedin, 2019). In terms of the effectiveness of OER, our Reflect Lab team considered and demonstrated that gamification as a process provides an opportunity to acknowledge and bring awareness to the importance of life lived, regardless of background, culture, ethnicity, or difference (see also Avidov-Ungar, O., & Hayak, M. 2023). Using this to drive positive change has the potential to transform education, but more importantly transform the lives of an entire generation by redefining social justice and advocating for unheard voices (Hayes, C., 2024). The aim of the Reflect Lab project was to support universities, and in particular lecturers, to implement inquiry-based learning in their practice, which is an important part of their innovative teaching (Hébert & Jenson, 2019).

For these social science teaching/learning laboratories, reflection labs were developed, tested, and analyzed through the students' reflections in the final sessions. The aim is to establish an innovative course structure that promotes self-directed learning in higher education institutions (HEI). Students were asked to conduct independent research into pressing political and social issues using social science methods in Reflect labs. During the implementation of the projects, the lecturers accompanied and supported this process and the critical discussions as learning leaders and used GBL at these points. In this way, the project provides a counterpoint to the often-criticized reduction of learning in higher education to the mere transfer of knowledge. In each class, a unit was used to test parts of the ReflectLab strategy: students were given stimulus material (cartoons, articles and games), had to investigate a topic for 3 h and shared their experiences. The rooms were equipped with WIFI and a projector; students used their iPhones or laptops to access the internet. In all rooms for 20–25 students, tables and chairs can be moved around and set up for small group work (in this way students were invited to network, not just to learn and play individually).

One of the intellectual outputs is an IT platform that can be used by teachers, students, and pupils in the teaching and learning process. The ReflectLab platform is still accessible to all interested parties and is used for exchange, information, and mutual support. Users of the platform can access all intellectual outputs and learning materials uploaded to the platform, share best practices, and communicate with each other via chat and video functions to share and support each other. All partners have been involved in the creation of some open resources by contributing to the database with e-tools, game descriptions, and training opportunities from their region and country.

For more details and open resources, there is an open access platform; one of the elements is the lecture manual with many methodological details related to the use of innovative learning models: inquiry, problem solving, critical thinking through reading and writing, and of course game-based learning—https://www.idd.uni-hannover.de/fileadmin/idd/Projekte/Reflect-Lab/IO6_en.pdf. Participants found it useful to be reflective teachers all the time, to be active learners, to be aware of students' behavioral changes during the lesson, and to make the right decision at which moment a game can be used most efficiently.

The main ideas from the participants' feedback (including in their reflection journals) from all these experiences relate positively to the main aspects of using gamification in education as described in the literature: gamification and the use of GBL to introduce stimulus materials, minutes of play can enhance learning and, on the other hand, improve a person's creativity when working (see Dickey, 2007; Webster & Martocchio, 1992); other motives for gamification are to increase motivation and strengthen social belonging among participants (see also Scheiner and Witt, 2013); increasing learner satisfaction through immediate feedback and individually achievable goals is another reason for gamification (McGonigal, 2011).

The main conclusion from all the experiences with gamification in higher education was the fact that one of the greatest benefits is the creation of rich learning experiences that arise from the application of gamification, motivated by the introduction of elements such as rewards, points, levels, and challenges that stimulate healthy competition and self-improvement. Starting from an observational and reflective perspective, the theories and models presented in this chapter and their popularity in gamification research need to be reviewed. We should then move to an explanatory perspective, analyzing the relationships between the commonalities of the identified theoretical foundations and the specific teaching and learning contexts.

Conclusions

The introduction of innovative inclusion and gamification strategies enables the identification of policy directions at the level of higher education institutions aimed at both streamlining the academic curriculum and its access methods and introducing changes at the level of teacher training curricula. In this context, strategies are needed for both the design of open educational resources (OER) and the development of open educational practices. (OEP). These strategies may include the expansion of pedagogical approaches that value gamification from the perspective of increasing student employability in learning, and the enhancement of online learning environments (which include problem solving, case studies, research reports, etc.).

Starting from the traditional view of college teaching methodology, which includes mainly expository techniques such as lectures and frontal teaching with very little dialog or interaction, suitable for conveying information but not stimulating interaction, additional thought or inspiration (Bligh, 1998), it seems that gamification and GBL are trying to become a new toolbox for the individualization of learning processes, a good way to achieve the goal of developing a learner-centered college.

To support our theoretical considerations, in this chapter we present a series of empirical studies that highlight the main conclusion of several works on gamification, namely that gamification has established itself as a dynamic and innovative strategy in education, offering a unique approach to improving the learning experiences of college students.

Through theoretically underpinned ideas, concrete examples and practical strategies from the collection of case studies presented (see the third section of this chapter), we aim to provide educators, college teachers, teacher sneakers, researchers, and course designers with an introductory guide to the effective implementation of gamification and GBL in universities with the aim of individualizing learning. We believe that these few pages will inspire higher education professionals to adopt and adapt this innovative pedagogical strategy to their specific needs in order to improve student participation, engagement, and learning outcomes.

References

Adams, N., Little, T. D., & Ryan, R. M. (2017). Self-determination theory. In M. L. Wehmeyer, K. A. Shogren, T. D. Little, & S. J. Lopez (Eds.), *Development of self-determination through the life-course* (pp. 47–54). Springer.

Adare-Tasiwoopaápi, S. & Silva, N. (2023). Gamification in higher education: A how-to instructional guide. https://doi.org/10.4324/9781003444954.

Alsawaier, R. (2018). The Effect of Gamification on Motivation and Engagement. *International Journal of Information and Learning Technology,* 35, 56–79. https://doi.org/10.1108/IJILT-02-2017-0009

Atenas, J., Havemann, L., Nascimbeni, F., Villar-Onrubia, D., & Orlic, D. (2019). Fostering openness in education: Considerations for sustainable policy-making. *Open Praxis, 11*(2), 167–183. https://doi.org/10.5944/openpraxis.11.2.947

Avidov-Ungar, O., & Hayak, M. (2023). The use of digital games by teacher educators in colleges of education. *Journal of Information Technology Education: Research, 22*(1), 373–387. https://doi.org/10.28945/5191

Backlund, P., Erlandsson, P. & Andersson, J. (2021). "A Skill Tree Method to Identify and Map In-game Skills to Out-of -game Contexts". Paper read at XVth ECGBL, University of Brighton, UK, September.

Bado, N. (2022). Game-based learning pedagogy: A review of the literature. *Interactive Learning Environments, 30*(5), 936–948. https://doi.org/10.1080/10494820.2019.1683587

Bamford, J., & Moschini, E. (2024). The third space, student and staff co-creation of gamified informal learning: An emerging model of co-design. *London Review of Education, 22*(1), 21. https://doi.org/10.14324/LRE.22.1.21

Bandura, A. (1977). *Social learning theory*. Prentice Hall.

Barz, N., Benick, M., Dörrenbächer-Ulrich, L., & Perels, F. (2024). The effect of digital game-based learning interventions on cognitive, metacognitive, and affective-motivational learning outcomes in school: A meta-analysis. *Review of Educational Research, 94*(2), 193–227. https://doi.org/10.3102/00346543231167795

Bell, K. (2018). *Game On! Gamification, gameful design, and the rise of the gamer educator* (Illustrated ed.). Johns Hopkins University Press.

Bligh, D.-A. (1998). What's the Use of Lectures? Intellect books: Exeter (5th edition).

Bozkurt, A. & Durak, G. (2018). A Systematic Review of Gamification Research: In *Pursuit of Homo Ludens. International Journal of Game-Based Learning.* 8. https://doi.org/10.4018/ijgbl.2018070102

Caniglia, G., John, B., Bellina, L., Lang, D. J., Wiek, A., Cohmer, S., & Laubichler, M. D. (2018). The global curriculum: A model for transnational collaboration in higher education for sustainable development. *Journal of Cleaner Production, 171*, 368–376.

Costello, R. (2020). Gamification strategies for retention, motivation, and engagement in higher education: Emerging research and opportunities. IGI Global, 2020. Accessed August 30, 2023. https://www.igi-global.com/book/gamification-strategies-retention-motivationengagement/235480.

Crețu, C. M., & Rogoz, N. (2014). Teachers' expectations regarding the accredited programs for professional development provided by universities. *In Procedia - Social and Behavioral Sciences, 142*, 660–667., ISSN 1877-0428. https://doi.org/10.1016/j.sbspro.2014.07.682

Cretu, C. M., Rogoz, N., & Chihaia, D. (2012). How to design and implement a validation methodology for virtual educational games. In Proceedings of the 11th European conference on E-learning (pp. 97–105).

Cretu, C., Chihaia, D., & Coroeru-Rogoz, N. (2011). rePlay. 3D gaming platform as instrument and strategy for psycho-pedagogical counselling in schools. In EDULEARN11 proceedings. (pp. 2669–2678). IATED.

Deci, E. L., & Ryan, R. M. (2008). Self-determination theory: A macrotheory of human motivation, development, and health. *Canadian Psychology/Psychologie Canadienne, 49*(3), 182–185.

Deci, E. L., & Ryan, R. M. (2000). The "what" and "why" of goal pursuits: Human needs and the self-determination of behavior. *Psychological Inquiry, 11*, 227–268. https://doi.org/10.1207/S15327965PLI1104_01

Deterding, S., Dixon, D., Khaled, R., & Nacke, L. (2011a). 'From game design elements to gamefulness: Defining gamification'. In Proceedings of the 15th international academic MindTrek conference: Envisioning future media environments, MindTrek 2011, Tampere, Finland, 28–30 September, 9–15.

Deterding, S., Sicart, M., Nacke, L., O'Hara, K., & Dixon, D. (2011b). Gamification: Using game-design elements in non-gaming contexts. In *Proceedings of the 2011 annual conference extended abstracts on human factors in computing systems—CHI EA'11. The 2011 annual conference extended abstracts, Vancouver, BC, Canada, 7–12 May* (pp. 2425–2428). ACM Press.

Dewi, A. E. R. (2024). Effectiveness of implementing inclusive education: Challenges and opportunities in culturally diverse classrooms. *Journal of Pedagogi, 1*(3), 1–7. https://doi.org/10.62872/k2k0zs91

Dickey, M. (2007). Game design and learning: A conjectural analysis of how massively multiple online role-playing games (MMORPGs) foster intrinsic motivation. *Educational Technology Research and Development*. 55. 253–273. https://doi.org/10.1007/s11423-006-9004-7

Downes, S. (2007). Models for sustainable open educational resources. *Interdisciplinary Journal of E-Learning and Learning Objects, 3*(1), 29–44.

Du, B., Chai, Y., Huangfu, W., Zhou, R., & Ning, H. (2021). Undergraduate university education in internet of things engineering in China: A survey. *Education Sciences, 11*(5), 202. https://doi.org/10.3390/educsci11050202

Durán, A. G. (2024). Gamification in the art world: An escape room to immerse yourself in the history and local artists of the City. In V. Membrive (Ed.), *Practices and implementation of gamification in higher education* (pp. 141–171). IGI Global Scientific Publishing. https://doi.org/10.4018/979-8-3693-0716-8.ch007

Dweck, C. S., & Leggett, E. L. (1988). A social-cognitive approach to motivation and personality. *Psychological Review, 95*(2), 256–273. https://doi.org/10.1037/0033-295X.95.2.256

Ehlers, U. D. (2011). Extending the territory: From open educational resources to open educational practices. *Journal of Open, Flexible, and Distance Learning, 15*(2), 1–10.

Elliott, E. S., & Dweck, C. S. (1988). Goals: An approach to motivation and achievement. *Journal of Personality and Social Psychology, 54*(1), 5–12.

Foster, A., & Shah, M. (2020). Principles for advancing game-based learning in teacher education. *Journal of Digital Learning in Teacher Education, 36*(2), 84–95.

Gao, Q., Wang, Q., & Wu, C. (2023). Construction of enterprise digital service and operation platform based on internet of things technology. *Journal of Innovation & Knowledge., 8*, 100433. https://doi.org/10.1016/j.jik.2023.100433

Garces, P., & O'Dowd, R. (2021). Upscaling virtual exchange in university education: Moving from innovative classroom practice to regional governmental policy. *Journal of Studies in International Education, 25*(3), 283–300. https://doi.org/10.1177/1028315320932323

Hayak, M., & Avidov-Ungar, O. (2020). The integration of digital game-based learning into the instruction: Teachers' perceptions at different career stages. *TechTrends, 64*(6), 887–898.

Hayes, C. (2024). Philosophy, theory, and praxis: Gamification pedagogy in global higher education. In V. Membrive (Ed.), *Practices and implementation of gamification in higher education* (pp. 252–274). IGI Global Scientific Publishing. https://doi.org/10.4018/979-8-3693-0716-8.ch012

Hébert, C., & Jenson, J. (2019). Digital game-based pedagogies: Developing teaching strategies for game-based learning. *Journal of Interactive Technology and Pedagogy, 15*.

Huang, R., Tlili, A., Chang, T. W., et al. (2020). Disrupted classes, undisrupted learning during COVID-19 outbreak in China: Application of open educational practices and resources. *Smart Learning Environments, 7*, 19. https://doi.org/10.1186/s40561-020-00125-8

Huang, B., & Hew, K. F. (2018). Implementing a theory-driven gamification model in higher education flipped courses: Effects on out-of-class activity completion and quality of artifacts. *Computers & Education, 125*(2018), 254–272. https://doi.org/10.1016/j.compedu.2018.06.018

Ibañez, F., Playfoot, J., Fabregat, M., Costa, M., Torres, S., Crețu, C. (2010). "rePlay Project - Gaming Technology Platform for Social Reintegration of Marginalised Youth", Proceedings of the 2nd International Conference on Computer Supported Education (CSEDU), pp 489–495.

Kim, S., Song, K., Lockee, B., & Burton, J. (2018). *Gamification in learning and education: Enjoy learning like gaming (advances in game-based learning)*. Springer.

Klabbers, J. H. (2009). *The magic circle: Principles of gaming & simulation*. Sense Publishers.

Landers, R. N., Bauer, K. N., Callan, R. C., & Armstrong, M. B. (2015). Psychological theory and the gamification of learning. In T. Reiners & L. C. Woods (Eds.), *Gamification in education and business* (pp. 165–186). Springer.

Lave, J. (1988). *Cognition in practice: Mind, mathematics, and culture in everyday life*. Cambridge University Press.
Lave, J. (1991). *Situating learning in communities of practice. Perspectives on socially shared cognition*. (Vol. 2, pp. 63–82).
Liu, Y. (2023). An innovative talent training mechanism for maker education in colleges and universities based on the IPSO-BP-enabled technique. *Journal of Innovation & Knowledge, 8*(4), 100424., ISSN 2444-569X. https://doi.org/10.1016/j.jik.2023.100424
Luarn, P., Chen, C. C., & Chiu, Y. P. (2023). The influence of gamification elements in educational environments. *International Journal of Game-Based Learning, 13*(1), 1–12.
Majuri, J., Koivisto, J., & Hamari, J. (2018) 'Gamification of education and learning: A review of empirical literature'. In *Proceedings of the 2nd international GamiFIN conference, GamiFIN* 2018. CEUR-WS, Pori, Finland, 21–3 May.
McGarr, O., & McDonagh, A., (2019). Digital competence in teacher education. Developing Student Teachers Digital competence. https://dicte.oslomet.no.
McGonigal, J. (2011). Reality is broken: Why games make us better and how they can change the world. New York: Penguin Press.
Moreno-Guerrero, A., Rodriguez-Jiménez, C., Gómez-Garcia, G., & Navas-Parejo, M. R. (2020). Educational innovation in higher education: Use of role playing and educational video in future teachers' training. *Sustainability, 12*, 2558. https://doi.org/10.3390/su12062558
Moreno, A. G. (2024). Enhancing the learning and application of knowledge in university students: An escape room proposal. In V. Membrive (Ed.), *Practices and implementation of gamification in higher education* (pp. 71–87). IGI Global Scientific Publishing. https://doi.org/10.4018/979-8-3693-0716-8.ch004
Nascimbeni, F., Burgos, D., Spina, E., & Simonette, M. J. (2020). Patterns for higher education international cooperation fostered by open educational resources. *Innovations in Education and Teaching International*, 1–11.
Ngui, T. K. (2019). Inclusive education in higher education institutions in Kenya. *Journal of Education and Practice, 10*(3), 45. https://doi.org/10.7176/JEP/10-3-05
Nousiainen, T., Kangas, M., Rikala, J., & Vesisenaho, M. (2018). Teacher competencies in game-based pedagogy. *Teaching and Teacher Education, 74*, 85–97. https://doi.org/10.1016/j.tate.2018.04.012
Organisation for Economic Co-operation and Development (OECD). (2015). Educational research and innovation. Open educational resources. A catalyst for innovation. https://read.oecd-ilibrary.org/education/open-educational-resources_9789264247543-en#page4.
OECD. (2025). Education and skills in Romania: Reviews of national policies for education. OECD Publishing. https://doi.org/10.1787/594cbb5d-en
Ohiri, S.-C., Okonkwo, J., & Somto, K.-E., (2024). A critical analysis of teachers' insights into the implementation practices in Owerri education zone 1 of Imo State. (Vol. 18, pp. 373–390).
Palha, S., Bouwer, A., Webb, K., van Smaalen, D., & Agterberg, D. (2024). Game-based pedagogy in teacher training: Results of a pilot course. *European Conference on Games Based Learning Proceedings, 18*(1), 677–684. https://doi.org/10.34190/ecgbl.18.1.2698
Plass, J. L., Mayer, R. E., & Homer, B. D. (2020). *Handbook of game-based learning*. MIT Press.
Prensky, M. (2001). *Digital game-based learning*. McGraw-Hill.
Prensky, M. (2006). 'Don't bother me Mom, I'm learning!': How computer and video games are preparing your kids for twenty-first century success and how you can help! . St. Paul, MN: Paragon House.
Robinson, K., & Aronica, L. (2015). Şcoli creative. Revoluţia de bază a învăţământuilui. Bucureşti: Publica.
Sailer, M., Hense, J., Mandl, H., & Klevers, M. (2017). Fostering development of work competencies and motivation via gamification. In M. Mulder (Ed.), *Competence-based vocational and professional education: Bridging the worlds of work and education* (pp. 795–818). Springer.
Scheiner, C., & Witt, M. (2013). The Backbone of Gamification – Theoretical Consideration of Play and Game Mechanics. 2372–2386. https://pdfs.semanticscholar.org/4caf/322b68508c28e82e4270c2c57399a015149e.pdf

Seghedin, E. (2019). *Promoting reflectivity in higher education. From theory to practice*, INTED2019 Proceedings, p. 9227.ISBN: 978-84-09-08619-1, ISSN: 2340-1079, doi: 10.21125/inted.2019.2287, 13th International technology, education and development conference, 11–13 March, 2019, Valencia, Spain, https://library.iated.org/view/SEGHEDIN2019PRO.

Siemon, D., & Linda, E. (2017). Gamification of teaching in higher education. In S. Stieglitz, C. H. Lattemann, R.-B. Susanne, R. Zarnekow, & T. Brockmann (Eds.), *Gamification using game elements in serious contexts* (pp. 153–163., ISSN 2196-8705 ISSN 2196-8713 (electronic) ISBN 978-3-319-45555-6). Springer. https://doi.org/10.1007/978-3-319-45557-0

Stentiford, L. , Koutsouris, G. (2022). Critically considering the 'inclusive curriculum' in *Higher education British Journal of Sociology of Education* 43(8), 1250–1272. https://doi.org/10.1080/01425692.2022.2122937

Subhash, S., & Cudney, E. A. (2018). Gamified learning in higher education: A systematic review of the literature. *Computers in Human Behavior, 87*, 192–206.

Sweller, J. (2003). Evolution of human cognitive architecture. In B. Ross (Ed.), *The psychology of learning and motivation* (Vol. 43, pp. 215–266). Academic Press.

Sweller, J. (2004). Instructional design consequences of an analogy between evolution by natural selection and human cognitive architecture. *Instructional Science, 32*(1/2), 9–31.

Taylor, G., Jungert, T., Mageau, G. A., Schattke, K., Dedic, H., Rosenfield, S., & Koestner, R. (2014). A self-determination theory approach to predicting school achievement over time: The unique role of intrinsic motivation. *Contemporary Educational Psychology, 39*(4), 342–358.

Tlili, A., Huang, R., Chang, T. W., Nascimbeni, F., & Burgos, D. (2019). Open educational resources and practices in China: A systematic literature review. *Sustainability, 11*(18), 486.

United Nations Educational, Scientific, and Cultural Organization (UNESCO). (2019). *Recommendation on open educational resources (OER).* https://www.unesco.org/en/legal-affairs/recommendation-open-educational-resources-oer.

Vandercruysse, S., Vandewaetere, M., & Clarebout, G. (2012). Game-based learning: A review on the effectiveness of educational games. In M. M. Cruz-Cunha (Ed.), *Handbook of research on serious games as educational, business, and research tool* (pp. 628–647). IGI Global.

Wagner, T. (2014). *Creating innovators: The making of young people who will change the world.* Trei Press.

Webster, J., & Martocchoio, J. J. (1992). Microcomputer playfulness: Development of a measure with workplace implications. *MIS quarterly, 16*, 201–227. https://doi.org/10.2307/249576

Weitl-Harms, S. & Spanier, A. & Hastings, J. & Rokusek, M. (2023). A Systematic Mapping Study on Gamification Applications for Undergraduate Cybersecurity Education. *Journal of Cybersecurity Education Research and Practice.* 2023. https://doi.org/10.32727/8.2023.12

Zachary, F.-W., Dian, T., & Peta, W. (2011). Orientation passport: Using gamification to engage university students. In *Proceedings of the 23rd Australian computer-human interaction conference* (OzCHI '11). Association for Computing Machinery, New York, NY, USA. (pp. 122–125). https://doi.org/10.1145/2071536.2071554.

Zhang, Z., Dong, Y., & Zhang, L. (2021). Analysis on the training path of foreign-related legal talents under the background of globalization. *Forest Chemicals Review*, 1050–1063.

Zhang, X., Tlili, A., Nascimbeni, F., Burgos, D., Huang, R., Chang, T. W., et al. (2020). Accessibility within open educational resources and practices for disabled learners: A systematic literature review. *Smart Learning Environments, 7*(1), 1. http://forestchemicalsreview.com. https://www.icevonline.com

Chapter 5
Initial Teacher Training for Inclusive Education and Gamification

Ioana Boghian and Venera-Mihaela Cojocariu

Abstract One of the current concerns of Romanian educational trainers/decision makers in education is the competence profile of the inclusive teacher in compulsory mainstream education. It includes specific and methodological knowledge, skills, and attitudes that enable him/her to carry out the pedagogical process for students with special educational needs (SEN) in order to create a specific and stimulating environment for learning. The studies show that the majority of teachers in the Romanian mainstream education system have insufficient knowledge regarding the implementation of the didactic process in classes of students with SEN, with mostly negative attitudes; moreover, younger teachers have a higher level of professional skills required to work with SEN students; however, although their attitude towards inclusive education is positive, if they had the choice, they would not include students with SEN. The causes of this reluctance are the insufficient emphasis on training for inclusive education in teacher training (at least in initial training), but also certain specificities of the context in which teaching takes place in mainstream schools, such as a large number of students in a class, the lack of a school counselor/support teacher in some schools, and the inefficiency in the implementation of certain teacher training programs due to the predominance of the theoretical aspect to the detriment of the practical. The solution to empowering teachers to work with students with special educational needs lies in their quality training for inclusive education as part of initial teacher education. In this sense, examples of good practice for inclusive education can be included in certain subjects of the psycho-educational training module and the pedagogical practice must have a clearly defined component focused on working with SEN students. Our approach aims to propose, based on theoretical considerations, a model for initial teacher

I. Boghian · V.-M. Cojocariu (✉)
Teacher Training Department, Vasile Alecsandri University of Bacău, Bacău, Romania
e-mail: boghian.ioana@ub.ro; venera@ub.ro

I. Boghian, G. Mareş (eds.), *Gamification and Inclusion*, Inclusive Learning and Educational Equity 12, https://doi.org/10.1007/978-3-031-98390-0_5

training that aims to enable future teachers to work with SEN students and implicitly overcome their reluctance in this area.

Keywords Gamification · Competence profile of the inclusive teacher · Students with special educational needs (SEN student) · Inclusive education

Introduction

Children with disabilities, of whatever type and degree, have long been considered undesirable, difficult, different, problematic, a nuisance to other children, and our hopes and efforts are aimed at overcoming this approach as quickly as possible. Due to a lack of knowledge and the associated mentality based on "a stereotype deeply rooted in the collective social and institutional mentality" (Turza & Duminică, 2015), it was assumed that children with disabilities should live, grow up and be educated separately from typical children. Until 1990, their education in Romania took place exclusively in institutions created specifically for this purpose, namely special schools. After 1990, against the background of an increasingly thorough analysis of the educational aspects in connection with children's/human rights, this topic has attracted wider interest. A slow process of transition from the paradigm of segregated education to the paradigm of inclusive education had begun. Since 1997, Law No. 128 on the Status of Teaching Staff (and its updated versions) has defined the itinerant or assistant teacher and his/her role. Later, with the introduction of the Methodology for the Organization of Educational Support Services for Children, Students and Adolescents with Special Educational Needs integrated into mainstream education (2011), efforts to support children with special educational needs begin to take effect. Art. 5 "The school integration of people with special educational needs takes place in units of general education" and Art. 7 "The specialized services necessary for the integration of children with SEN are provided by itinerant and support teachers in collaboration with all the factors involved" create the specific methodological context for the realization of inclusive education in Romania. Subsequently, the new *Legea învăţământului preuniversitar* (Law of Pre-university education) no. 198/2023 has defined in section 2 the way in which special education is currently organized (in mainstream school, special education, hospitals, at home) and the categories of beneficiarie (Ministerul Justiției, 2023a: 24–25, 2023b).

In this respect, one of the current concerns of teachers and decision-makers in education is the competence profile of the integration teacher in compulsory mainstream education. It includes specific and methodological knowledge, skills, and attitudes that enable them to carry out the teaching-pedagogical process for students with special educational needs (SEN) in order to create a specific and stimulating environment for learning (Goraş-Postică & Guţu, 2018; Balan et al., 2017; Horga et al., 2016; Vrăşmaş, 2001, 2004, 2007).

The concept of inclusive education was explained in the Salamanca (Spain) Declaration on Special Needs Education, which was adopted at the World Conference on Access and Quality organized by UNESCO and the Spanish Ministry of Education from 7 to 10 June 1994. It sets out the approach to inclusive education (from a political and legal perspective) by enrolling all children with special educational needs in mainstream schools, unless there are compelling reasons to do otherwise. This adds to teachers' skills the ability to plan, manage, and facilitate classroom interaction, taking into account the different needs and abilities of learners. With more confident and skilled teachers, the inclusive education program will have a positive impact on community awareness. This would increase the proportion of disabled children attending school in the light of education for all and more and more disabled or differently abled children would work and contribute to social development.

Inclusive education means the full inclusion of children with different abilities (from giftedness to disabilities of some degree) in all aspects of school life that other children can access and enjoy.

The inclusive approach embraces schools and classrooms that are considered normal precisely because they truly embrace change to meet the needs of all children as a positive valorization and appreciation of differences (Loreman et al., 2005). *The Individuals with Disabilities Education Act* (IDEA) in the United States, as amended in 1997, clearly states that schools are required to educate children with disabilities in regular classrooms.

Integration and inclusion are two terms that are not synonymous, so it is confusing to use them from the same conceptual or methodological perspective. While by (school) integration we mean "the process of adaptation of the person with SEN to the norms and requirements of the school they attend, the establishment of positive affective relationships with the members of the school group (school community/class) and the successful implementation of school activities," (school) inclusion means "the continuous process of improving the services offered by the educational units in order to include all members of the community in the educational process, regardless of their characteristics, disadvantages or difficulties" (Ministerul Justiției, 2011: 3). The term inclusion implies the identification and minimization of barriers to the learning and participation of students with special educational needs in the educational process, as well as the maximization of resources allocated for this purpose (Booth & Ainscow, 2002). Inclusion in schools is "about equality of opportunity for all students [...] with particular reference to the functioning of different groups of students" (Office for Standards in Education - OFSTED, 2001). The simple distinction that can be made is that inclusion means coming from outside. Inclusion programs aim to integrate children with different abilities into the existing classrooms and structures of a school. They strive to normalize and help a child fit into an existing school model. The difference to inclusion is that it assumes that all children are part of the mainstream school from the start of their schooling.

Inclusive education is "the permanent process of improving the school institution with the aim of using existing resources, particularly human resources, to support the participation of all people within a community" in the educational process' (OFSTED, 2001: 5). It is therefore based on the humanistic and optimistic premise that every child has the right to be educated in a mainstream school, including children with special needs. A child with special needs should not be segregated and enrolled in special schools, except perhaps in extreme cases. Their needs can be met in a mainstream school if it has the necessary infrastructure and sufficiently trained staff. The goal of every teacher in an inclusive classroom is to observe the needs of the students and the differences between them and to find the optimal approaches to make learning meaningful for each student by referring to their uniqueness. An educational opportunity for all, inclusive education is the implementation of a policy and process that allows all children to participate in all programs. The policy that all children should be accepted without restriction in all educational settings and in all program categories is based on the idea of equality of all children, but also on the acceptance of their natural diversity.

The process of inclusion refers to the concrete ways in which the system can succeed in making itself welcoming to all children. In relation to the inclusion of children with disabilities, this approach means shifting services from caring for the disabled child to educating and supporting the child's personal development. Inclusive education goes one step further by defining these children as children with special educational needs who require a special kind of attention and engagement (as opposed to the old view where children were seen as deficient). The change in perspective in understanding education is nothing more than understanding this change in the sense of "making the program for children with disabilities an integral part of the general education system, rather than a system within the general education system" (Kusuma & Ramadevi, 2013: 27).

At the level of the education system and policy, there should be an administrative and budgetary priority line aimed precisely at the practical implementation of inclusive education by respecting the principle of inclusive education, enrolling all children in mainstream schools, and including the component of inclusive education for all categories of teachers in the curriculum of initial training for the teaching profession. UNESCO (2001, 1994) states that all children, regardless of their difficulties or differences, can learn together if their teachers know how to respond to their needs; adapt to different learning styles, learning speeds, and learning outcomes; organize the learning environment; select appropriate didactic strategies; use resources appropriately; and maintain partnerships and links with local communities.

Another approach to inclusive education is summarized in Bristol City Council's Equality and Education Policy, which describes it as follows: "The process by which all those providing education develop their culture, policies and practices for inclusive settings where a focus on the student's needs is ensured. They are enabled to create a sense of community and belonging to the special needs of these children and also to provide new opportunities for those who may have struggled in the past. This does not mean that they treat all students equally. Rather, it is about embracing their diversity and uniqueness in terms of their experiences and needs" (Kusuma & Ramadevi, 2013: 26).

OFSTED (2001) argues that effective schools are educationally inclusive. This is evident not only in their performance but also in their "ethos and willingness to offer new opportunities to students who have previously struggled" (OFSTED, 2001: 18).

Booth and Ainscow (2002) have concluded that inclusion involves a system of closely interrelated elements, of which the essential ones might be a new kind of school culture, effectiveness, transformational leadership, schools as learning organizations, teacher learning at the intersection of inquiry and reflection, collaborative planning, student involvement, and celebration of every success.

Inclusive education is based on the general principle that school should welcome all children regardless of physical, intellectual, social, emotional, linguistic, and other aspects. It should welcome disabled and gifted children alike; street children and affluent families; children from remote or nomadic populations; children from linguistic, ethnic, or cultural minorities; and children from other disadvantaged countries or marginalized areas/groups.

If we look at the essential aspects of inclusive education, we can highlight the following (Kusuma & Ramadevi, 2013: 27):

- It is an endless series of processes in which children and adults with disabilities have the opportunity to participate fully in the school community and in the activities offered to people without disabilities.
- It ensures the education of children with disabilities in a school of their choice, together with children without disabilities.
- It provides educational services and special support to children with disabilities and their parents.
- It provides special support to teachers who are not yet equipped to work with students with disabilities and to administrators who have relationships with children with disabilities who are in the same program as other children.
- It promotes friendships between disabled children and all other children.

Inclusive education therefore means more than the physical presence of a child in the classroom, following the same curriculum as people with disabilities, taking the same exams as people without disabilities and obtaining the same certificate. According to the NCF Review (2005), inclusive education means that all students, whether young people with or without disabilities, can learn together under regular pre-school regulations, in community educational contexts with an appropriate network of support services.

Nowadays, most teachers recognize the value of inclusion and analyze it from the perspective of effective pedagogical practice based on two aspects: collaboration between classroom teachers and teachers specializing in the education of children with special educational needs, and the development and application of a planned integrated package of pedagogical interventions (Logan et al., 1995). Of particular importance are regular reflections that lead to the revision and refinement of strategies that actively include students with disabilities.

In conclusion, we can highlight a number of principles of inclusive education (Ghirxi et al., 2019: 15) that can guide the work of any teacher interested in respecting and capitalizing on diversity in the classroom:

- Every student has the right to education and to equal opportunity in the process.

- No student shall be excluded from or discriminated against on the basis of ethnicity, color, gender, language, religion, socioeconomic status, political or other opinion.
- All students can learn in their own way and at their own pace and benefit from education.
- Schools must adapt to the needs of the students (and not the students to the needs of the school).
- Individual differences between students are a source of diversity and, implicitly, of enrichment.

The term gamification was first used by Shirky and Terrill in 2008 (Christopoulos & Mystakidis, 2023). The term has its grammatical origin in the verb gamify. Gamification stands for the approach of using game elements in non-game situations (website, online community, in the educational system or in business), with promising effects on students' learning engagement and motivation (Magnago & Nunes, 2024; Mateus et al., 2024; Ruiz-Navas et al., 2024; Tomé Klock et al., 2024; Jadán-Guerrero et al., 2023), including their well-being (Christopoulos & Mystakidis, 2023). Indeed, it is the approach of introducing game-like experiences into real life to support the accumulation/training/consolidation of skills (Tomé Klock et al., 2024).

Overall, the most frequently emphasized positive effects of well-designed and implemented gamification relate to cognitive and emotional benefits (e.g., problem solving, communication, collaboration, resilience to challenges). If we add the stimulation of intrinsic motivation, the result is that gamification can create a genuine and constant commitment to learning in the long term, which is a prerequisite for academic achievement (Christopoulos & Mystakidis, 2023). When we associate gamification with inclusive education, we recognize formative opportunities to increase the inclusion and participation of students with diverse profiles and needs by fostering an experiential and collaborative learning environment. Researchers (Magnano & Nunes, 2024; Sharma & Kumar, 2024; Jadán-Guerrero et al., 2023) highlight the growing number of studies looking at the impact of gamification in inclusive education. They show how it can "appeal to all students, including those with disabilities and other learning difficulties" (Magnano & Nunes, 2024, p. 2902). Gamification is the pedagogical approach by which the practical application of inclusive education can be designed and implemented, a support to inclusive education, a way in which gamified activities can be adapted/modified to the user's characteristics to improve outcomes for students with different special educational needs.

Peer review studies (Ruiz-Navas, S. et al., 2024) show an evolution of research on gamification from a general approach (2015) (concept, design) to gamification and its design in different contexts (2016–2017), then the focus on gamification in education in general and in different particular contexts (2018–2020) and later (2020–2022) the extension to gamification in more and more specific situations, such as in the online environment or with students with special educational needs. A research trend is highlighted that emphasizes the need to develop gamification applications where the most current point is precisely where gamification meets inclusion and moves from gamification to adaptive gamification, with all its positive effects: personalization, motivation, respect for individual rhythm, adaptation to a specific type of need (e.g., autism, dyslexia, dysgraphia, ADHD, anxiety, learning disabilities, intellectual disabilities, speech and language disorders, sensory disabilities, unwanted behaviors—Sharma & Kumar, 2024; Jadán-Guerrero et al., 2023).

At the same time, gamification promotes inclusion through the way it is developed and is a tool for this (Manzano-León et al., 2023; Mateus et al., 2024). It promotes a sense of belonging and commitment, responsibility and the possibility of making decisions, collaboration, and the elaboration of original solutions through the use of theoretical knowledge in practical contexts, confronting real problems and practicing how to overcome them (very important dimensions in general, but especially when we refer to working with students with special educational needs).

A series of studies on this topic allows us to list concrete, actionable strategies for educators and administrators to use gamification effectively for inclusion or that can be developed/adapted for inclusion: group competitions, escape room, students vs. teachers, competition against self (Sharma & Kumar, 2024); Habitica, Fitbit, Snapchat (Tasyürek, D., 2024; Duolingo, BeeUp, Sony Wonderbook, ClassDojo (Vlad, 2021).

In the Romanian education system, dealing with the use of gamification and training teachers in this direction is a recent concern. Mostly it is integrated in the in-service training or self-education approach. In the last 10 years, numerous projects have been carried out with European funding, which have enabled the opening of teacher training on this topic or the concrete implementation of these approaches in the educational process.

To summarize, we present several such projects carried out in different geographical areas of Romania and at different levels of the educational system:

1. *GamED* (Gamification for Developing Essential Competencies in Youth Work—gamED Gamification for Developing Essential Skills in Youthwork (gamED) - Romanian Angel Appeal - Romanian Angel Appeal, Erasmus 2020-3-RO01-KA205-095067) (2020–2022). The Romanian Angel Appeal Foundation in collaboration with five other partners: World College Services of the Mediterranean (WUSMED) and Blue Room Innovation from Spain, Instituto Politecnico de Setubal and Produções Fixe from Portugal and the "Vasile Alecsandri" University of Bacău from Romania. The aim is to improve the quality of programs that focus on developing key skills for a successful life while teaching young people important values such as fairness, social justice, non-discrimination, and community engagement, through the acquisition of basic gamification and game design skills that support youth workers in the development and delivery of innovative educational programs.
2. *Gamest* (GAMification Techniques for entrepreneurial vet Teachers) gamest – gamest Erasmus+2019-1-RO01-KA202-06321 (high-school and university education) (2019–2021). Partners: "Dunărea de Jos" University of Galați, Romania; FVB SRL Ancona, Italy; Solski Center Novo Mesto, Slovenia; Prism Consulting

SRL Padova, Italy; The University of Santiago de Compostela, Spain. The general objective of the project was to support the promotion of high-quality and innovative teaching based on the application of gamification strategies. One of the outputs is the volume *Gamification—An Innovative Teaching Method* (Vlad, 2021).

3. *Gamification of digital* learning, GDL: Gamification of Digital Learning Erasmus+ Project, Erasmus+KA220 (high-scool education) (2022–2023). The project was coordinated by LogoPsyCom from Mons, Belgium, a private company specialized in projects for skills development, vocational training, revalidation and inclusion of young people with learning disabilities. Partners: Euphoria Net Srl Rome, Italy, "Mihai Băcescu" Technical College, Limassol Private High School, Cyprus, and Lodz Vocational High School from Poland.
4. *Inclusion through gamification*, Proiect Inclusion Through Gamification - Impact in Gorj, Erasmus+KA210—a small partnership in the field of school education (pre-school and primary education) (2021–2023), with partner teams from Romania, Slovakia, and Turkey. They proposed examples of gamification developed and tested with students, using platforms such as Kids Educational Games | RamoGames.com, Arcademics - Math Games, Language Arts Games, and More, Wordwall, Jigsaw Planet, CoolMath4Kids.
5. *Gamify Your Teaching, GAMIFY_O3 Didactic Materials_RO.pdf, Erasmus + KA202-014975 (2015–2017)* implemented by a consortium of seven European countries: Romania, Italy, Lithuania, Poland, the United Kingdom, Spain and Greece. The beneficiaries were entrepreneurship trainers and vocational education teachers using gamification.

From such a perspective, if we ask what is the impact of the functioning of an inclusive school, we might find that (New Brunswick Association for Community Living, 2011): the practice of developing inclusive schools involves understanding inclusion as an ongoing process rather than a one-time event; strengthening and supporting the participation of all students, teachers, parents, and community members in the activities of the school; providing an accessible curriculum, an appropriate training program for teachers and all students, fully accessible information, an accessible learning environment and support (material, psychological, educational); ensuring a functioning partnership between schooland family; continuity and collaboration between general education and education for children with SEN; building the capacity to create and use personalized intervention plans; maintaining good capacity to plan integrated pedagogical approaches and those for team communication and gamification.

Gamification plays a fundamental role in creating and sustaining a more inclusive and equitable education. This requires adequate infrastructure and teacher training to implement it effectively, as well as a welcoming school environment to meet the needs of students with special educational needs (Filho et al., 2024, Magnano & Nunes, 2024; Tomé Klock et al., 2024; Christopoulos & Mystakidis, 2023).

In summary, inclusive education with gamification is quality education that works for each individual child and enables them to maximize their own potential (UNICEF, 2006).

Methodology

The study we propose is a literature review. Its aim is to develop a model for initial teacher education that will enable future teachers to work with students with disabilities.

Research objectives:

O1 - To identify teachers' attitudes towards students with special educational needs (SEN) and the origins and causes of these attitudes;

O2 - To identify the specific characteristics of the competence profile of the inclusive teacher;

O3 - Identify a set of solutions that enable teachers to work with students with SEN and gamification, and implicitly change their attitudes towards students with SEN;

O4 - Develop and propose a model for initial teacher training aimed at enabling future teachers to work with students with SEN and gamification, and implicitly overcome their reluctance to do so.

Results and Discussions

The results achieved are further presented in accordance with the objectives set:

Results for O1—identification of teachers' attitudes towards students with SEN and their causes

Some of the studies (Charitaki et al., 2024; Wahsheh, 2024; Kazmi et al., 2023; Levi-Sudai & Neagu, 2022; Desombre et al., 2021; Neagu & Nistor, 2020; Gidlund, 2018; Bukvić, 2014; Kusuma & Ramadevi, 2013; Ljubetić & Kostović Vranješ, 2008; Ashby, 2010) show that the majority of teachers in mainstream education have insufficient knowledge about the implementation of the didactic process in classes of students with SEN, with mostly negative attitudes; also younger teachers have a higher level of professional skills required to work with SEN students; although their attitude towards inclusive education is positive, if they had the choice, they would not include students with SEN in their class. The most frequently cited reasons for this reluctance are the insufficient importance given to training for inclusive education in teacher training, certain specificities of the context in which mainstream education takes place: a large number of students in a class; the lack of school counselors/support teachers in some schools; the large number of children who need to be counseled by each individual school counselor, respectively the practical impossibility of providing support to a teacher who needs it for a child with SEN; and the ineffectiveness of certain teacher training programs on inclusive education due to the predominance of the theoretical aspect to the detriment of the practical (Jurca et al., 2023). We highlight some opinions from the literature on the topic discussed here: "Inclusion involves a variety of practices aimed at improving outcomes. What good teachers do is think carefully about children and develop teaching practices that ensure they can reach all children" (Kusuma & Ramadevi, 2013: 28). "Ultimately, effective teaching is a relationship between two people; teachers achieve good results because they engage in that relationship. Inclusion offers a variety of learning opportunities. It represents the structuring of schools as a community in which all children can learn" (Ashby, 2010), yet for many teachers, the inclusion of students with disabilities in mainstream schools is not beneficial to either category of children (with and without disabilities). Gamification, although but recently associated increasingly more often with inclusivity, has been shown to promote the inclusion of students with disabilities, particular needs, and abilities, by supporting an inclusive environment, where everyone feels seen, encouraged and able to perform better (Mateus et al., 2024; del Olmo-Muñoz et al., 2023; Manzano-León et al., 2023).

Our attempt to overcome such unproductive theoretical and practical hypostases has led us to systematize the benefits of inclusion and gamification teaching and learning strategies for both categories of beneficiaries (Bukvić, 2014) (Table 5.1):

Table 5.1 The double benefits of inclusion in mainstream schools

Advantages of inclusion and gamification for children with SEN	Advantages of inclusion and gamification for children without disabilities
Children with SEN show a higher level of social interaction with peers without SEN in an inclusive, gamified learning environment than in a segregated context. The social and communication skills of children with different abilities are improved in the inclusive, gamified environment	They can be the beneficiaries of particular experiences in the classroom. These contexts can be used in a variety of ways to provide additional learning experiences that benefit all children (e.g., by inviting guest speakers from outside the school)
Children with SEN or gifted children can benefit from the variety of teaching, gamified strategies in the classroom.	Children without SEN or gifted children can benefit from the variety of teaching, gamified strategies in the classroom
In inclusive, gamified learning settings, friendships develop more frequently between children with SEN and children without SEN	They can learn to appreciate and respect children with different disabilities. They can build friendships with peers with SEN or gifted peers
Inclusion and gamification help to improve the general knowledge of children with SEN	Engagement in peer tutoring situations (improved self-esteem, acquisition of learning content) and sharing/using academic content
Inclusion and gamification teachingand learning strategies encourage children with SEN to showcase their talents and make the most of them	They may have the opportunity to learn additional skills such as Braille or sign language. They are encouraged to showcase their talents and make the most of them
The main motto of inclusive education, i.e., "learn to live together" can be achieved more easily, and more effectively through the use of gamification in the educational context	

It is precisely for this reason that Majoko (2019) emphasizes the need for some essential clarifications: inclusion means changing schools to improve the education system for all students. It means changes in the curriculum, changes in the way teachers teach and how students learn, and changes in the way students with and without special needs interact and relate to each other, with the value of respect being fundamental in this interaction.

Results for O2—identifying the specific characteristics of the competence profile of the inclusive teacher

The identification of these particularities is based on the central role of the teacher in the inclusion process. The teacher, from the perspective of inclusive education, must preactively transform into a reformer of the process/classroom and adapt the philosophy behind the educational process and its practices. Every teacher who has worked in regular classrooms feels that working in an inclusive environment can be a difficult and complex matter. in general, teachers believe that inclusion requires a high level of pedagogical and organizational competence.

We highlight a number of specific dimensions of an inclusive classroom in which the specific aspects of the inclusive teacher's competence profile can manifest themselves (Filho et al., 2024, Luo & Li, 2024; Magnano & Nunes, 2024; Opeña & Pontillas, 2024; Tomé Klock et al., 2024; Christopoulos & Mystakidis, 2023; Crețu, 2023; Woodcock et al., 2022; Arvelo-Rosales et al., 2021; Florian & Camedda, 2019; Majoko, 2019; Florian, 2012; Pantic & Florian, 2015):

- *Promoting positive attitudes/relationships in all children*—the fundamental aim of education is to instill values and create respect for all people, regardless of their differences. The teacher's task is to develop an appropriate attitude towards building a healthy relationship between children with and without disabilities. If the relationship between them is good, then it is relatively easy to manage inclusive education;
- *Collaboration with parents in the inclusive classroom:* studies show (Hornby, 2010) that a functioning partnership between the family and the school is particularly beneficial for children with various disabilities and the success of these children in mainstream schools. Parents' in-depth knowledge of their own child's needs and disabilities can help schools and teachers make better decisions about appropriate learning tasks, learning environments and teaching styles;
- *Collaboration with colleagues:* working in inclusive classes is based on the interaction of a whole team of professionals: specialist teachers, psychologists, speech therapists. By working with them, the teacher can receive additional help, experience and ideas, practical advice and support, and even joint planning of teaching situations can be achieved. This is a good example of team teaching;
- *Inclusive environment:* it must be welcoming and friendly; children should feel comfortable and enjoy coming to school; colorful diagrams could be used to explain any abstract concepts, and the classroom could resemble a research lab. From an administrative point of view, the school should provide the necessary facilities such as ramps (for children with physical disabilities) or a handrail (for children with visual impairments);

- *Teaching with the help of new information and communication technologies:* teachers need to integrate ICT into an effective teaching and learning process by addressing existing disabilities, developing strategies to extend learning opportunities and applications for the different learning levels, using gamification and adapting them to the different categories of SEN. ICT provides tools that help both students without and students with disabilities in their school work. By engaging students in collaborative activities, gamification, ICT can help to create appropriate and unique experiences in school. Effective teaching and learning activities can be provided through sources such as gamification, internet, learning platforms, audio (only) or visual (only) sources connected to the internet;
- *Collaboration with paraprofessionals* (Chireshe, 2011; Donnely & Watkins, 2011): they help schools and teachers collect data on and provide services to children with various disabilities, their diagnosis, management, and rehabilitation. Sometimes the most inclusive and effective use of paraprofessionals is to prepare materials for instruction and assist in completing tasks in the classroom.

Inclusive Education and Teacher Competence

Inclusive education is a global movement that aims to create an education system that values all children by designing a classroom that welcomes all students regardless of disability, social context, sexuality, ethnicity, etc. Today's concept of children with special needs has replaced the negative labels of the past. The modern concept views children as unique and their uniqueness can be observed in one or more dimensions: Vision, hearing, communication, adaptive behavior, etc. Research conducted worldwide aims to increase the suitability and usefulness of inclusive education, the benefits of transition from special schools to inclusion in neighborhood schools, a transition whose goal is to benefit all children (Slee & Allan, 2001; Julka, 2007).

The *competence of the inclusive teacher* is the ability to plan, manage, and facilitate classroom interaction in a way that is appropriate and takes into account the diverse needs and abilities of learners. The teacher deals with the different energy levels, ensures appropriate student participation and creates pairs and working groups that have a positive impact on learning, motivating them and ensuring that different learning styles are addressed and their different needs are met.

What competencies do teachers need to have to be competent inclusion teachers? (Kusuma & Ramadevi, 2013: 34):

- The ability to solve problems, to informally assess a student's abilities rather than relying solely on a standardized curriculum.
- The ability to appreciate children's individual interests and use their intrinsic motivation to develop the necessary skills.
- The ability to set high, but alternative, appropriate expectations for students, including the development and use of alternative assessments.

- The ability to set appropriate expectations for each student, regardless of ability.
- The ability to modify student assignments: Designing instructional activities at different levels so that all students have a role to play; This teaching skill can be applied not only at the elementary or secondary school level, but also at the college level and involves more instruction based on interactive activities and fewer lecture-based activities.
- The ability to learn how to value all types of skills that students bring to the classroom, not just academic skills.
- The ability to create daily success for all students. This includes counteracting the message that all students receive when certain students are regularly pulled out of the classroom for special activities.

Other skills that will help teachers in an inclusive environment (Azade, 2001):

- Awareness that they are responsible for each student in the class; teachers need to figure out or learn how to work with each child rather than assuming that someone else will tell them how to teach a child.
- Knowledge of a variety of teaching strategies and how to use them effectively; this includes the ability to adapt materials and restate goals for a child's needs.
- Collaborate with parents and special educators to find out what skills a child needs and to determine the best teaching approach.
- Looking at each student in the classroom from the perspective of their potential to improve, rather than from the perspective of a problem or challenge that needs to be solved.
- Flexibility and a high tolerance for ambiguity.
- Awareness of the importance and role of parents, the community and NGOs in educating children with diverse needs.
- Guidance and support to others in the use of different methods of implementing inclusive education.
- Advising both students with special needs and students without special needs on the inclusion and integration of a child with special needs in their class.
- Calling in support staff for advice.
- Purchasing special educational material relevant to working with students with special educational needs.
- Gathering useful information and recording it for the assessment of the student's progress.
- Supporting a special education teacher in their work with students with SEN.
- Develop a feedback system that provides data on relevant issues relating to students with special needs, teachers, parents, and other staff.

Teachers must redefine their role for inclusive education, and teacher educators must share this responsibility with future teachers to see every student as a regular and essential element of the educational act. A set of generic skills and competencies in this sense includes basic teaching skills, classroom management, professional guidance and communication, referrals, individualized instruction, interactive skills, orientation strategies for entry into mainstreaming, goal setting, regulation of programs, use of teaching strategies, promotion of classroom climate, resource management, and evaluation and monitoring.

As teachers are seen as key to educational change, their feelings of frustration and inadequacy are potential barriers to inclusive education. Teachers are not very familiar with the details of various disabilities, their diagnosis, management, and rehabilitation. They need programs to develop their skills in dealing with students with different needs. These programs should also be followed by the heads of school institutions, as they are crucial for the recruitment of support teachers, the acquisition of didactic material specifically for inclusive education, the equipment and infrastructure needed to work with children with SEN.

It seems that the real key to inclusion in this context is pedagogical decision-making. Indeed, proponents of inclusion tend to emphasize inclusive education not as a product but as a process (Robertson, 1999; Booth & Ainscow, 2002; Jocobson, 2000; Marshall et al., 2002).

Inclusive processes are becoming essential in research on school effectiveness and development. National institutes, regional rehabilitation centers, and other educational institutions can also play a role in strengthening capacity to promote inclusive education.

Results for *O3—identifying a set of solutions that enable teachers to work with students with SEN and gamification, and implicitly change their attitudes towards students with SEN*

The general solution for empowering teachers is to train them in inclusive education as part of their initial teacher training.

Among the specific solutions that can be considered are:

- The introduction of some examples of good practice for inclusive education and gamification in specific subjects from the psycho-educational training module.
- Ensuring a clearly defined component within pedagogical practice that focuses on working with students with SEN through the use of gamified teaching-learning activities.

Utilizing the training modules/disciplines included in initial and in-service teacher training.

- The implementation of blended curriculum design strategies (including differentiated, gamified teaching where students' individual learning can be personalized and adapted to their abilities and interests).
- Differentiated planning (which includes thinking sophisticatedly about different ways each lesson or activity can be modified, and gamified to better meet the needs of students. A teacher can differentiate the content they expect students to learn. The teacher can consider aspects such as students' current abilities, their interest and how they learn best).
- The preparation and enhancement of the inclusive class—an inclusive class is one in which the teacher ensures a positive relationship between the classmates of students with special needs and those without special needs. Several factors are critical to the success of an inclusive class: collaboration between main-

stream and special education teachers, well-developed individualized education plans and programs, team planning and communication, provision of integrated services, ongoing training, and staff development.

The inclusive classroom, then, is a child-centered classroom in which students are engaged in problem-solving activities in various types of activities that provide opportunities for students with different abilities. Learning centers could be established and used: a language center; a media center where one listens to recorded stories or creates multimedia presentations on the computer; a music center with different types of musical instruments for students to practice on depending on their talent and interest; a math center with manipulative operations; gamified activities adjusted to suit the particularities of typical students, and students with SEN. Whatever the activity, the associated objectives are clarified before students begin the activity.

Teachers can use a range of techniques to help build classroom communities (Kusuma & Ramadevi, 2013: 38): Games that create a sense of belonging and community, community songs and books, openly addressing individual differences, assigning classroom tasks that create a sense of belonging and community, and preparing students to find ways to help each other. During these activities, the teacher reminds students of the acceptable noise level, the learning objectives and the tasks to be completed. During the activities, the teacher focuses on the specifics of the learning center, taking into account different intelligences, different abilities, and learning styles. Learning begins with the teacher giving instructions to the whole class and ends with discussions about what has been learned.

According to Bhaumik et al. (2011), the following considerations are key to the success of the inclusive classroom:

(a) Students must be active, not passive learners,
(b) Children should be encouraged to make their own decisions as often as possible. The teacher gives students time to experiment and test solutions because deep learning comes from taking risks and learning from mistakes,
(c) Parental involvement is crucial.
(d) Students with disabilities must be given the opportunity to learn at their own pace and use alternative assessment strategies.
(e) Students must be successful, learning objectives must be specific, achievable, measurable and involve a degree of challenge.

In this conceptual and methodological context, a series of integrative practices can be outlined, recommended in particular in the national reports (Nevada Partnership, 2020), to which we have elaborated some possible pedagogical action alternatives, including gamification (Table 5.2):

Results for O4—The initial teacher training model focused on enabling future teachers to work with students with special educational needs and gamification, and implicitly on overcoming their reluctance in this regard

The development of such a model requires a holistic perspective on the complexity of working with students with SEN. Such a perspective requires an appropriate

Table 5.2 Inclusive, gamification practice

What is the recommendation?	What can be done?
– Less face-to-face instruction/teaching, with the whole class	– More work in groups or individually
– Less passivity of students	– Activation of students by participation in solving group tasks and use of gamified learning activities
– Less rewarding of silence in the classroom	– Acceptance/stimulation of the free manifestation of states/feelings during the teaching-learning process; use of gamified activities to foster free expression of states and feelings
– Less time for activities where students are busy with books, and at their desks	– More time for active, experimental, collaborative, gamified learning activities to promote students' active engagement in the learning process
– Less effort by teachers to teach a large amount of learning content superficially	– More effort by teachers to lead students to a deeper study of smaller number of books and topics; gamified activities specific to text study and interpretation
– Less memorization of facts and details	– Greater emphasis on higher order thinking skills in teaching/learning the key concepts and principles of a subject; gamified teaching-learning-assessment methods to support higher academic achievement levels in students
– Less emphasis on competition and grades	– Greater promotion of cooperation, collaboration and the results achieved, through gamified activities, and not only
– Less use/decreasing reliance on standardized tests	– The complementary increase in alternative assessment methods (projects, products, reflection journals, portfolios, observation sheets, kahoot quizzes, and other digital and/or traditional gamified approaches to assessment)
– More time spent reading complete, original books	– Less time spent accessing and using incomplete, fragmented, or non-original texts
– More choice for students	– Fewer prompts from teachers; the use of gamification elements such as instructions, rules, timeframe to provide stduents with a structured learning, goal-oriented context
– More emphasis on the multiple and collaborative roes of teachers, parents, admministrators, and community members in instruction and assessment of student outcomes	– Reduction of the teacher's sole role in instruction and assessment of student outcomes, more gamification as a way to enhance student engagement in achieving learning goals
– Adopting, emphasizing and shaping the principles of democracy in schools	– Reducing the authoritarian approach in schools; the use of gamified activities to empower students to make their own choices and take responsibility for their learning, as well as their learning outcomes

deductive connection between all components of the curriculum and the development of a theoretical-conceptual platform that provides the necessary openness to action.

Based on the literature review, we have outlined a possible model for the initial training of teachers working with students with special needs with the use of gamification. It involves a four-level approach: 1. theoretical-conceptual; 2. teleological; 3. content; 4. procedural. Each level links teachers and students from the perspective of the targeted approach and reveals a dual and interrelated approach (1. teacher training for inclusive education → educating students from the perspective of inclusive education; 2. the goals of professional training for inclusive education → the goals of educating students from the perspective of inclusive education; 3. academic content → school content; 4. specific strategies and techniques for professional training for inclusive education → specific strategies and techniques for educating students from the perspective of inclusive education, including gamification). The way in which the top-down determination of the model is ensured can only be usefully complemented by the way in which feedback is provided between stakeholders. Thus, the manifestations and developments in the procedural plan (strategies and techniques specific to inclusive education—both those specific to teacher training and those used in the process of inclusive education with students) will generate changes in the substantive plan (academic and school) and subsequently influence the teleological and even the theoretical-conceptual dimension. The decisive actor remains the teacher—with his complex professional and human structure, which is initially shaped and can be constantly (re)shaped, with his competences (which are particularly important for inclusive education) and his determining attitudes towards people and students with SEN (see Fig. 5.1).

The model implies the combination of inclusive education and gamification practices at all levels. Gamification promotes inclusion by providing teachers with flexible tools to adapt their teaching practices to the needs of all students. Inclusion is supported through gamified activities as these help create an inclusive learning environment where each learner can progress at their own pace, while focusing on achieving learning objectives.

Conclusions and Recommendations

The need for education is today greater than ever. This is why all current developments in the educational sciences are geared towards the specifics of today's society, with its global problems. Therefore, inclusive education and gamification for inclusion (adaptative gamification) (Ruiz-Navas, S. et al., 2024) represent two of the great challenges of today's society, both from a structural and functional point of view (Dewi, 2024; Magnano & Nunes, 2024; Pagano, 2024; Sharma & Kumar, 2024; Jadán-Guerrero et al., 2023; Derzhavina et al., 2021; Schuelka, 2018; Mag et al., 2017).

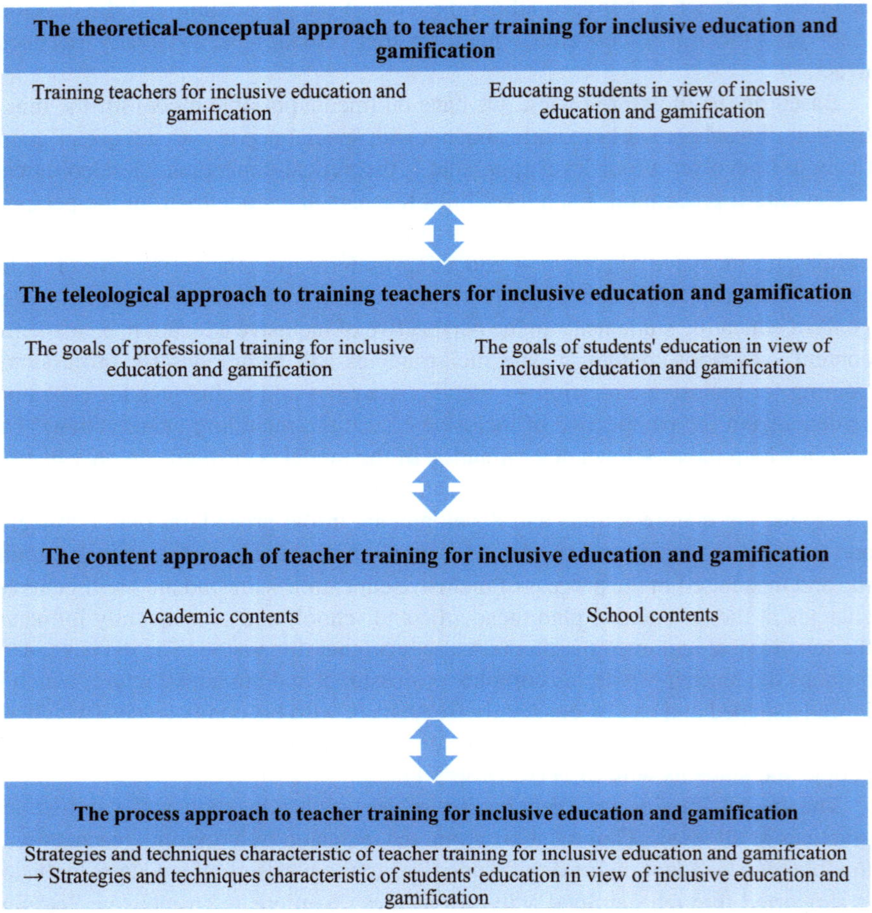

Fig. 5.1 A model for initial teacher training to enable future teachers to work with SEN students and gamification

The dimension of interpersonal differences between students, linked to the issue of equal access to educational opportunities and the democratization of education, means that the specific approaches of adaptative gamification and inclusive pedagogy are evolving, gaining much more audience and relevance and responding to a real, growing need, especially for teachers, both in terms of their initial training and their continuing education.

Inclusive pedagogy (Florian & Beaton, 2017) and gamification in education, in convergence with all other formative approaches, express a high humanism that values each person as they are and that invests faith, hope, and effort in their educability and perfection. The fundamental measures of an inclusive approach are acceptance and access to the other and ensuring participation in quality education.

These are also three main directions of teacher training to ensure the smooth running of activities with students with SEN: 1. shaping the right attitude of teachers towards students with SEN (Saloviita, 2018). "Gamification can overcome stereotypes and prejudices by allowing individuals to exhibit their abilities and talents in a secure environment" Mateus et al., 2024, p.6) atât atunci când e vorba despre elevi, despre elevi cu SEN cât și despre profesori; 2. ensuring the necessary conditions for the organization and access of students with SEN in the school (Ainscow, 2020; Hayes & Bulat, 2017); 3. empowering teachers to carry out specific activities (Filho et al., 2024; Magnano & Nunes, 2024; Tomé Klock et al., 2024; Christopoulos & Mystakidis, 2023; Kelly et al., 2022; Kefallinou, 2016). The greatest benefit of such an approach is that, over time, it can lead to a shift in thinking about adaptative gamification and inclusion that models not only for students with disabilities, but also for all students, educators, parents, families, and community members.

Although the teacher plays a crucial role in the success of gamification and inclusive education (and this is precisely why our interest in this study is in teacher education), what the teacher can do is predetermined by the educational system in which he or she works, the existing legal, paradigmatic, organizational and material context. If the legal context is adequately structured (as in the case of the Romanian system), it is still necessary to work on the other aspects that are more difficult to overcome.

The projects on gamification carried out in Romania over the last 10 years have led to the creation of numerous support materials, developed with the help of partners from other European countries (with expertise in the field), but adapted to the specific needs of students and teachers in the Romanian education system. The materials not only open the view on this important tool of gamification, but are also a variety of suggestions for other good practices that can be adapted and further developed from now on.

Taking into account the objective realities (the diversity of students, the presence of students with special educational needs and the socio-historical design of the educational system and its organization), we believe that there are a number of levers with which we can intervene in the training of teachers to use them for a didactic process in an inclusive classroom and in a gamification process. We believe that the following types of training contexts can be included in the basic training curriculum of any teacher who can benefit from greater extensions and content under the conditions of certain specializations:

- *Formal procedures:*
  - Introducing a discipline dedicated to this topic—inclusive education (in preschool/primary/secondary/high school/university/adult education) and a module on gamification in this process.
  - The creation of specific academic modules for inclusive education as part of the disciplines already present in initial teacher education curricula (a module within the Psychology of Education—on SEN and its pedagogical approach; a module within the Fundamentals of Pedagogy—on the forms and components of education and the possibilities of achievement with students with SEN; a module within the Theory and Methodology of Teaching—on strategies to work with students with SEN, with a differentiated and personalized

approach; a module within the Theory and Methodology of Assessment—on how forms and methods of assessment can be restructured and used in the activity with students with SEN; a module within the Teaching Practice—observation of specific approaches in an inclusive class and effective teaching, etc.).
  - The infusion approach, where for each topic and discipline, whenever a specific context for inclusive education and gamification can be created, teachers transfer the general aspects of the topic covered to the context of the inclusive classroom.

- *Non-formal procedures (projects):*
  - Carrying out interpersonal knowledge and relationship activities
  - Carrying out activities of a workshop nature for teamwork and the creation of joint products (literary, artistic, technological, musical): Students, parents, teachers, community members, and adults with disabilities who have integrated socially and professionally
  - Organization of joint artistic programs: Students, parents, teachers, community members and adults with disabilities who have integrated socioprofessionally
  - Debates/workshops organized jointly with teachers, parents, different categories of specialists, and members of the local community

Such approaches could lead both to the consolidation of the specific professional competences of all teachers and to their extension towards the competences of the integrative teacher. The tacit assumption of all the aforementioned solutions is, of course, that the college teachers who provide initial teacher education are themselves equipped to work with SEN students in an inclusive classroom, are able and willing to engage with them.

The importance of initial training in this sense remains essential, as does the nature of the culture at system and institutional level, as they are generators and carriers of the fundamental values of inclusive education: positive valorization and appreciation of differences, trust, respect, collaboration, and kindness.

References

Ainscow, M. (2020). Promoting inclusion and equity in education: Lessons from international experience. *Nordic Journal of Studies in Education Policy, 6*(1), 7–16. https://doi.org/10.1080/20020317.2020.1729587

Arvelo-Rosales, C. N., Alegre de la Rosa, O. M., & Guzmán-Rosquete, R. (2021). Initial training of primary school teachers: Development of competencies for inclusion and attention to diversity. *Education Sciences, 11*(8), 413. https://doi.org/10.3390/educsci11080413

Ashby, C. (2010). The trouble with normal: The struggle for meaningful access for middle school students with developmental disability labels. *Disability and Society, 25*(3), 345–358.

Azade, Y. A. (2001). *Role of inclusive education in proceedings of the workshop on appropriate model of education of children with special needs*. Rehabilitation Council of India.

Balan V., Bortă L., & Botnari V. (2017). Educaţie incluzivă: Unitate de curs, Ministerul Educaţiei, Culturii şi Cercetării al Rep. Moldova, Ediţie revizuită şi completată, Tipogr. Bons Offices, Chişinău.

Bhaumik, S., Watson, J., Barrett, M., Raju, B., Burton, T., & Forte, J. (2011). Transition for teenagers with intellectual disability: Carers' perspectives. *Journal of Policy and Practice in Intellectual Disabilities, 8*, 53–61.

Booth, T., & Ainscow, M. (2002). *Index for inclusion developing learning and participation in schools*. CSIE.

Bukvić, Z. (2014). Teachers competency for inclusive education. *The European Journal of Social and Behavioural Sciences, VI*(IV), 1585–1590.

Charitaki, G., Kourti, I., Gregory, J. L., Ozturk, M., Ismail, Z., Alevriadou, A., & Demirel, C. (2024). A comparative analysis of teachers' attitudes towards including all students in six countries. *Educational Research and Evaluation*, 1–41. https://doi.org/10.1080/13803611.2024.2406516

Chireshe, R. (2011). Special needs education in-service teacher trainees' views on inclusive education in Zimbabwe. *Journal of Social Science, 27*, 157–164.

Christopoulos, A., & Mystakidis, S. (2023). Gamification in education. *Encyclopedia, 3*(4), 1223–1243. https://doi.org/10.3390/encyclopedia3040089

Creţu, D. M. (2023). Preparing future teachers for inclusive education—conceptual frameworks and curriculum opportunities. Research and education, no. 9, 71-83. Preparing future teachers for inclusive education—Conceptual frameworks and curriculum opportunities—research and education. Accessed 8 Nov 2024.

Derzhavina, V. V., Nikitina, A. A., Makarov, A. L., Piralova, O. F., Korzhanova, A. A., Gruver, N. V., & Mashkin, N. A. (2021). Inclusive education importance and problems for students social integration. *Propósitos y Representaciones*. https://doi.org/10.20511/pyr2021.v9nSPE3.1130

Desombre, C., Delaval, M., & Jury, M. (2021). Influence of social support on teachers' attitudes toward inclusive education. *Frontiers in Psychology, 12*, 736535. https://doi.org/10.3389/fpsyg.2021.736535

Dewi, A. E. R. (2024). Effectiveness of implementing inclusive education: Challenges and opportunities in culturally diverse classrooms. *Journal of Pedagogi, 1*(3), 1–7. https://doi.org/10.62872/k2k0zs91

Donnelly, V., & Watkins, A. (2011). Teacher education for inclusion in Europe. *Prospects, 41*, 341–353.

Filho, T. A. G., de Santos, J. L. D., Melo, M., de Marques, R. J., Marques, F. R. V., da C, L. H. d. S., Lima, de, L. A. T., Bissaro, D. Z., Chagas, A. M., Rodrigues, C. P., Silva, da, L. H. P., Sanches, R. d. S. A., & França, L. N. (2024). School inclusion: The role of gamification as an educational mechanism for students with disabilities. *Seven Editora*, 891–899. Retrieved from https://sevenpublicacoes.com.br/editora/article/view/4243

Florian, L., & Camedda, D. (2019). Enhancing teacher education for inclusion. *European Journal of Teacher Education, 43*(1), 4–8. https://doi.org/10.1080/02619768.2020.1707579

Florian, L., & Beaton, M. (2017). Inclusive pedagogy in action: Getting it right for every child. *International Journal of Inclusive Education, 22*(8), 870–884. https://doi.org/10.1080/13603116.2017.1412513

Florian, L. (2012). Preparing teachers to work in diverse classrooms: Key lessons for the professional development of teacher educators from Scotland's Inclusive Practice Project. *Journal of Teacher Education, 63*, 275–285.

Goraş-Postică, V., & Guţu, S. (2018). Educaţia incluzivă în Republica Moldova: Repere legislativ-reglatorii actualizate şi inegalităţi perpetuate. Studia Universitatis Moldaviae. Chişinău.

Jadán-Guerrero, J., Avilés-Castillo, F., Buele, J., & Palacios-Navarro, G. (2023). Gamification in inclusive education for children with disabilities: Global trends and approaches—a bibliometric review. In O. Gervasi et al. (Eds.), *Computational science and its applications—ICCSA 2023 workshops. ICCSA 2023* (Lecture notes in computer science) (Vol. 14104). Springer. https://doi.org/10.1007/978-3-031-37105-9_31

Jocobson, L. O. (2000). Valuing diversity-student-teacher relationships that enhance achievement. *Community College Journal of Research and Practice, 28*(1), 49–67.

Ghirxi, J., Borg, D., Camenzuli, J., Pace, M., & Schembri Muscat, A. (2019). *A policy on inclusive education in schools. Route to quality inclusion*. The Ministry of Education and employment of Malta. A-Policy-on-Inclusive-Education-in-schools.pdf. Accessed 4 Nov 2024.
Gidlund, U. (2018). Teachers' attitudes towards including students with emotional and Behavioural difficulties in mainstream school: A systematic research synthesis. *International Journal of Learning, Teaching and Educational Research, 17*(2), 45–63. https://doi.org/10.26803/ijlter.17.2.3
Hayes, A.M., & Bulat, J. (2017). Disabilities inclusive education systems and policies guide for low- and middle-income countries. : RTI Press. https://www.ncbi.nlm.nih.gov/books/NBK554622/. Accessed 8 Nov 2024.
Horga, I., Apostu, O., Balica, M., UNICEF coordinator in Romania, Costache, L., Fartușnic, C., & Vrășmaș, T. (2016). *Educație pentru toți și pentru fiecare: accesul și participarea la educație a copiilor cu dizabilități și/sau CES din școlile participante la Campania UNICEF Hai la școală!* Alpha MDN.
Hornby, G. (2010). Preparing teachers to work with parents and families of learners with SEN in inclusive schools. In C. Forlin (Ed.), *Teacher education for inclusion: Changing paradigms and innovative approaches* (pp. 93–101). Routledge.
Julka, A. (2007). *Meeting special needs in school. A manual*. National Council of Educational Research and Training.
Jurca, A. M., Baciu, D., Lustrea, A., Sava, S., & Borca, C. V. (2023). Exploring attitudinal dimensions of inclusive education: Predictive factors among Romanian teachers. *Education Sciences, 13*, 1224. https://doi.org/10.3390/educsci13121224
Kazmi, A. B., Kamran, M., & Siddiqui, S. (2023). The effect of teacher's attitudes in supporting inclusive education by catering to diverse learners. *Frontiers in Education, 8*, 1083963. https://doi.org/10.3389/feduc.2023.1083963
Kefallinou, A. (2016). *Empowering teachers to promote inclusive education—literature review.* The European Agency for Special Needs and Inclusive Education https://www.researchgate.net/publication/308750303_Empowering_Teachers_to_Promote_Inclusive_Education_A_Literature_Review#. Accessed 8 Nov 2024.
Kelly, J., Mckenzie, J., Watermeyer, B., Vergunst, R., Karisa, A., & Samuels, C. (2022). 'We need to go Back to our schools, and we need to make that change we wish to see': Empowering teachers for disability inclusion. *International Journal of Disability, Development and Education, 71*(4), 633–649. https://doi.org/10.1080/1034912X.2022.2141696
Kusuma, A., & Ramadevi, K. (2013). Inclusive-education teacher competencies. *Shanlax International Journal of Education, 1*(3), 24–40.
Levi-Sudai, P., & Neagu, G. (2022). The Attitudes of Teachers towards Disadvantaged Young Students: Israel–Romania Comparative Analysis. Sustainability 14, no. 19: 12468. https://doi.org/10.3390/su141912468.
Ljubetić, M., & Kostović Vranješ, V. (2008). Pedagogical (in) competence of teachers. *Educational science, 10*(1), 209–230.
Logan, K. R., Diaz, E., Piperno, M., Rankin, D., MacFarland, A. D., & Bargamian, K. (1995). How inclusion built a community of learners. *Educational Leadership*.
Loreman, T., Deppler, J., & Harvey, D. (2005). *Inclusive education: A practical guide to supporting diversity in the classroom*. Routledge Falmer.
Luo, Y., & Li, H. (2024). An evidence-based inclusive pedagogical approach in action and its insights for enhancing the professional competence of inclusive education teachers in China. International Journal of. *Chinese Education, 13*(1). https://doi.org/10.1177/2212585X241242529
Mag, A. G., Sinfield, S., & Burns, T. (2017). The benefits of inclusive education: New challenges for university teachers, MATEC web of conferences 121, 12011, MSE 2017. The benefits of inclusive education: new challenges for university teachers. Accessed 8 Nov 2024.
Magnago, W., & Nunes, P.de C. (2024). Gamification and inclusive education: Promoting the engagement of all students. *ARACÊ, 6*(2), 2902–2911. https://doi.org/10.56238/arev6n2-147

Manzano-León, A., Aguilar-Parra, J. M., Rodríguez-Moreno, J., & Ortiz-Colón, A. M. (2023). Gamification in initial teacher training to promote inclusive practices: A qualitative study. *International Journal of Environmental Research and Public Health, 19*(13), 8000.

Majoko, T. (2019). Teacher key competencies for inclusive education: Tapping pragmatic realities of Zimbabwean special needs education teachers. *SAGE Open, 9*(1), 1–14.

Marshall, J., Ralph, S., & Palmer, S. (2002). 'I wasn't trained to work with them': Mainstream teachers' attitudes to children with speech and language difficulties. *International Journal of Inclusive Education, 6*(3), 199–215.

Mateus, C., Campis, R., Jabba, D., Erazo, A. M., & Romero, V. (2024). Gamification as a tool for inclusion. In F. Altınay, Z. Altınay, & K. Meltzoff (Eds.), *Intellectual and learning disabilities—inclusiveness and contemporary teaching environments*. Books on Demand. https://doi.org/10.5772/intechopen.106310

Neagu, G., & Nistor, G. (2020). The attitude of teachers towards the process of school inclusion of students with special educational needs secondary data analysis. *Revista de Asistență Socială, XIX*(3), 45–62. www.swreview.ro. Accessed 8 Nov 2024

New Brunswick Association for Community Living. (2011). Creating an inclusive school. A Reflection Tool for Administrators, Educators and Other School Staff. http://nbacl.nb.ca/wp-content/uploads/2015/02/Creating_An_Inclusive_School_Tool_-_Web.pdf. Accessed 29 Oct 2024.

Office for Standards in Education (OFSTED). (2001). *Managing support for the attainment of pupils from minority ethnic groups*. OFSTED.

del Olmo-Muñoz, J., Bueno Baquero, A., Cózar-Gutiérrez, R., & González-Calero, J. A. (2023). Exploring gamification approaches for enhancing computational thinking in young learners. *Education Sciences, 13*(5), 487.

Opeña, M. V., & Pontillas, P. V. (2024). Teachers' 21st -century skills and their competence on inclusive education in Opol districts. *International Journal of Multidisciplinary Research and Analysis, 7*(8), 3975–3987. https://doi.org/10.47191/ijmra/v7-i08-39

Pagano, U. (2024). Towards inclusive education: The evaluation challenge. *Science & Philosophy, 12*(1), 168–188. Towards Inclusive Education: The Evaluation Challenge | Pagano | Science & Philosophy. Accessed 8 Nov 2024.

Pantic, N., & Florian, L. (2015). Developing teachers as agents of inclusion and social justice. *Educational Inquiry, 6*, 331–351.

Robertson, C. (1999). Initial teacher education and inclusive schooling. *Support for Learning, 14*(4), 169–173.

Ruiz-Navas, S., Ackaradejraungsri, P., & Dijk, S. (2024). Are there literature reviews about gamification to foster inclusive teaching? A scoping review of gamification literature reviews. *Frontiers in Education, 9*, 1306298. https://doi.org/10.3389/feduc.2024.1306298

Saloviita, T. (2018). Attitudes of teachers towards inclusive education in Finland. *Scandinavian Journal of Educational Research, 64*(2), 270–282. https://doi.org/10.1080/00313831.2018.1541819

Schuelka, M. J. (2018). Implementing inclusive education. K4D Helpdesk Report. Brighton, UK: Institute of Development Studies. 374_Implementing_Inclusive_Education.pdf. Accessed 8 Nov 2024.

Sharma, V., & Kumar, J.A. (2024). Gamification: A new era of inclusion in education, (PDF) gamification: A new era of inclusion in education.

Slee, R., & Allan, J. (2001). Excluding the included: A reconsideration of inclusive education. *International Studies in Sociology of Education, 11*(2), 173–192.

Tasyürek, D. (2024). Best gamification examples and practices to boost user engagement, 10 Best Gamification Practices to Boost User Engagement - Storyly.

Tomé Klock, A. C., Palomino, P. T., Rodrigues, L. A. L., Toda, A. M., Simanke, S., Spors, V., Santana, B. S., & Hamari, J. (2024). Gamification towards and alongside equity, diversity and inclusion: Looking back to move forward. *New Media & Society*. https://doi.org/10.1177/14614448241254028

Turza, M., Duminică, G. (coord.) (2015). Izolați printre noi - Dimensiuni ale participării copiilor cu cerințe educaționale speciale în sistemul de educație românesc. : Rentrop & Straton.
Vlad, C. (2021). *Gamification—an innovative teaching method.* Galati University Press. Gamification_book Gamest.pdf
Vrășmaș, E. (2004). *Introducere în educația cerințelor speciale.* CREDIS.
Wahsheh, N. (2024). The inclusion of students with disabilities: Teachers' attitudes. *Multidisciplinary Science Journal, 6*(12), 2024258. https://doi.org/10.31893/multiscience.2024258
Woodcock, S., Sharma, U., Subban, P., & Hitches, E. (2022). Teacher self-efficacy and inclusive education practices: Rethinking teachers' engagement with inclusive practices. *Teaching and Teacher Education, 117*. https://doi.org/10.1016/j.tate.2022.103802
UNESCO (2001). Overcoming exclusion through inclusive approaches in education. A Challenge and A Vision. Conceptual Paper for the Education Sector.
UNESCO. (1994). The Salamanca statement and framework for action. In: Final report of the world conference on special needs education: Access and quality, Salamanca, Spain.
Vrășmaș, E. (2007). *Dificultăți de învățare în școală.* V&I INTEGRAL.
Vrășmaș, T. (2001). *Învățământul integrat și / sau incluziv.* Aramis.

Further Reading

XXX Ministerul Justiției. (2023a). *Legea învățământului preuniversitar* nr. 198/2023, publicată în M.O. 5.07.2023. https://edu.ro/sites/default/files/_fi%C8%99iere/Minister/2023/Legi_educatie_Romania_educata/legi_monitor/Legea_invatamantului_preuniversitar_nr_198.pdf. (accessed 4 November 2024).
XXX Ministerul Justiției. (2023b). *Statutul personalului didactic* Legea nr.198/2023, Statutul personalului didactic – Legea 198/2023 – Vivid Education. (accessed 4 November 2024).
XXX (2020). Nevada Partnership for Inclusive Education https://nvpie.org/. (accessed 4 November 2024).
XXX (2013). *Support for children with special educational needs* (SEN), European Commission, Bruxelles.
XXX (2012). Diversity, inclusion and equity: Insights form special needs provision. OECD, https://www.oecd.org/education/school/26527517.pdf. (accessed 4 November 2024).
XXX Ministerul Justiției. (2011). Metodologia privind organizarea serviciilor de sprijin educațional pentru copiii, elevii și tinerii cu cerințe educaționale speciale integrați în învățământul de masă, ORDIN5574_2011_Ordin_si_Metodologie_servicii_sprijin_educațional_tinerii_CES_integrați_în_înv_de_masă.pdf. (accessed 4 November 2024).
XXX UNICEF (2006). Child friendly schools. Manual. UNICEF, https://www.unicef.org/documents/child-friendly-schools-manual. (accessed 4 November 2024).

Chapter 6
Learning Behavior in the Context of Educational Gamification

Nadia Laura Serdenciuc

Abstract The present approach analyzes the impact of a gamified educational environment on learning behavior and examines the changes that individuals experience when they engage in a gamified environment. In today's society, gamification drivers are used as tools to redefine learning environments, tapping into people's natural inclinations for competition and recognition and reshaping learner behavior. Gamification stimulates curiosity, is a source of reward, and enables simulations. It transforms the entire educational process and turns learning tasks into challenging adventures. To keep learners motivated and increase their engagement with the task, gamification design facilitates real-time customization and provides a progressive approach to individual development. The ability to customize their learning experience by selecting tasks, choosing specific skills to solve a problem, and unlocking different levels of difficulty based on task completion gives students the opportunity to experience different levels of autonomy. Considered as a trend or a methodological strategy, gamification generates particular psychological experiences linked to the well-being of the beneficiaries. This theoretical approach aims to show both the positive outcomes and the possible negative effects of using gamification features in the educational process on learning behavior. Our aim is to provide a context for understanding the possible directions of educational interventions to promote some expected behaviors while the learner is immersed in the world of game.

Keywords Gamification · Game mechanics · Gamification in education · Learning experiences in a gamified set-up

N. L. Serdenciuc (✉)
Teacher Training Department, Faculty of Educational Sciences,
Ştefan cel Mare University of Suceava, Suceava, Romania
e-mail: nadia.serdenciuc@usm.ro

I. Boghian, G. Mareş (eds.), *Gamification and Inclusion*, Inclusive Learning and Educational Equity 12, https://doi.org/10.1007/978-3-031-98390-0_6

Introduction

Man's inherent tendency to understand the complexity of his environment, coupled with the desire to optimize his responses to life's challenges, has given rise to a constant quest for knowledge. The endeavor to find the most appropriate ways to explore the realms of the new, both from an internal and external perspective, has made humans an active agent of their personal growth. Motivated by their curiosity and fueled by their playful spirit, people have created environments that encourage both broad perspectives and intense exploration, facilitating personal development.

The playful approach to serious topics has not compromised the depth or breadth of knowledge gained. Instead, the learning process has been enhanced by promoting the affective component that strengthens cognitive engagement and motivation. This has led to more efficient and sustainable learning outcomes.

We were interested in investigating the relationship between gaming and learning, focusing on the impact of gaming on personal growth. Considering that play can be both spontaneous and organized, with the latter often associated with targeted pedagogical interventions, we decided to investigate the potential of learning through play and its pedagogical impact in a structured play environment. Our attention was drawn by the concept of structured play, so we decided to explore the potential of games as a valuable tool to create an engaging and effective learning experience.

Pedagogy provides practitioners with a variety of didactic strategies that facilitate the inclusion of games in learning. The use of games in classroom activities helps beneficiaries develop skills and attitudes and acquire knowledge by engaging them in fun and engaging activities that prepare them for real-life situations. Beyond the use of games in educational activities, the question is whether the educational environment can be structured in such a way that game is not just a distinct or supplementary tool in didactic activities, but an integral part of the educational environment. This approach shifts the focus from the use of games in learning to the use of a gamification perspective in education, without losing the educational objectives in the context of a more intense engagement that requires a different kind of effort from learners.

The growing trend towards gamification in education reflects a change in the way society views the potential of game-based activities, beyond their simple association with childhood or their dominant use in entertainment.

An entire industry has emerged dedicated to the development of games geared to the interests and maturity level of users, aimed at activating their personal resources and addressing various psychophysical components, while offering the opportunity to form new facets of identity that are thought-provoking. We are also seeing a growing interest in restructuring different activities in different domains within a gamification approach to maximize formative potential, shape or reshape users' behavior and tailor their experiences to desired outcomes, ultimately leading to increased productivity of the overall activity.

Based on these premises, we seek to identify the key factors behind the growing interest in gamification in today's society. With a clearer understanding of the concepts involved, we aim to use a theoretical approach from the literature to explore the potential of restructuring the educational environment based on a gamification approach to learning, ensuring alignment between gamification specificity and the coordinates created by the dynamics of interdependence between curriculum components. We will analyze learner behavior in a gamified environment and identify signs of their success as well as potential challenges for educators. In order to harness learners' immersion in the world of gaming with the aim of achieving educational goals from a student-centered perspective, we will explore the possible approaches for educational interventions.

Gamification in Contemporary Society

To understand the importance of gamification in today's society, we will examine some perspectives on the scope of the concept, identifying elements that have been added to the structure of games under the influence of the evolving media industry and that have led to an expansion of the approach to various fields of activity from a gamified perspective: entertainment, business, marketing, health, education, etc.

The year 2008 marks the first documented use of gamification and the concept became widely used after 2010 (Deterding et al., 2011), as it is associated with the intention of "shaping users' behavior in a desirable direction" (Dicheva et al., 2015). As "a popular technique used in a variety of contexts," the purpose of gamification is to motivate people to behave in a certain way (Landers, 2015).

Deterding et al. (2011) locate the origins of the term gamification in the digital media industry. In the search for a "game with purpose" that is linked to a desirable type of interaction and activates playfulness through the curiosity, exploration, and reflection of participants, human-computer interaction (HCI) researchers were interested in expanding this field of exploration and using it as an important source of inspiration for the "reuse" of games beyond entertainment at home.

As a result of a specific investigation of several game properties proposed by game theorists, Bedwell et al. (2012) selected a set of nine categories covering a wide range of possible game properties: Action Language, Assessment, Conflict/Challenge, Control, Environment, Game Fiction, Human Interaction, Immersion, and Rules/Goals. Each of these attributes has been explained by the authors in relation to games mediated through a screen. Action Language includes a user's method of interaction with the system (pressing a particular button) and the interface that allows them to do so (game pad, keyboard, mouse). Assessment includes the measurement of success (scoring) within a game and the player's progress in achieving game objectives (in addition to the content of the feedback given to the player during the game, this also includes some hints or instructions). The conflict/challenge attribute refers to the level of difficulty of the game, the type of problems presented that may trigger conflict, and the degree of uncertainty in defining these problems (surprise). Control is the player's ability to influence the game. The environment is represented by the physical setting in which the player finds themselves and their perception of the game world. Game fiction includes fantasy (elements that deviate from the real world) and mystery (a gap between known and unknown information). Human interaction refers to the interactions between human participants involved in a game (the digital world mediates social interaction between participants who are in different physical locations but in a shared virtual space. Immersion is represented by the player's perception of their place in the game world. Rules/goals represent the reasons why the player interacts with the game world and acts in a certain way.

Our time is marked by challenges, because the transition from one phase to the next in social development in all areas means overcoming moments of uncertainty, the search for a balance between action and reflection and the pursuit of optimization. Challenges are recognized as characteristics of game, and harnessing this attribute to foster the motivation of people engaged in tackling challenging tasks can better prepare them for real-life confrontations. Therefore, the intention to shift the focus to a formative approach follows a natural continuum that allows for the integration of game-based elements into the pedagogical design of learning activities.

Gamification is not a reality that works by itself. It is closely linked to an activity or work process and has the potential to redesign the structural components and redefine the sequence of actions by putting the user at the center to provide a "fun and enjoyable experience" (Wood & Reiners, 2015). Theorists often explain gamification in the context of "using game-based elements in a non-game-based environment" (Deterding et al., 2011; Wood & Reiners, 2015; Dicheva et al., 2015), where the goal is to increase the engagement of subjects in all sequences of an activity, due to the different interaction dynamics created by certain game elements.

Various areas of business and society are integrating gamification techniques due to their transformative effect (Christopoulos & Mystakidis, 2023). Gamification is a popular topic in industry and also in academia (Majuri et al., 2018) and is used in various fields: productivity, finance, health, education, sustainability, news and entertainment (Deterding et al., 2011), business, marketing, corporate management, wellness initiatives, education (Dicheva et al., 2015), retail, health, work, and education (Ortiz et al., 2016). According to Caponetto et al. (2014), gamification can be seen as an engine to drive basic things like "learning, employee performance, customer engagement and even crowdsourcing initiatives."

Understanding Concepts: Game, Gamification, and Gamified Educational Environment

One of the first known meanings of the term game referred to "an activity practiced for diversion or amusement" (according to Merriam-Webster.com Dictionary, 2024). The definition of the term gradually evolved to include elements specific to the context of its development: "a physical or mental activity or contest that has rules and that people engage in for pleasure" (Britannica Dictionary.com, 2024), "an entertaining activity or sport, especially one played by children, or the equipment needed for such an activity" (Cambridge Dictionary, 2024), "an activity or sport usually involving skill, knowledge, or chance, in which you follow fixed rules and try to win against an opponent or to solve a puzzle" (Collins Dictionary.com, 2024).

Beyond these definitions, which explain the meaning of the concept on the basis of a superordinate category (activity) and also highlight the specific differences that distinguish game from other types of activity, the specialized literature offers a variety of perspectives that broaden our understanding of its scope and identify specific elements as key features of the dynamics of the activity described.

Al-Azawi et al. (2016) have identified a number of specific elements that define a game: fun, separation (involves different spatial and temporal coordinates), uncertainty (generated by the difficulty of predicting the outcome), non-productivity (lacks a specific utility), rules (different from daily life), and fictitious (implies reference to and awareness of an alternative reality).

Both games and gamification contain game elements, according to Landers (2015), who also notes a difference between the two concepts: whereas in a game we are dealing with a mixture of all elements, gamification refers to the "identification, extraction and application of individual game elements or limited, meaningful combinations of these elements."

Based on a literature review, Wood and Reiners (2015) draw our attention to the following concepts that have a similar meaning to gamification: behavioral games, funware, applied gaming, playful design, also emphasizing the difference between the intention of restructuring activities with game-based elements, and the simple use of games to achieve serious outcomes (serious games). In the latter case, the outcome is considered a "side effect" of a game (Oja & Riekki, apud Wood & Reiners, 2015), whereas gamification is mostly about creating a specific game-based context in which participants are intrinsically motivated to achieve the goals (Groh, apud Wood & Reiners, 2015). Serious games are about "the design of fully-fledged games for non-entertainment purposes," while gamified applications use elements of game (Dicheva et al., 2015). When comparing game-based learning and gamification, Kapp (2012) emphasizes that learners in gamified environments do not play all the time because gamification uses only a few game elements, while educational games (used in game-based learning) form a distinct unit with a beginning, gameplay and an end, used by learners to acquire knowledge and develop skills.

Gamification originates from the field of digital media and aims to change people's behavior, whereby three aspects come into play: mechanics (related to the presentation of data and algorithms—points and badges), dynamics (represented by the "runtime behavior of mechanics" reflected in task completion and players' choises) and aesthetics (desired reactions—the "feeling of being challenged", the "feeling of community"), according to Basten (2017), who stresses that organizations interested in applying gamification should avoid reducing gamification to just "awarding points only."

The educational environment provides the appropriate framework for learning. In search of the answer to the question: "What makes a specific context to be challenging for learning?", Hutchinson (2003) analyzes some attributes: the motivational triggers of the learners, the specificity of the physical environment, the safety, the sense of belonging, self-esteem boosters, the relevance of learning, the actions and attitudes of the learning facilitators, the design of the curriculum. We can easily see that only one of the listed characteristics points to tangible elements associated with a learning context (the specificity of the physical environment); the other elements are generated by the actions and attitudes of learning facilitators in formal, non-formal or informal contexts. Together, these elements function as a unified whole, regardless of their specific nature, while at the same time assuming interdependencies within the structure. The application of gamification principles in this specific setting changes the educational environment, has an impact at the level of individual attributes and also changes the meaning of their interdependencies. Considering the specificity of gamification in connection with the attributes of the educational environment, some differences in the integration of game elements can be identified: the emergence of new motivational triggers leading to increased engagement; the variety of elements representing the physical environment (sometimes special equipment is required to access technological resources); new safety rules; an increased sense of belonging created by a deeper emotional connection between participants; new boosters of self-esteem (related to tasks completed, levels completed and points gained); a change in participants' perception of the relevance of learning; specific actions by learning facilitators to better orient participants in the gamified environment and a supportive attitude that focuses on learners and allows "the freedom to fail"; a new curriculum design (that improves the permeability of interdependencies between curricular components to integrate game potential into the planning and implementation of learning experiences).

The functioning of this playful environment must be carefully managed by the learning facilitator, because the implicit changes brought about by the presence of game elements do not in themselves guarantee positive effects or efficient implementation. They need to be applied in a way that is tailored to the specific characteristics of the learner.

We are interested in analyzing the effects of gamification on learning behavior. In doing so, we consider gamification as the incorporation of game elements into a specific activity without overshadowing the objectives to be achieved by carrying out that activity.

Gamification in Education

Education is interested in appreciating human curiosity (as the basis of its exploratory Interests) and its spirit of play (Christopoulos & Mystakidis, 2023). As these two emotions are essential for games, the integration of gamification into an educational environment is obvious.

Based on a literature review on gamification, Majuri et al. (2018) mention that the most common contexts for empirical research on gamification are education and learning. We can even identify some techniques that games and educational activities have in common: feedback, task arrangements in terms of their complexity, personalization (Dicheva et al., 2015). By analyzing different studies dealing with gamification in education, Oliveira et al. (2023) identify a common intention: the redesign of educational environments to take advantage of the motivational benefits achieved through games. The integration of gamification into the educational intervention adds "a playful, creative and challenging" perspective to the learning strategy (Manzano-León et al., 2022).

Due to their "remarkable motivational power," which arises from the fact that participants set mechanisms in motion for the sheer joy of playing and because of the opportunities to win, games are often used as learning tools as part of teaching activities (Dicheva et al., 2015). The authors point to the value of using games in education, not only in terms of reinforcing knowledge, but also in terms of developing skills such as problem solving, collaboration, and communication. Gamification techniques can make learning more engaging and effective (Caponetto et al., 2014). Gamification in education suggests using game thinking and game design elements to "improve learner engagement and motivation" (Dicheva et al., 2015).

General Implications of Gamification Approach in Education

Similar to a didactic method, gamification is not a valuable tool per se, but its success depends on its contextual use. Wood and Reiners (2015) point out that gamification not only encapsulates game rules and mechanisms for increasing participant engagement and changing behavior in desirable ways, but it can also cause harm if not used properly. There are some differences in the impact of integrating game elements into educational activities "in both proximal and distal learning outcomes" due to the correspondence between the game elements used and the contexts of their application (Landers, 2015).

Oliveira et al. (2023) mention engagement and motivation among the benefits of using gamification in education and affirm that gamification can also have the opposite effects by interfering with some students' learning.

Based on an analysis of 17 studies on negative effects related to gamification in education published between 2012 and 2016, Toda et al. (2018) identified four negative effects: indifference (some learners felt indifferent to the gamified application—"neither entertaining nor boring"), loss of performance (not understanding the rules or not wanting to be penalized during a gamified activity can lead to performance drop, but also focusing more on the gamified mechanics than on the assessment has a negative impact on the results obtained), undesirable behavior (such as demotivation due to excessive competition, frustration at not achieving the badges, lack of satisfaction with the bonus system) and declining effects (decreasing motivation and engagement over time). The authors suspect that these effects are due to the lack of methods or frameworks for planning and effectively using gamification.

Undesirable effects of gamification occur when game elements become "more important than the core function" of an activity, resulting in users being distracted from the purpose of the task and in some cases perceiving a disadvantage (a demotivating factor - in the case of observed cheating by some users) Basten (2017).

Christopoulos and Mystakidis (2023) not only point out the advantages of integrating games in the educational context from the beneficiaries' point of view: active participation, collecting feedback data to regulate their behavior, monitoring the whole process to gain better control over their own actions, but also draw our attention to some possible disadvantages: placing too much emphasis on rewards could compromise intrinsic motivation; there is a possibility of losing focus on the learning objectives due to a dysfunctional integration of gamification into the learning context. If access to the gamified version of a learning situation is mediated by technological resources, it is possible that some students from marginalized backgrounds may find themselves in a disadvantaged position.

The Challenge of Putting Together Gamification and Curricular Components

Efforts to integrate gamification into education bring with them the challenge of finding a real balance between entertaining participant engagement and achieving learning objectives without risking the latter being overshadowed by the excitement generated by the game mechanics.

The impact of gamification on players in educational contexts depends on the specificity of the learning experiences (individual or in a learning community), the age of the participants and the stage of their cognitive development, as Christopoulos and Mystakidis (2023) suggest, emphasizing the need to link gamification to the objectives of the curriculum to achieve a true integration of game mechanics into the teaching activity. The authors strongly advocate the need to follow ethical guidelines from a societal perspective during the design phase. The use of technology in the process of integrating game mechanics into the educational environment can lead to significant resource requirements, which also require a certain level of user competence.

Dicheva et al. (2015) use the term educational gamification design principles to explain the mechanics of a gamification approach in education based on the results of a mapping study, citing the following elements: goals, challenges, customization, progress, feedback, competition and collaboration, accrual grading, access, freedom of choice, freedom to fail, storytelling, new identities and/or roles in onboarding, time restriction. Goals must be specific and clearly formulated, have a moderate level of difficulty and offer an immediate perspective. Challenges refer to clear and operational learning tasks that are presented in a gradual complexity. Progress must be visible (through points, progress bars, levels, virtual goods/currency). Feedback must include immediate rewards in short feedback cycles (not based on general long-term benefits). The competitive approach and social engagement are reflected in badges, leaderboards, levels, and the use of avatars. This includes individual and team competitions and participation in work or team projects. Accrual grading focuses on the points earned. Performance is validated by visible status, which strengthens reputation, social credibility, and recognition. The ability to unlock new content gradually expands participants' access to other game options. To link participants' options to the desire to achieve set goals, the gamified approach includes freedom of choice (the ability to take alternative paths to success). There is also a safe way to proceed: a low risk of submission and the possibility of multiple attempts to ensure the freedom to fail. The emotional environment related to the sequence of events is possible in a gamified approach because of its narrative coordinate. The narrative context offers the opportunity to search for specific meanings and feel part of the story. The onboarding view is the basis for participant engagement and the time limit is a contextual element that also provides a challenge and activates individual or collective resources (using a countdown system). The results of the study show that the following design principles are most frequently used: visual engagement, freedom of choice, freedom to fail, and rapid feedback. The authors affirm that gamification in education requires a specific technological infrastructure combined with an appropriate didactic framework.

Majuri et al. (2018) have described three game benefits associated with gamification solutions that have been highlighted in various empirical studies: achievement/progression (operationalized by points/score, challenges/missions, badges/medals, trophies, leaderboards, levels, quizzes, status bars, performance feedback, timer/speed, increasing difficulty), social (cooperation/teamwork, social networks, competition, peer/rating, customization, multiplayer), immersion (avatar/virtual reality, narrative/dialog, virtual word, in-game rewards, role-playing), non-digital elements (location data, real world/financial rewards, movement tracking, physical objects as game resources) and a miscellaneous category (help, virtual currency, full game versions, adaptive difficulty, game rounds, safe practice environment, reminders, penalties).

Christopoulos and Mystakidis (2023) highlight some game mechanics designed to facilitate play and emphasize the need to carefully balance game elements in an educational context to avoid undermining participants' focus on learning objectives: avatars (role play, identity choice, customization), levels (with difficulty scaling, milestone markers, modular learning), badges (to represent skills, milestones achieved, social recognition), challenges/quests (problem solving, narrative engagement, task variety), leaderboards (to represent competition, recognition, benchmarking), rewards (intrinsic/extrinsic), turns (act as attention regulators, are linked to sequential learning, are integrated into competitions or collaborative learning experiences), points (are feedback markers, represent resources for rewards), non-player characters (have a guiding function, are information mediators and promote engagement). Through the use of avatars in education, participants demonstrate their special status, and engagement is further enhanced by the ability to customize avatars. In educational environments, points earned reflect learning progress and keep the player motivated. In some games, longer or shorter periods of time are inserted between the player's actions: turns that are also understood as "one action play" during a game round. In an educational context, levels can reflect different learning segments of the content. By progressively reaching each level, players show that they have mastered certain techniques and are ready for the next challenge. Badges play the role of symbols and in education are linked to the achievement of goals that mark learning progress. The focus on earning badges encourages players to think critically and stimulates problem-solving skills, as earning a particular badge is based on a game strategy developed during a learning process while enhancing the learning itself. A quest is linked to the achievement of a goal. By completing a specific task, students move from one action point to another. Rewards relate to extrinsic motivation, which arouses the interest of participants, or intrinsic motivation, which creates long-term commitment from participants. There are different types of rewards: achievements, feedback messages, the awarding of items, the unlocking of content. Participants are ranked in leaderboards according to their performance: overall performance or performance on specific tasks. Non-player characters have the task of offering quests or helping players to complete the stages of the story, they act like agents offering support and guidance.

Gamification requires a permanent updating in terms of new challenges because, as users improve their skills, the tasks they face might appear too simple and, if the algorithm offers no novelty, their positive effects can decrease (Basten, 2017). The author affirms that the performance of users might decline if removing game elements "even below the level before gamification was introduced."

Learning Behavior Specificity in a Gamified Educational Set-Up

Gamified environments are designed to influence user behavior. If we refer to a pedagogical environment and analyze the actors directly involved in the pedagogical process, we recognize a repertoire of behaviors associated with the teacher, as well as corresponding behaviors of the learners. It is difficult to distinguish between the different behaviors of the participants when applying the criteria of a direct correspondence with the specificity of the learning process.

When analyzing learning phases, a distinction can be made: behaviors that create the conditions for learning, behaviors that indicate that learning is in progress, or behaviors that show that learning has already taken place. Given the relationship between learning and change and the fact that behavior is an indicator of change, we can analyze learner behavior from the point of view of the type of changes that are produced in the learner's personality: behaviors related to cognitive changes, behaviors reflecting emotional and attitudinal changes, and actions reflecting the acquisition of new behavioral patterns.

Although the learning process involves individual internal experiences, interaction with others serves as an external stimulus that can influence the timing, intensity and meaning that the learner ascribes to the change. We can thus distinguish between behaviors that reflect an individual, independent approach to learning and those that reflect membership in a learning community in which the dimension of shared collective learning experiences is evident.

We can also identify behaviors associated with metacognitive processes that determine a certain attitude as a result of reflection on the learning situation, leading to positive effects in terms of learning and performance or negative effects in terms of an unengaged attitude caused by various disruptive factors. Depending on their attitude towards learning, learners may exhibit behaviors that signal either deep interest and engagement or disinterest and detachment from the learning situation.

The integration of game elements into the learning context undoubtedly leads to a change in the dynamics of the participants' behavior during the lesson.

Christopoulos and Mystakidis (2023) highlight the elements of learning mechanics associated with educational activities that contribute to the development of some cognitive, technical or social skills: actions (required to complete certain tasks/observation, discussions, investigations, role-playing), educational tutorial (helps participants to acquire knowledge or consolidate their skills while performing actions at their own pace, using different resources or with the teacher's guidance), demonstration (which allows the teacher's actions to be observed and duplicated), assessment/feedback (a way for participants to track their learning progress) offered during and after the activity, reflection/discussion (as a source of evaluation of different aspects of the game: elements that the participants liked best, challenging tasks or actions, the match between the choice of games and the motivation and needs of the students).

Majuri et al. (2018) found that some participants benefit from motivation through gamification, while others do not. This is related to various contextual factors that influence participants' experiences with gamification: demographics, personality factors, different associations with the task. The authors confirm that there is also a possible influence of each participant's learning style on their perception of gamification challenges.

Landers (2015) has elaborated a theory of gamified learning and explains that gamification cannot replace learning, but it can enhance it. Analyzing the relationship between the teaching content and the learning outcomes from a systemic approach (input—process—output), the author proposes a dual perspective: a less mediated one (where the teaching content is directly operationalized into learning outcomes) and a more mediated one (based on the results of educational research that confirms that behavior and attitudes influence learning). The full mediated cycle includes Instructional content—behavior/attitudes—learning outcomes. There is another coordinate that implies changes at the level of behaviors and attitudes: game characteristics. By acting directly on the attitudinal component, game characteristics have an implicit influence on learning outcomes. The relationship between the game characteristics and the behaviors/attitudes developed becomes a source of improvement in learning. By influencing behaviors/attitudes, game features moderate the efficiency of learning.

Based on a literature review and analysis of some case studies, Stott and Neustaedter (2013) identify four features in game design that are considered more successful when used in learning environments: freedom to fail, rapid feedback, progression, and storytelling.

Freedom to fail encourages players to take risks, explore and take the focus off the end results and put it on the learning process. The authors show that this feature parallels a core principle of modern pedagogy: formative assessment and the drive to raise their level. Rapid feedback, which is often used in games, plays an important role in learning and increases its efficiency. Progression in game design refers to levels passed or missions accomplished, while in pedagogy we have the concept of "scaffolded instruction." Narrative elements are often integrated into game design because the facts necessary for participants are easier to learn through a story. Stories can describe actions and tasks in a realistic context and thus influence learner participation and motivation.

Gamification techniques used in educational contexts mediate the interaction between students and learning content and address "transversal attitudes and behaviors such as collaboration, creativity, and self-guided study" (Caponetto et al., 2014). Beyond collaborative skills, gamification has the potential to foster problem-solving skills, resilience and intrinsic motivation (Christopoulos & Mystakidis, 2023), create a deeper connection to learning and develop a much more nuanced perspective than "learning for fun." The authors emphasize increased engagement, multiple initiatives, goal setting, and achievement based on transforming fun learning experiences into meaningful and relevant experiences.

In line with different approaches to gamification, Majuri et al. (2018) identified some common psychological outcomes: perceived enjoyment, fun, engagement, motivation, and perceived usefulness. In terms of outcomes related to participant behavior in gamified educational contexts, the authors shed light on grades, participation in a system, and speed of completion of tasks and assignments. They also note that gamification solutions very rarely focus on social interactions and behavioral goals and rarely serve to promote collaboration.

Based on a literature review, Christopoulos and Mystakidis (2023) correlate gamification elements that could generate key motivational drives in participants and identify six player types: Achiever (focused on achievement and excellence), Explorer (driven by curiosity, eager to explore), Socializer (motivated by the need to connect with others), Killer/Disruptor (winning type by gaining attention), Builder/Creator (driven by creativity, enjoying craft and art), Philanthropist (searching for meaning, altruist). The authors describe each type from the perspective of a gamified educational context. Those most likely to find themselves in the Achiever role are more focused on collecting rewards that make their status visible to others. They have a need to be competent and are therefore willing to invest time and effort in completing tasks, even if they are difficult. Explorers are interested in understanding the structure and workings of the game in order to use it as an advantage to develop personal strategies that help them outperform others. Socializers seek emotional and social connections during game, value teamwork and sometimes use their leadership skills. In educational contexts, they prefer collaborative learning. Killers are highly competitive players who are out to win in order to increase their reputation and defeat their opponents. The authors also mention that some participants (disruptors) are intent on satisfying their need for attention even if their efforts challenge others through disruptive behavior in an educational setting. Builders enjoy working alone or with others on activities that involve creation, and they are usually interested in arts and crafts. Philanthropists are altruistic participants who seek meaning in their actions. All of these player types can be distinguished by a set of behaviors associated with their particular way of engaging in and perceiving game situations.

Even though player types are described on the basis of some dominant characteristics, the authors emphasize the need to consider the different roles that players experience in a gamified setup in a combined mode, without limiting participants to expressing themselves in only one role coordinate (Christopoulos & Mystakidis, 2023). The players' behavior serves both as an indicator of their personality traits and as a source of insights for identifying pedagogical approaches that use game elements to achieve the desired pedagogical outcomes.

Oliveira et al. (2023) discuss the need for "a tailored gamification in education" referring to the intention to personalize the design of structured learning situations in order to improve students' experiences and better respond to their needs. The authors analyzed several studies that addressed the impact of personalizing gamification in education and concluded that most of them considered the following aspects for tailored gamification: human aspects that include both personal characteristics ("gamer type," "learning style," "goal orientation," "personality traits," "age," "gender," "demographic aspects," "instructor preferences," "psychological needs satisfaction," "motivation stage") and personal changes (in terms of the dynamics of personality traits over the course of life experiences), as well as cultural aspects. As for the benefits of a customized gamification approach in education, the authors mention that "users spend more time in the learning environment," but also note that a "non-tailored" version of gamification proves to be more effective when it comes to student motivation.

Immersion in the world of game is closely related to the "game aestetics," according to Christopoulos and Mystakidis (2023) and triggers emotional reactions in the player's interactions with the game sequences. Based on the results of a literature review, the authors highlight the following coordinates: sensations (generated by visual or tactile stimuli and the perception of time), fantasy (the use of imaginative worlds and protagonists), narrative (a particular continuity of events that elicit emotional responses and provide a context for anticipation and empathy), audio (music, sound effects, voice-over), challenge (used as a learning tool or context to integrate theory and practice), fellowship (a particular type of engagement related to a sense of community). Jennett et al. (2008) consider that the experience of immersion in games is an "outcome of a good game experience" that reflects the user's level of involvement and is often used to describe involvement in a computer game. The experience of immersion can be analyzed in terms of control and emotional involvement. When players make decisions in the game, they emphasize the game features that give them the ability to control their playtime, the freedom to quit the game at any time and the ability to shift their attention from one element of the game to another element outside the game when necessary. While an intensely immersive experience is entertaining, it can distort the perception of time by focusing attention on a limited number of elements and minimizing the need to use the ability to decide when to end the game session. While a high level of immersion can be disruptive when using game elements in an educational setting, too little cannot effectively activate the motivational component and does not lead to the desired behavioral changes. Even though gamification involves the use of game elements in learning, participants may have varying degrees of immersion in the gamified experience, which explains their reaction to game elements. An overly immersive experience can lead to a downplaying of the importance of the educational objectives.

In gamified learning environments, teachers need to closely observe student behavior as an indicator of their engagement in the proposed learning context. Based on these observations, they should select appropriate pedagogical interventions by using different game elements or reducing them when necessary to promote engagement or prevent destructive behaviors.

Conclusions

The use of gamification in education presents teachers with a number of challenges in the design, implementation and monitoring of learning experiences. In addition to subject-specific competencies and pedagogical skills, this also requires a range of skills to integrate game elements into different learning contexts and to design the pedagogical environment in a way that positively influences student motivation and engagement. Teachers need to select appropriate strategies that facilitate the acquisition of curriculum content while providing an enjoyable learning experience that creates a sense of emotional comfort, stimulates children's curiosity, and encourages their initiatives to enthusiastically take on the various challenges created by a playful learning environment.

References

Al-Azawi, R., Al-Faliti, F., & Al-Blushi, M. (2016). Educational gamification vs. game based learning: Comparative study. *International Journal of Innovation, Management and Technology, 7*(4/2016), 132–136. https://doi.org/10.18178/ijimt.2016.7.4.659

Basten, D. (2017). Gamification. *IEEE Software, 34*(05), 76–81.

Bedwell, W. L., Pavlas, D., Heyne, K., Lazzara, E. H., & Salas, E. (2012). Toward a taxonomy linking game attributes to learning: An empirical study. *Simulation & Gaming, 43*(6), 729–760. https://doi.org/10.1177/1046878112439444

Caponetto, I., Earp, J., & Ott, M. (2014) Gamification and education: A literature review. In *European conference on games based learning* (vol. 1. p. 50). Academic Conferences International Limited.

Christopoulos, A., & Mystakidis, S. (2023). Gamification in education. *Encyclopedia, 3*(4), 1223–1243.

Deterding, S., Dixon, D., Khaled, R., & Nacke, L. (2011). From game design elements to gamefulness: Defining "gamification". In *Proceedings of the 15th international academic MindTrek conference: Envisioning future media environments* (pp. 9–15). https://doi.org/10.1145/2181037.2181040

Dicheva, D., Dichev, C., Agre, G., & Angelova, G. (2015). Gamification in education: A systematic mapping study. *Educational Technology and Society, 18*(3), 73–88.

Game. Britannica Dictionary.com Dictionary. https://www.britannica.com/dictionary/game. Accessed 22 Nov 2024

Game. Cambridge Dictionary, https://dictionary.cambridge.org/dictionary/english/game. Accessed 22 Nov 2024

Game. Collins Dictionary, https://www.collinsdictionary.com/dictionary/english/game. Accessed 22 Nov 2024

Game. Merriam-Webster.com Dictionary, Merriam-Webster, https://www.merriam-webster.com/dictionary/game. Accessed 22 Nov 2024

Hutchinson, L. (2003). Educational environment. *BMJ, 326*(7393), 810–812.

Jennett, C., Cox, A. L., Cairns, P., Dhoparee, S., Epps, A., Tijs, T., & Walton, A. (2008). Measuring and defining the experience of immersion in games. *International Journal of Human-Computer Studies, 66*(9), 641–661.

Kapp, K. M. (2012). What is gamification. In *The gamification of learning and instruction: game-based methods and strategies for training and education*, 1–23.

Landers, R. N. (2015). Developing a theory of gamified learning: Linking serious games and gamification of learning. *Simulation & Gaming, 45*(6), 752–768. https://doi.org/10.1177/1046878114563660

Majuri, J., Koivisto, J., & Hamari, J. (2018) Gamification of education and learning. A review of empirical literature. In *Proceedings of the 2nd international GamiFIN conference, GamiFIN 2018*. CEUR-WS.

Manzano-León, A., Aguilar-Parra, J. M., Rodríguez-Moreno, J., & Ortiz-Colón, A. M. (2022). Gamification in initial teacher training to promote inclusive practices: A qualitative study. *International Journal of Environmental Research and Public Health, 19*(13), 8000. https://doi.org/10.3390/ijerph19138000

Oliveira, W., Hamari, J., Shi, L., Toda, A. M., Rodrigues, L., Palomino, P. T., & Isotani, S. (2023). Tailored gamification in education: A literature review and future agenda. *Education and Information Technologies, 28*(1), 373–406.

Ortiz, M., Chiluiza, K., & Valcke, M. (2016). Gamification in Higher Education and STEM. In *Proceedings of EDULEARN16 Conference,* Barcelona, Spain, ISBN/978-84-608-8860-4.

Stott, A., & Neustaedter, C. (2013). Analysis of gamification in education. *Surrey, BC, Canada, 8*(1), 36.

Toda, A. M., Valle, P. H. D., & Isotani, S. (2018). The dark side of gamification: An overview of negative effects of gamification in education. In A. Cristea, I. Bittencourt, & F. Lima (Eds.), *Higher education for all. From challenges to novel technology-enhanced solutions. HEFA 2017. Communications in Computer and Information Science* (Vol. 832, pp. 143–156). Springer. https://doi.org/10.1007/978-3-319-97934-2_9

Wood, L. C., & Reiners, T. (2015). Gamification. In M. Khosrow-Pour (Ed.), *Encyclopedia of information science and technology* (Vol. IV, 3rd ed., pp. 3039–3047). IGI Global.

Part I
Gamification and Inclusion in Education: Challenges and Solutions

Chapter 7
Differentiation and Inclusive Approach in Teaching Activities from Higher Education. Using Gamification in a Constructivist Teaching-Learning Context with Gifted Students

Rogoz Nicoleta

Abstract The future of education in the twenty-first century is linked to the quality and diversity of educational opportunities. The organization and support of teaching methods requires imagination, creativity, and innovation. In this regard, the most useful materials are Open Educational Resources (OER), as they are considered to have several advantages: The digital format allows for reuse, sharing, adaptation, and redistribution for educational settings other than the original one (Organization for Economic Co-operation and Development—OECD, PISA 2018 draft global competence framework, 2015). Curriculum design in higher education (HE) responds to the current need for differentiation and involves designing the curriculum according to the needs, abilities, and real expectations of the beneficiaries. Differentiation defines a framework of analysis that emphasizes the importance of subject knowledge in curriculum design. In this context, design can be seen as "the process of meaningfully constructing and linking the components of a curriculum so that fundamental questions such as what needs to be taught, how and why, what resources are needed and how learning should be assessed are clarified" (UNESCO-IBE, Glossary of curriculum terminology, 17, 2013). This chapter aims to answer two research questions: What are the effective ways of differentiation and integrative approaches to the curriculum in universities? What is the importance of using gamification in differentiating the teaching and learning of gifted students? The results of the analysis can be used to improve the efficiency of differentiated and inclusive curriculum development mechanisms at the education system level.

R. Nicoleta (✉)
"Alexandru Ioan Cuza" University from Iași, Iași, Romania
e-mail: nicoleta.rogoz@uaic.ro

I. Boghian, G. Mareş (eds.), *Gamification and Inclusion*, Inclusive Learning and Educational Equity 12, https://doi.org/10.1007/978-3-031-98390-0_7

Introduction

Differentiated instruction is promoted as a model for creating more inclusive classrooms by addressing individual learning needs and maximizing learning opportunities. Achieving this through pedagogical practices is no longer a goal of higher education, except in conjunction with what social inclusion means through a curriculum adapted to culturally, linguistically, racially, ethnically, religiously, etc. minority groups. This type of inclusion enables universities to find solutions for adapting students to the labor market and social life. While differentiated instruction was originally interpreted as a set of teaching practices that enable differentiation at the teaching, learning, or assessment level, current theories consider differentiated instruction as a pedagogical model with philosophical and practical components rather than just the act of differentiation. Therefore, it is important to analyze how current theories influence the perception of differentiated instruction. At the same time, it is a priority to find out at what component levels this can be introduced, what factors explain the differences in the adoption of differentiated instruction, how differentiated instruction can be implemented in inclusive classrooms, what specific differentiation is for gifted students, and how open educational resources (OER) can be introduced to facilitate gamification as a learning resource.

Differentiation and Inclusion. Semantic Meanings Concerning Curriculum Design in Universities

Differentiation in Teaching-Learning. The Importance of Gamification Strategies

Debates about the introduction of differentiation and inclusion practices in universities discuss the need to adapt the curriculum to the different contexts from which students come. From this perspective, "when we think about the inclusive curriculum and what might constitute inclusion, a common understanding might be that an inclusive curriculum recognizes and helps all students to adapt" (Stentiford & Koutsouris, 2022). In the way differentiation in teaching and learning is carried out, the existence of curriculum models that influence the goals we pursue are considered. These models include "classical humanism, progressivism, reconstructionism and learning technology" (Norwich, 2013).

According to the model of classical humanism, knowledge is seen as a corpus of information that must be passed on from teachers to students. From the perspective of this model, there are certain standards for what is considered "good" and legitimate in terms of knowledge, and follows the ideology of the ruling class. This model has its roots in ancient Greek philosophy. These meanings associated with knowledge "have been challenged many times since the second half of the 20th century, as evidenced in the critical pedagogy of P. Freire (1970), the neo-Marxist analysis of curriculum, the state, political economy and culture of M. Apple (1979), and Michael Young's influential call for an understanding of the constructed and politicized nature of knowledge and its role in reproducing inequalities in knowledge and control" (Young, 1971). However, M. Young argued that "some forms of knowledge (which he refers to as 'powerful knowledge') are 'better' (i.e. epistemic, moral or esthetic) than others and should be taught as part of the curriculum" (White, 2018). Therefore, this type of knowledge is distinguished from the "knowledge of the powerful" (i.e., knowledge authorized by those in power) (Young, 2008; Young & Muller, 2013).

Progressivism refers to a more person-centered approach whose origins date back to the Enlightenment and which "criticizes the traditional authoritarian and hierarchical model." From this perspective, the child/young person is seen as someone who must discover their own knowledge and develop through their own experiences. This model emphasizes freedom, self-expression and learning as discovery, with the influence of society seen as a corrupting force. Progressivism represents the perspective of the sociology of education and offers a critique of the neoconservative and classical approaches (Moore & Young, 2009). However, the postmodern perspective has gained prominence in recent decades (Slattery, 2013; Usher & Edwards, 1994).

The reconstructivist model differs from the progressive model because it is less focused on the individual and emphasizes the importance of society in determining individual progress. This perspective is supported by the author J. Dewey (1916) through education for democracy. The contexts in which learning takes place become important, not just the aspects that characterize the child in terms of their dispositions or personal experiences. Therefore, the curriculum is created with reference to the norms and values of society to determine the individual's commitment and determination to achieve meaningful social change (Stanley, 1992).

The learning technology model aims at a rational and algorithmic approach to learning and proposes a "technical problem-solving framework" (Norwich, 2013, p. 57). From this perspective, learning is approached utilitarian and a single model is applied to all types and areas of learning. Educational goals and learning outcomes are seen as specific and measurable. It is useful to set performance indicators and targets or create league tables to assess the alignment of educational plans with what is considered relevant to the workplace (Beck, 1999; Wheelahan, 2010).

From this perspective, the role of the teacher becomes important as he defines tasks in a differentiated teaching-learning context that reflect problems to be solved by going through algorithms. Therefore, the teacher strives to find new ways to frame the problem so that it is fully perceived through the game and other digital resources. This facilitates the understanding and identification of solutions that can be implemented in the gamification strategies.

Certain aspects become important that emphasize the role of gamification strategies in differentiating teaching and learning: (1) integrating gamification strategies into a broader educational context so that they serve as a tool adapted to an educational approach; (2) emphasizing the role of gamification strategies as facilitators of learning and not only as motivational stimuli due to their entertaining nature; (3)

taking into account the needs and interests of the target audience (students) so that the results of engagement can be useful in different situations; and (4) gamification strategies facilitate the understanding of concepts and are considered as complementary tools to the teaching method (Heidmann, 2015).

Designing the Academic Curriculum Regarding Inclusion

The design of a differentiated and inclusive college curriculum includes the reference to individual educational paths for students. In this sense, there is freedom to edit the curricula at the level of each college/faculty and to structure their content at the level of the two essential components: the compulsory component (field-specific, specialized, complementary courses) and the optional component. In addition to these two components, there are a number of electives that are relevant to lifelong learning.

The reference to the legal framework for the procedure for the regular evaluation of a college's degree programs prompts us to focus on the design of curriculum content as a quality assurance tool in conjunction with the curriculum. Therefore, the differentiated college curriculum can refer to adjustments at the level of conditions for successful learning expressed through competencies, objectives, teaching methods, content, learning activities, and assessment methods.

The Specifics of Differentiated Curriculum for Talented Students. The Perspective of Constructivism

Characteristics of Constructivist Teaching: Learning—Assessment

Designing a differentiated curriculum is about responding to the specific learning and educational needs of the beneficiaries they work with. Teachers design and implement strategies to differentiate the curriculum to support the specific individual learning needs of students. In most cases, these are mainly adaptations at the content level—more exercises and more applied tasks are suggested for low-achieving students, while more complex content is taught for high-achieving students (Brevik et al., 2018).

Differentiation and personalization enable the activation of different types of intelligence and learning styles based on the way students engage with the learning content. A differentiated curriculum therefore involves adapting the curriculum to the real needs of the beneficiaries, taking advantage of their critical thinking, imagination, flexibility, adaptive behavior, problem-solving skills, curiosity and need for collaborative learning (both face-to-face and in the virtual environment), initiative, and entrepreneurship.

In the literature analyzed at the international level, differentiation practices target four elements within the educational process, namely content, process, product, and socio-affective environment. Moreover, these adaptations are required in accordance with three categories of needs expressed by beneficiaries—those related to their availability, interest, and learning profile (Tomlinson & Imbeau, 2010).

The differentiation of the curriculum relates to certain relevant dimensions: Educational objectives/competences; educational content (information, skills and attitudes); the teaching process (teaching-learning methodology); the educational environment (physical environment—space, objects, etc. and psychological environment—socio-affective climate, forms of relationships, teacher personality, student personality, types of rewards or punishments, etc.); assessment (functions, forms, methods and instruments, etc.). For this target group (gifted students), it is necessary to develop digital competences by introducing content into the classroom facilitated by the application of gamification strategies. The virtual learning environment emphasizes engagement in a fast-paced learning rhythm and enables a dynamic process of curriculum adaptation.

The college's decision-making curriculum represents the educational offer proposed by the college, which is based on the learning needs and interests of the students and, on the other hand, takes into account the specificities of the college, the needs and traditions of the local community. Therefore, we can say that the CDU becomes an expression of the uniqueness of a school organization and describes how the needs of the beneficiaries are met.

When designing the college curriculum, the criteria of vertical and horizontal coherence are taken into account, especially when we refer to the key competences (Council of the European Union, Council Recommendation on key competences for lifelong learning, 2018/C 189/01). Therefore, the consideration of benchmarks for the design of differentiated college curricula is necessary for planning. Based on this, we consider the existence of a continuum of differentiated college curricula relevant in relation to the electives and optional subjects that are present in the offer of universities and faculties. A careful analysis of these subjects at Bachelor's and Master's level would make it possible to design an offer that meets the requirements of the labor market and the real needs of the beneficiaries.

Good management of the differentiated curriculum would facilitate the improvement of academic performance as well as the training of specialists characterized by a set of specific transversal and professional competences. The existence of clear benchmarks for the relevance of the curriculum to students emphasizes academic autonomy and the efficiency of inclusion practices. The freedom and responsibility of the college regarding the structure and content of the differentiated college curriculum (optional courses, elective courses, extracurricular activities) are emphasized.

Optional and elective subjects become an expression of college autonomy and decentralization at the curricular level. It becomes necessary to consider benchmarks for the design of a differentiated college curriculum and for the implementation of gamification and inclusion practices:

(a) A student-centered approach that focuses on learning and learning outcomes and has profound implications for curriculum design, delivery, and assessment requires the promotion of a flexible curriculum. This curriculum involves diversifying and adapting learning situations for students according to their age/developmental level, interests, and abilities, while respecting diversity (ethno-cultural, linguistic, religious, etc.).
(b) Building differentiated learning pathways and implementing explicit measures to personalize education as a guarantee of equal opportunities in education. These efforts take into account the adaptation to the learning style and pace, the amount of knowledge accumulated, the skills developed, the depth of understanding and the degree of expression in terms of attitude, the socio-cultural environment of belonging, etc.
(c) The emphasis on competences as a central element in the organization of the basic documents of the curriculum, frameworks, study programs of different disciplines/modules or extracurricular activities. The emphasis on competences is not only required for teaching and learning, but also for assessment. Therefore, it would be necessary to promote the assessment of competences as part of the process of designing the educational profile of graduates.

Designing a differentiated curriculum at the course, seminar, or laboratory activity level puts the teacher in a different position, and the decision maker will refer to the results achieved in terms of how the hours available to the teacher were used (either for creating support contexts for at-risk students or for extending and developing the acquisition of gifted students).

In adapting content for gifted students, teachers must consider both the quantitative aspect (which corresponds to the amount of knowledge) and the qualitative aspect (which concerns the appropriateness of the content to the rhythm, learning style, depth of understanding, and ability to make interdisciplinary connections). This approach involves the assessment of certain psychological processes, such as synthesis, analysis, independent learning (the psychological processes involved); interpersonal and intrapersonal communication processes (the characteristics and risks of integration in microgroups); and affective processes (focusing on higher emotions, feelings, passions).

Reporting on the treatment of gifted students includes innovative curricular approaches. Thus, some universities in the USA, Canada, Australia, the Netherlands, Germany, Denmark, etc. have included discretionary honors programs in the curriculum that are "designed for gifted and motivated students who have the willingness and ability to pursue more than the normal programs" (Clark & Zubizarretta, 2008, Hébert & McBee, 2007, cited in Wolfensberger, 2012, p. 11). Honors programs (HP) are considered models of best practice in the administration of transdisciplinary curricula that focus on science, technology, engineering, and mathematics (STEM) fields. Precisely for this reason, it is necessary to rethink the format of digital competences and the content to be assimilated, taking into account their relevance to a labor market environment marked by digital transformation. Several aspects become important: the specificities of the learning environment and the competences developed; the creation of thematic modules that can be completed at one's own pace and reflect the transdisciplinary nature; the identification of assessment strategies that use gamification and the valorization of learning outcomes in the social environment. At the European level, transdisciplinary programs have been developed where teams of students act as consultants to solve problems for companies/organizations/local communities/authorities or to evaluate such programs, notably in the Netherlands, Denmark, Norway, and Belgium. These programs provide transformative learning experiences, paying close attention to students' individual passions and interests. In the context of honors programs, the gifted student is described as someone who has a high potential for talent, creativity, and the motivation to engage in academic activities beyond what the formal college curriculum offers.

According to the author T. Wagner (2014, p. 204), "Educational institutions are deeply and inherently conservative, especially at the high school and college level." This aspect forces us to reflect on the importance of knowledge as a foundation for innovation. The traditional approach based on the transmission of information is completely inadequate, as students do not have enough opportunities to ask questions, think about new content, discover relevant information, and become curious about possible alternatives to solve problems in different subject areas.

To ensure success in the process of understanding content, acquiring knowledge, and developing basic skills and competencies (Erickson, 2006; Tomlinson et al., 2008; Wiggins et al., 2005), the differentiation process requires teaching students the essential aspects of the topic being taught according to their level of understanding and ability to apply them to problem solving (Tomlinson & Imbeau, 2010). In differentiating the teaching process, the teacher's role is to adapt the teaching methodology used. The didactic strategies used should target several developmental plans for the beneficiaries, such as improving their self-confidence and independence in thinking (Tomlinson & Imbeau, 2010). Therefore, the most appropriate methods are those from the category of methods to promote creativity (Philips 6.6, brainstorming, 6.3.5, panel discussion, Synectics method, etc.) or critical thinking (Structured Brainstorming, 3-step interview, SINELG—Efficient Interactive System for Reading Thoughts, FRISCO method, etc.). The application of these methods facilitates the development of important factors of creative thinking—originality (novelty, uniqueness, unpredictability, element of surprise) or fluency (the large number of ideas generated in a short time) (Stoica Constantin, 2004).

Another important aspect of curriculum differentiation is the creation of an appropriate learning environment that is a psychological environment conducive to the development of maximum potential: Ensuring supportive and safe permissive conditions; mutual stimulation by promoting the transfer of opinions, assessments, observations, suggestions, experiences; encouragement of original expression, divergent thinking and risk-taking for the production of novelty; acceptance and respect for the differences and distinctions between individuals; transparency and empathetic communication; the balance between competitive and cooperative behavior (Crețu, 1997, p. 74).

The authors Chamberlin and Powers (2010) highlight seven key principles that underpin differentiated teaching:

- "Teachers teach students what is essential" so that they learn to make the connection between teaching, learning, and assessment, with assessment playing the role of providing an overview of the student's level of understanding, interests or learning style.
- Teachers respond by taking into account the differences between students.
- Students actively participate in academic activities.
- "Teachers and students work together in the learning process."
- Teachers are flexible in combining group activities and discussions with those conducted with the whole class.
- Activities are designed to meet students' preferences.
- "The space, time, and materials used are adapted to the students' needs" (Turner et al., 2017).

The more the differences between students are taken into account, the more inclusion is facilitated at the level of college institutions. The characteristics of the constructivist environment thus determine a certain interpretative way of perceiving learning. Learning is "seen as a process that is progressively constructed in different contexts and requires personal interpretations by the learner." At the same time, learning claims the attribute of pragmatism, as the learner undertakes a constant reconfiguration of the knowledge acquired in the educational context. To achieve this goal, constructivist learning becomes a collaborative, contextualized process in which assessment is a form of feedback activation (Rogoz, 2014).

In this context, we can update the eight conditions that are necessary for constructive learning and that enable the achievement of inclusion:

- Presentation of complex learning situations in connection with authentic situations
- Definition of social interactions
- Valuing content and knowledge that is relevant to the student
- Matching content to the student's cognitive developmental level
- Use formative, ongoing assessment
- Perceive the teacher as a guide and facilitator of learning
- Taking responsibility for the student's learning
- Continuous review of content and presentation from multiple perspectives (Doolittle, 1999; Doolittle, 2001; Rogoz, 2014)

These conditions for the optimization of learning make it possible to create an objective image of constructive education, which can be recognized more by the process it determines than by its content. Reflection on the process becomes a priority because we can anticipate the degree of immersion, the students' engagement in learning, the way they construct their knowledge, the way they use the learning contexts, and the way they apply the results of their learning in social life or in the labor market. The environments for validating the competencies developed by students during pre-college education are becoming a priority, and this prioritization is determined by the new trends and challenges of today's society. The profile of the graduate is repositioned within the framework of new analytical elements that can be carried out by decision-makers, education professionals, teachers, or representatives of institutions in society interested in offering educational products/services. The graduate's profile is repositioned within the framework of new analytical elements that can be carried out by decision-makers, educational experts, teachers, or representatives of institutions in society interested in providing educational products/services.

We can summarize the specific characteristics of constructivist learning as follows (Rogoz, 2014):

- It is constructed learning—students approach learning situations by applying permanent transformations to assimilated knowledge; they are involved in constructing knowledge and creating mental models on the basis of which they can acquire and assimilate knowledge.
- It is active learning—students build their understanding, with the teacher's role being to coach, moderate and provide suggestions that form the basis for the experiments. After each learning phase, it is very important to reflect and look for effective methods of self-assessment that will serve as a measure of progress.
- It is reflective learning—students continuously engage in a process of reflection/self-monitoring about the learning process and the way they process new experiences; the teacher assists in the formulation of evaluation questions (both in relation to the content retained and the learning methods used); the teacher creates contexts in which students are placed either in situations where they reflect on the learning content or on the strategies that are considered effective in the learning process and that can subsequently ensure transfer to everyday life.
- It is collaborative learning—learning happens through interaction with others and is based on the development of social and emotional skills; the role of the teacher is to create different contexts in which collaborative learning can take place (which involves not only the exchange of content, but also of strategies—learning methods). The role of the teacher is to create different contexts in which collaborative learning can take place (which includes not only sharing content but also strategies—learning methods).
- It is an inquiry-based learning—it involves the use of inquiry methods based on problem solving; students use a variety of solutions and answers to think about; in addition, a learning context is created through investigation/research and experimentation where students are put in the role of a researcher who tests hypotheses, validates them and draws relevant conclusions regarding scientific truths.
- It is a learning in evolution/progress—it consists in a constant validation and revalidation of correct solutions in learning, following the algorithmic steps that lead to the integration of knowledge into acquisition systems; the teacher's role is to help students distinguish between consonant and dissonant information, eliminate learning gaps and choose effective methods to define a process of personal and academic/school development.

With regard to assessment, it is important to differentiate at the product level, which is defined in terms of learning outcomes following active participation in the learning process. The importance of assessment for curriculum design increases when referring to certain recommendations, namely:

(a) Conduct initial assessments to obtain information about students' level of engagement in the learning process, their interest in the subject being taught and elements of their learning profile
(b) Conduct formative assessments taking into account the characteristics of gifted students: availability/commitment to tasks, interest and learning profile
(c) Create summative assessments by creating contexts in which students have the opportunity to express themselves in different ways to show what they know, what they have acquired according to their particularities and needs, to express themselves through a particular form of language, within a particular time frame, etc. (Tomlinson & Imbeau, 2010)

Curriculum differentiation requires a developed expertise that follows trends and changes in education as well as developments in the areas of subjects taught (both theoretical and practical).

The current regulations on the inclusive curriculum make it necessary to reflect on the innovative capacity of universities. From the perspective of college capabilities, we believe it is necessary to involve educational policy makers in efforts to update the positioning of this type of curriculum in curriculum documents. In this context, we present a number of arguments from the perspective of curriculum development.

When we refer to the integrative curriculum approach, we need to understand how competencies are linked to integrated areas as well as to different groups of students. Therefore, the discussions in the specialized literature support a careful analysis of the existing relationship between "transformative competences" (OECD, 2019), cross-curricular competences, transversal competences, professional competences and the eight key competences prioritized in relation to the European standards. It is necessary to train teachers in the use of differentiated approaches and experiences so that they can facilitate students' adaptation to the changing world. These approaches would facilitate (a) the development of skills to understand the ideas and feelings of others; (b) the development of skills to adopt a participatory and flexible behavior in relation to social differences; (c) the training of social entrepreneurship skills, skills to use information and communication technologies in virtual environments; and (d) the development of the ability to select existing online sources that belong to the category of open educational resources.

In this context, we emphasize the importance of the differentiated academic curriculum for the development of key competences. This type of curriculum, considered as an elective, invites students to choose according to their interests and needs (UNESCO, IBE, 2013, p. 25). The learning outcomes of CD can be easily transferred not only at the level of formal curriculum but also at the level of non-formal and informal curriculum. The approach and valorization of these outcomes would facilitate the adaptation of students to a professional environment that is in a constant state of change.

The Efficiency of Open Educational Resources (OER) in Teaching. Premises for the Use of Gamification in Engaging Gifted Students

The approach to gifted students involves identifying curricular opportunities that meet their individual needs. Therefore, "gifted individuals need access to a broad, balanced, and challenging curriculum and to educational approaches that have the potential to transform their lives and prepare them for future challenges" (Davis et al., 2011; Eyre & Lowe, 2002; Goodhew, 2009; Gosfield, 2008; Smutny, 2003).

There is a body of evidence supporting the effectiveness of educational programs for gifted students, provided they are theoretically and empirically sound (Bernal, 2003; Castellano & Diaz, 2002; Epstein, 1979; Kevin, 2005; Ng & Nicholas, 2010; Olenchak & Renzulli, 1989; Shore & Delcourt, 1996; Van Tassel-Baska, 2005).

One of the most important differentiation practices is that which makes it possible to create a stimulating learning environment through the use of special teaching methods. It has been demonstrated that "strategies such as 'differentiated' instructional approaches or computerized independent learning approaches improve the learning ability of gifted students" (Gross & Van Vliet, 2005; Van Tassel-Baska, 2003). In other words, traditional teaching methods or "pencil and blackboard" teaching are considered ineffective in terms of their impact on the teaching and learning processes of gifted students. Therefore, the introduction of open educational resources such as podcasts and video games is recommended. In 2006, the Federation of American Scientists (FAS) published a highly regarded report stating that complex games provide a stimulating environment for learning. The report "encouraged private and government support for expanding research in complex game environments for learning" (Hines et al., 2009). Studies have emphasized "the potential of digital games in terms of conceptual understanding" (Barab et al., 2007; Klopfer et al., 2009), the "development of skills and process practices" (Kafai et al., 2010; Steinkuehler & Duncan, 2008), epistemological understanding (Squire & Jan, 2007; Squire & Klopfer, 2007), and player engagement in tasks (Barab et al., 2009; Dieterle, 2009; Ketelhut, 2007).

Reports by the National Research Council (NRC) and other authors (e.g., Honey & Hilton, 2010; Martinez-Garza et al., 2013; Young et al., 2012) have "recognized "this potential, but they also acknowledge that there is no systematic evidence for games as learning tools."

For example, it has been noted that "one of the most important factors in successful educational games is the ability of the game to maintain the motivation and interest of the individual learner by adapting the learning and game experience to the learner's needs, preferences, goals and abilities" (Kickmeier et al., 2011). There is a need to change the design to make it attractive and engaging so that it can accommodate individual differences. The future of education in the twenty-first century is linked to the quality and diversity of educational opportunities. The organization and support of teaching and learning requires imagination, creativity, and innovation.

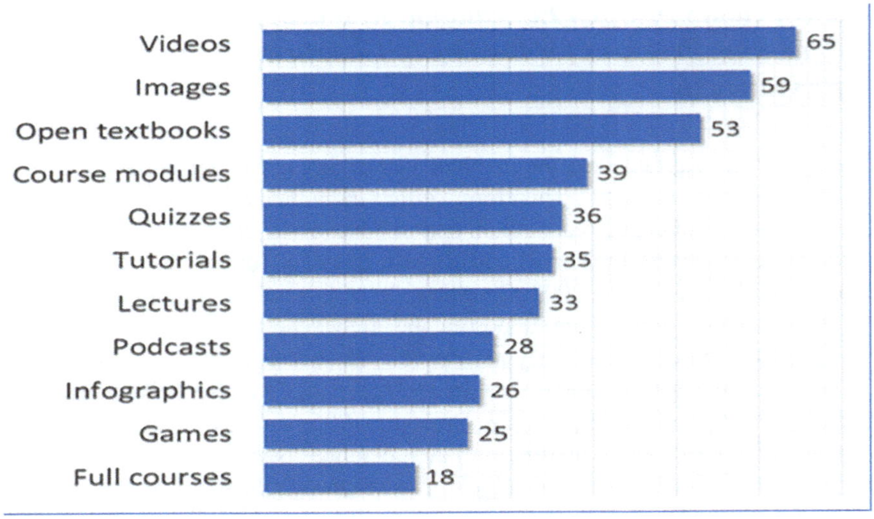

Fig. 7.1 Open Educational Resources and their use frequency (Source: OECD (2015), Educational Research and Innovation. Open Educational Resources. A Catalyst for Innovation, https://read.oecd-ilibrary.org/education/open-educational-resources_9789264247543-en#page4)

The most appropriate teaching, learning, and research materials are Open Educational Resources (OER) as they are considered to have the following advantages: digital learning resources can be used in an educational setting—digital format; the digital format allows reuse, sharing, adaptation and redistribution for a different educational context than the original. It is recommended to identify effective strategies for the integration of OER with minimal use (complete courses, games, infographics, podcasts, lectures, tutorials) (Fig. 7.1).

The use of open educational resources in working with gifted students would enable them to improve their soft skills. Therefore, it would be necessary to "provide learning technologies and gamification through serious games as a learning technique that can help them succeed in a labor market embedded in the global economy" (Apandi, 2022). In this context, gamification suggests "incorporating the entertaining and engaging elements of games into real-world or non-game productive activities" (Deterding et al., 2011; Nah et al., 2013; Werbach & Hunter, 2012; Zichermann & Cunningham, 2011). Gamification provides gifted students with a form of active learning that can incorporate humorous elements into games (Icard, 2014). In this way, interpersonal skills are developed that facilitate collaborative learning. This encourages a co-creative process that also stimulates critical thinking. Engaging in collaborative tasks through games results in "stimulating students to effectively transform knowledge into social capital due to peer recognition" (Herz, 2001). The main ways to integrate gamification into teaching and learning are non-online supported courses, Massive Open Online Courses (MOOC), blended/flipped learning courses, online learning sites, gamified platforms/systems, and mobile learning. These approaches to the academic curriculum increase student immersion in assignments and promote competition that enables students to complete learning activities (Chee-wei et al., 2017; Figueroa, 2016; Nicholson, 2015).

In the Romanian context, we find that research is initially focused on the use of gamification to promote inclusion within student groups. We are in a phase of digital transformation of college environments that facilitates the following inclusion strategies through gamification:

(1) The implementation of interventions at different levels through the development of institutional innovation capacities and the training of professional groups from the perspective of developing teaching skills in electronic learning systems
(2) The development of learning communities and networks to facilitate the transfer of knowledge in non-formal educational environments or workplaces
(3) The development of a curriculum that promotes values such as fairness, social justice, non-discrimination, and community inclusion
(4) The development of a range of digital competences among teachers to harness the potential of digital technologies for the improvement and innovation of education, with a focus on the inclusion of students with special educational needs

Conclusions and Recommendations

By considering four relevant dimensions—content, process, product and socio-affective environment—differentiation and inclusion practices facilitate the development of competencies that correlate with the demands of the labor market on students. The relevance of designing the academic curriculum with differentiation in mind and introducing gamification into the teaching and learning process for gifted students therefore encourages their engagement in completing tasks and developing their critical and creative thinking skills. At the same time, collaborative learning contexts are facilitated in the online environment, taking into account students' individual needs, abilities, preferences, and goals. Contemporary pedagogical approaches derived from the principles of learning theories such as constructivism facilitate integrative pedagogical interventions. Therefore, issues related to cutting-edge technologies such as virtual and augmented reality, interactive videos, video games, and other open educational resources constitute a relevant methodological framework for the use of differentiated and integrative approaches. With this in mind, we consider some relevant recommendations for creating an infrastructure for making the academic curriculum more flexible through differentiation practices and the integration of gamification strategies appropriate for gifted students: developing guides for teachers and students involved in gamified learning systems; creating opportunities for student participation in networked research activities across the curriculum; designing learning contexts that allow students to engage in the production, evaluation, and dissemination of knowledge using interdisciplinary approaches; creating online learning communities that foster motivation, enjoyment of teamwork, collaboration, communication, critical and creative thinking; developing reflective skills by approaching content from multiple perspectives.

The challenge for educators and researchers, then, is to find a coherent psycho-pedagogical framework that enables the use of technology to increase the effectiveness of the inclusive curriculum at the level of higher education institutions. At the same time, personalization is required according to the students' profiles, the game themes, the educational context, the culture and preferences of the learners, the learning styles, the level, the motivation to play, and the experience with games.

References

Apandi, A. M. (2022). Gamification meets mobile learning: Soft-skills enhancement. In Information Resources Management Association (Ed.), *Research anthology on developments in gamification and game-based learning* (pp. 1280–1299). IGI Global. https://doi.org/10.4018/978-1-6684-3710-0.ch061

Barab, S. A., Scott, B., Siyahhan, S., Goldstone, R., Ingram-Goble, A., Zuiker, S., & Warren, S. (2009). Transformational play as a curricular scaffold: Using videogames to support science education. *Journal of Science Education and Technology, 18*, 305–320. https://doi.org/10.1007/s10956-009-9171-5

Barab, S. A., Zuiker, S., Warren, S., Hickey, D., Ingram-Goble, A., Kwon, E.-J., et al. (2007). Situationally embodied curriculum: Relating formalisms and contexts. *Science Education, 91*, 750–782. https://doi.org/10.1002/sce.20217

Beck, J. (1999). Makeover or takeover? The strange death of educational autonomy in neo-liberal England. *British Journal of Sociology of Education, 20*(2), 223–238. https://doi.org/10.1080/01425699995425

Bernal, E. M. (2003). To no longer educate the gifted: Programing for gifted students beyond the era of inclusionism. *Gifted Child Quarterly, 47*, 183–191. https://doi.org/10.1177/001698620304700030

Brevik, L. M., Gunnulfsen, A. E., & Renzulli, J. S. (2018). Student teachers' practice and experience with differentiated instruction for students with higher learning potential. *Teaching and Teacher Education, 71*, 34–45. https://doi.org/10.1016/j.tate.2017.12.003

Castellano, J. A., & Diaz, E. I. (2002). *Reaching new horizons: Gifted and talented education for culturally and linguistically diverse students*. Allyn & Bacon.

Chamberlin, M., & Powers, R. (2010). The promise of differentiated instruction for enhancing the mathematical understandings of college students. *Teaching Mathematics and Its Applications., 29*, 113–139. https://doi.org/10.1093/teamat/hrq006

Chee-wei, T., Pei-duo, Y., Ling, L., Chung-kit, F., Chun-kiu, L., & Yanru, C. (2017). Teaching computational thinking by gamification of k-12 mathematics: Mobile app math games in mathematics and computer science tournament. In *Proceedings of Computational Thinking Education 2017* (pp. 55–59). The Education University of Hong Kong.

Clark, L., & Zubizarreta, J. (Eds.). (2008). *Inspiring exemplary teaching and learning: Perspectives on teaching academically talented college students*. Lincoln..

Crețu, C. (1997). *Psihopedagogia succesului*. Polirom.

Davis, G. A., Rimm, S. B., & Siegle, D. (2011). *Education of the Gifted and Talented* (6th ed.). Pearson.

Deterding, S., Dixon, D., Khaled, R., & Nacke, L. (2011). From game design elements to gamefulness: Defining "gamification". In *Proceedings of the 15th International Academic MindTrek Conference: Envisioning future media environments Tampere* (pp 9–15). ACM.

Dewey, J. (1916). *Democracy and education: An introduction to the philosophy of education.* Macmillan.

Dieterle, E. (2009). Neomillennial learning styles and River City. *Children, Youth & Environments, 19*, 245–278. Retrieved from http://www.jstor.org/action/showPublication?journalCode=chilyoutenvi

Doolittle, P. (2001). The need to leverage theory in the development of guidelines for using technology in social studies teacher education. *Contemporary Issues in Technology and Teacher Education., 1*, 501–516.

Doolittle, P. E. (1999). *Constructivist Pedagogy*, http://edpsycherver.ed.vt.edu/workshops/tohe/1999/pedagogy.html

Epstein, C. B. (1979). *The gifted and talented: Programs that work.* National School Public Relations Association.

Erickson, H. L. (2006). *Concept-based curriculum and instruction for the thinking classroom.* Corwin Press.

Eyre, D., & Lowe, H. (2002). *Curriculum provision for the gifted and talented in the secondary school.* David Fulton Publishers.

Figueroa, J. F. (2016). Gamification and game-based learning: Two strategies for the 21st century learner. *World Journal of Education Research, 3*(2), 507–522.

Freire, P. (1970). *Pedagogy of the oppressed.* Continuum.

Goodhew, G. (2009). *Meeting the needs of gifted and talented students.* Continuum International Publishing Group.

Gosfield, M. W. (2008). *Expert approaches to support gifted learners.* Free Spirit Publishing Inc.

Gross, M. U. M., & Van Vliet, H. E. (2005). Radical acceleration and early entry to college: A review of the research. *Gifted Child Quarterly, 49*, 154–171. https://doi.org/10.1177/001698620504900205

Hébert, T. P., & Mcbee, M. T. (2007). The impact of an undergraduate honors program on gifted university students. *Gifted Child Quarterly, 51*(2), 136–151.

Heidmann, O. (2015). How to create a serious game? *EAI Endorsed Transactions on Game-Based Learning, 2*, 150608. https://doi.org/10.4108/eai.5-11-2015.150608

Herz, C. J. (2001). Gaming the system: What higher education can learn from multiplayer online worlds. *The Internet and the University, Educause Forum on the Future of Higher Education.* Retrieved from http://www.educause.edu/ir/library/pdf/ffpiu019.pdf

Hines, P. J., Jasny, B. R., & Mervis, J. (2009). Adding a T to the three R's. *Science, 323*, 53. https://doi.org/10.1126/science.323.5910.53a

Honey, M. A., & Hilton, M. (Eds.). (2010). *Learning science through computer games and simulations.* National Academies Press.

Icard, S. B. (2014). Educational technology best practices. *International Journal of Instructional Technology and Distance Learning, 11*(3), 37–41.

International Bureau of Education (UNESCO-IBE). (2013). *Glossary of curriculum terminology.* UNESCO-IBE.

Kafai, Y. B., Quintero, M., & Feldon, D. (2010). Investigating the "'Why'" in Whypox: Casual and systematic explorations of a virtual epidemic. *Games and Culture, 5*, 116–135. https://doi.org/10.1177/1555412009351265

Ketelhut, D. J. (2007). The impact of student self-efficacy on scientific inquiry skills: An exploratory investigation in River City: A multi-user virtual environment. *Journal of Science Education and Technology, 16*, 99–111. https://doi.org/10.1007/s10956-006-9038-y

Kevin, B. (2005). Using public relation strategies to advocate for gifted programming in your school. *Gifted Child Today, 28*, 32–37.

Kickmeier, M., Mattheiss, E., Steiner, C., & Dietrich, A. (2011). A psycho-pedagogical framework for multi-adaptive educational games. *IJGBL, 1*, 45–58. https://doi.org/10.4018/ijgbl.2011010104

Klopfer, E., Scheintaub, H., Huang, W., Wendel, D., & Roque, R. (2009). The simulation cycle: Combining games, simulations, engineering and science using StarLogo TNG. *E-Learning and Digital Media, 6*, 71–96. https://doi.org/10.2304/elea.2009.6.1.7

Martinez-Garza, M., Clark, D. B., & Nelson, B. (2013). Digital games and the U.S. National Research Council's science proficiency goals. *Studies in Science Education, 49*, 170–208. https://doi.org/10.1080/03057267.2013.839372

Moore, R., & Young, M. (2009). Reconceptualising knowledge and the curriculum in the sociology of education. In K. Maton & R. Moore (Eds.), *Social realism, knowledge and the sociology of education: Coalitions of the mind* (pp. 14–34). Continuum.

Nah, F., Telaprolu, V., Rallapalli, S., & Venkata, P. (2013). Gamification of education using computer games. In S. Yamamoto (Ed.), *HCI 2013, Part III* (Vol. 8018, pp. 99–107). LNCS.

Ng, W., & Nicholas, H. (2010). A progressive pedagogy for online learning with high-ability secondary school students: A case study. *Gifted Child Quarterly, 54*, 239–251. https://doi.org/10.1177/0016986209355973

Nicholson, S. (2015). *A recipe for meaningful gamification. Gamification in Education and Business* (pp. 1–20). Springer.

Norwich, B. (2013). *Addressing tensions and dilemmas in inclusive education: Living with uncertainty*. Routledge.

Olenchak, F. R., & Renzulli, J. S. (1989). The effectiveness of the school wide enrichment model on selected aspects of elementary school change. *Gifted Child Quarterly, 33*, 36–46. https://doi.org/10.1177/001698628903300106

Organisation for Economic Co-operation and Development (OECD). (2015). *PISA 2018 draft global competence framework*. OECD Publishing.

Organisation for Economic Co-operation and Development (OECD). (2019). *Future of Education and Skills. OECD Learning Compass 2030. Conceptual learning framework. Transformative Competences for 2030*. https://www.oecd.org/content/dam/oecd/en/about/projects/edu/education-2040/concept-notes/Transformative_Competencies_for_2030_concept_note.pdf

Rogoz, N. (2014). *Proiectarea curriculumului constructivist. Noi tendințe și sugestii metodologice*. Ed. Universității Alexandru Ioan Cuza.

Shore, B. M., & Delcourt, M. A. B. (1996). Effective curricular and program practices in gifted education and the interface with general education. *Journal for the Education of the Gifted, 20*(2), 138–154.

Slattery, P. (2013). *Curriculum in the postmodern era: Teaching and learning in the age of accountability* (3rd ed.). Routledge.

Smutny, J. F. (2003). *Designing and developing programs for gifted students*. SAGE Publishers.

Squire, K. D., & Jan, M. (2007). Mad city mystery: Developing scientific argumentation skills with a place-based augmented reality game on handheld computers. *Journal of Science Education and Technology, 16*, 5–29. https://doi.org/10.1007/s10956-006-9037-z

Squire, K. D., & Klopfer, E. (2007). Augmented reality simulations on handheld computers. *Journal of the Learning Sciences, 16*, 371–413. https://doi.org/10.1080/10508400701413435

Stanley, W. (1992). *Curriculum for Utopia: Social reconstructionism and critical pedagogy in the postmodern era*. State University of New York Press.

Steinkuehler, D., & Duncan, S. (2008). Scientific habits of mind in virtual worlds. *Journal of Science Education and Technology, 17*, 530–543. https://doi.org/10.1007/s10956-008-9120-8

Stentiford, L., & Koutsouris, G. (2022). Critically considering the 'inclusive curriculum' in higher education. *British Journal of Sociology of Education, 43*(8), 1250–1272. https://doi.org/10.1080/01425692.2022.2122937

Stoica Constantin, A. (2004). *Creativitatea pentru studenți și profesori*. Institutul European.

The Council of the European Union. (2018). *Council Recommendation of 22 May 2018 on key competences for lifelong learning (Text with EEA Relevance)* (2018/C189/1). https://eur-lex.europa.eu/legal-content/EN/TXT/PDF/?uri=CELEX:32018H0604(01)

Tomlinson, C. A., & Imbeau, M. B. (2010). *Leading and managing a differentiated classroom*. ASCD.

Tomlinson, C. A., Kaplan, S. N., Renzulli, J. S., Purcell, J. H., Leppien, J. H., Burns, D. E., Strickland, C. A., & Imbeau, M. B. (2008). *The parallel curriculum: A design to develop learner potential and challenge advanced learners*. Corwin Press.

Turner, W.-D., Solis, O.-J., & Kincade, D.-H. (2017). Differentiating instruction for large classes in higher education. *International Journal of Teaching and Learning in Higher Education, 29* (3), 490–500. http://www.isetl.org/ijtlhe/ ISSN 1812-9129.

Usher, R., & Edwards, R. (1994). *Postmodernism and education*. Routledge.

Van Tassel-Baska, J. (2003). *Curriculum planning and instructional design for gifted learners*. Love Publishing Co.

Van Tassel-Baska, J. (2005). *Acceleration: Strategies for teaching gifted learners*. Prufrock Press Inc.

Wagner, T. (2014). *Formarea inovatorilor. Cum creşti tinerii pentru a schimba lumea de mâine*. Ed. Trei.

Werbach, K., & Hunter, D. (2012). *For the win: How game thinking can revolutionize your business*. Wharton Digital Press.

Wheelahan, L. (2010). *Why knowledge matters in the curriculum: A social realist argument*. Routledge.

White, J. (2018). The weakness of 'powerful knowledge'. *London Review of Education, 16*(2), 325–335. https://doi.org/10.18546/LRE.16.2.11

Wiggins, G. P., Wiggins, G., & McTighe, J. (2005). *Understanding by design*. Ascd.

Wolfensberger, M. V. C. (2012). *Teaching for excellence. Honors pedagogies revealed*. Waxmann Publishing Co.

Young, M. (1971). *Knowledge and control: New directions for the sociology of education*. Collier Macmillan.

Young, M. (2008). *Bringing knowledge back in*. Routledge.

Young, M., & Muller, J. (2013). On the powers of powerful knowledge. *Review of Education, 1*(3), 229–250. https://doi.org/10.1002/rev3.3017

Young, M. F., Slota, S., Cutter, A. B., Jalette, G., Mullin, G., Lai, B., et al. (2012). Our princess is in another castle: A review of trends in serious gaming for education. *Review of Educational Research, 82*, 61–89. https://doi.org/10.3102/0034654312436980

Zichermann, G., & Cunningham, C. (2011). *Gamification by design*. O'Reilly Media.

Chapter 8
Serious Games in Education for Students with Special Needs

Matej Zapušek and Jože Rugelj

Abstract Serious games offer innovative ways to enhance the educational experience of students with special needs by creating safe, engaging, and adaptive learning environments. This chapter explores the application of the SADDIE methodology in the context of students with disabilities. Based on an extensive literature review, the chapter summarizes evidence-based guidelines for the development of games tailored to different special needs, including intellectual disabilities, hearing and visual impairments, dyslexia, autism spectrum disorders, and ADHD. The findings emphasize the crucial role of participatory and iterative design processes, the development of intuitive user interfaces, adaptive content and multisensory feedback mechanisms, as well as the integration of collaborative elements to promote social skills and inclusion. Specific adaptations are explored, such as the use of spatial audio for visually impaired learners and the inclusion of emotion recognition scenarios for students with autism. By addressing both general principles and specific adaptations, the chapter highlights the transformative potential of serious games in promoting cognitive, social, and motor skills. It also emphasizes the need to integrate advanced technologies such as virtual reality and adaptive artificial intelligence to improve accessibility and effectiveness, thus establishing serious games as a crucial component of inclusive education.

Keywords Serious games · Special needs education · SADDIE methodology · Active learning · Inclusive education

M. Zapušek (✉) · J. Rugelj
University of Ljubljana, Ljubljana, Slovenia
e-mail: matej.zapusek@pef.uni-lj.si; joze.rugelj@pef.uni-lj.si

I. Boghian, G. Mareş (eds.), *Gamification and Inclusion*, Inclusive Learning and Educational Equity 12, https://doi.org/10.1007/978-3-031-98390-0_8

Introduction

Serious games are defined as games whose primary purpose extends beyond entertainment to include education, training, and the dissemination of information (Michael & Chen, 2005). A game is considered educational when it incorporates intentional learning objectives; however, it is equally important that the game remains enjoyable and retains the core elements that make it engaging. Numerous studies have demonstrated that the inherent characteristics of games can be effectively leveraged to enhance the learning process. These features include fostering intrinsic motivation, providing continuous and immediate feedback, introducing learning content with progressively increasing complexity and allowing for adaptation to the learner's current skill level. One of the most important features of serious games is their potential to establish immersive learning environments that facilitate active participation, enabling learners to acquire knowledge through action and interaction. They also support the simulation of real-world scenarios, which not only aids in knowledge transfer but also provides a risk-free environment where learners are encouraged to experiment and learn from their experiences and where mistake is considered as an opportunity to learn not as something disastrous. Moreover, by integrating visual, auditory, and tactile components, serious games promote multisensory engagement, thereby enhancing learner involvement and improving the retention of educational content. In addition, serious games can foster activities that encourage social interaction, thereby supporting collaborative learning and the development of communication skills (Prensky, 2001).

Due to these characteristics, serious games hold significant potential for supporting the education of students with special needs, as they can effectively address their unique challenges and requirements. An important conceptual aspect that is closely related to serious games is the relationship between gamification, game-based learning, and inclusion. Gamification refers to the application of game design elements—such as points, rewards, leaderboards, and levels—in traditionally non-game contexts with the primary goal of increasing motivation, engagement, and persistence. Game-based learning, on the other hand, uses interactive gameplay to embed educational content into the mechanics of a game to promote active learning, experimentation, problem solving, and social interaction (Plass et al., 2020). Both gamification and game-based learning focus on personalized and customizable learning experiences and are therefore particularly well suited to address the diverse educational needs of students with special needs. From an inclusion perspective, these approaches enable students with different abilities to meaningfully participate in shared activities and promote positive interactions, empathy, and a greater appreciation of diversity. Consequently, serious games developed according to these principles are powerful tools for creating inclusive learning environments in which all students can actively participate and succeed. These games offer advanced modes of individualization, enabling specific adaptations and diverse modes of interaction that cater to a wide range of abilities, needs, and limitations (Yildirim & Surer, 2021). They provide a friendly, safe, predictable, and stimulating environment where students can feel comfortable and experiment without fear of negative consequences (Cai & Cao, 2021). Moreover, serious games can target specific cognitive abilities, such as attention, working memory, and executive functions, enhancing these critical skills through structured play (Shin et al., 2018). They can also be used to improve motor skills, supporting the development of both gross and fine motor mechanics (Kusumaningsih et al., 2022). The ability to simulate real-life scenarios enables students with special needs to practice essential social skills such as conflict resolution, emotional expression, and recognition of facial expressions (Goh et al., 2021). It is also possible to control and adapt sensory stimuli, along with the use of adaptive interfaces, which ensures engagement in the learning process regardless of physical limitations (Yildirim & Surer, 2021). Furthermore, a particularly valuable feature of serious games is their capacity to foster self-regulation, helping students develop strategies to manage emotions, impulses, and stress effectively (Terlouw et al., 2021). These attributes make serious games an essential tool for creating inclusive and supportive educational experiences tailored to the diverse needs of students with special needs.

At the University of Ljubljana, Faculty of Education, members of the Chair of Computer Science and Computer Science Didactics collaborate closely with the Department of Special and Rehabilitation Pedagogy to explore innovative ways to leverage ICT technologies in supporting the learning processes of students with diverse special needs. The authors of this paper have been extensively researching the development of a methodology for designing serious games, which we have named SADDIE. This acronym represents the sequential stages of the methodology, guiding practitioners through the process of conception, design, implementation, evaluation, and integration of serious games into the learning environment. Over the years, the SADDIE methodology has been successfully employed as a framework for game-based learning, facilitating the development of teacher competencies aligned with the DigCompEdu framework and creating serious games specifically designed for computer science education (Zapušek & Rugelj, 2023). We posit that this methodology can also be effectively adapted to address the unique educational challenges faced by students with special needs. However, for this purpose, the SADDIE framework requires meaningful adaptations and enhancements to accommodate the specific requirements of designing serious games tailored for students with diverse special needs. These adaptations would ensure that the methodology aligns with the specialized pedagogical, cognitive, and accessibility considerations necessary to support this learner group effectively.

This manuscript presents a comprehensive literature review exploring how serious games can address challenges associated with specific special needs, including intellectual disabilities, deafness and hearing impairments, blindness and visual impairments, physical disabilities, learning deficits such as dyslexia, autism spectrum disorders, and ADHD. The study examines examples of effective applications of serious games in supporting these needs and evaluates various design frameworks and methodologies. The primary objective is to synthesize these findings into a set of guidelines for applying the SADDIE methodology to the development of serious games tailored for students with special needs.

The findings of this study are significant for a wide audience, including serious game developers, special education professionals, therapists, and parents of students with special needs. The chapter is structured as follows: it begins by introducing the concept of game-based learning and emphasizing the benefits of using games in educational contexts. It then examines the application of serious games in the education of students with special needs, presenting research findings on their use for the specific needs mentioned above. Finally, it provides guidance on the development of serious games within the SADDIE methodology, ensuring that these games effectively address the educational goals and diverse needs of students. This chapter aims to bridge the gap between research and practice by providing actionable recommendations for creating impactful learning tools for students with special needs.

Game-Based Learning

Game-based learning is a pedagogical approach that uses the interactive mechanics, motivational elements, and problem-solving structures of games to create engaging, experiential learning environments (Prensky, 2001). This method integrates learning content into play and encourages active learning, critical thinking and collaboration (Gee, 2003). It provides a safe space for learners to experiment, fail and try again, promoting deep learning through situated practice and reflection (Aldrich, 2009). Game-based learning combines theoretical knowledge with practical application and is consistent with the intrinsic motivation and cognitive strategies that games inherently promote (Squire, 2011).

The thoughtful introduction and integration of game-based learning into educational contexts offer numerous advantages. A substantial body of research highlights its positive impact on motivation and engagement in learning activities. Motivation is a critical determinant of the learning process, as it directly influences how effectively and persistently individuals acquire knowledge. It also fosters deeper cognitive processing of information, is positively correlated with self-regulation, and significantly enhances the achievement of intended learning outcomes (Pintrich, 2003). Well-designed games can effectively foster intrinsic motivation by leveraging game features that align with sound pedagogical principles. These features include the creation of authentic, interactive experiences that actively engage learners, tailoring content to the needs and characteristics of the target audience and incorporating relatable characters that allow learners to form meaningful connections. Furthermore, games provide opportunities for progression, sustaining learners' interest through carefully structured tasks and objectives. Meaningful and immediate feedback tailored to individual performance further enhances the learning experience. Additionally, games incorporate elements traditionally associated with extrinsic motivation, such as point collection, rewards, levels, and achievements. When these elements are thoughtfully designed and meaningfully integrated into the game's context, they can effectively stimulate situational interest, which often evolves into intrinsic motivation over time (Gee, 2003).

A very important characteristic of games that can be usefully employed in an educational context is their ability to stimulate a state of "flow" (Prensky, 2001). This is a state of intense concentration and immersion in an activity in which the individual experiences a high level of engagement, enjoyment and satisfaction, surrendering to the activity and forgetting about time and external distractions. This enables the individual to learn very effectively as he or she is fully focused on the subject matter (Csikszentmihalyi, 1990). Games have several characteristics that affect the creation of a flow state. A well-designed game contains challenges that maintain a balance in terms of difficulty so that it does not become too easy and boring for the player, but at the same time is not too difficult and does not cause feelings of frustration, which is the basis for establishing a flow state. The game mechanics of educational games are designed to include clear goals in terms of what needs to be achieved in the game to progress, and immediate feedback to help the player monitor their progress and adapt to the given challenges. This type of immediate insight into one's successes and failures, and thus one's progress, also helps to create a state of game flow. Games also often contain interactive elements and an engaging storyline that allow the player to become fully immersed in the game and feel part of the game and therefore induce the state of flow (Squire, 2011). Research by Kiili (2005) found that educational games that incorporate the above elements to achieve a state of flow increase engagement in learning and therefore positively influence performance. Students who experienced a state of flow while playing educational games showed a greater understanding of the learning material and retained their knowledge better in the long term.

The personalization capabilities offered by serious games represent a critical feature that can be effectively applied in educational contexts. By allowing learning experiences to be tailored to the unique needs and characteristics of each learner, serious games can significantly enhance the educational process. Personalization features such as adjustable pacing, dynamic adaptation to the learner's performance, and non-linear progression allow the content to align with individual interests, making learning more engaging and effective. Furthermore, adapting the content helps to reduce the cognitive load on learners, facilitating better focus and comprehension (Toukiloglou & Xinogalos, 2022). These methods collectively improve the quality of learning, promote the retention of acquired knowledge, enhance learner satisfaction, and consequently boost engagement and motivation (Kickmeier-Rust & Albert, 2012). Research by Melero et al. (2015) underscores the benefits of personalized learning paths that account for prior knowledge and allow learners to progress through a curriculum tailored to their specific needs. This approach leads to improved comprehension of the material and a more thorough mastery of learning objectives. The effectiveness of personalization is further reinforced by techniques borrowed from intelligent tutoring systems, including reinforcement learning, neural networks, and domain ontologies. These techniques enable dynamic adjustments to task difficulty based on analyses of the learner's prior knowledge, in-game actions, and specified learning goals. Such adaptations significantly enhance the quality of learning outcomes (Hare & Tang, 2022).

Integrating serious games into the educational process has also proven to be an effective tool for developing critical thinking and problem-solving skills. Serious games can be used to create a variety of authentic simulations of real-life situations and other activities that require active student participation. In this context, the games encourage participants to first identify problems, hypothesise, collect data and test different solution strategies. They can then evaluate the consequences of their decisions and analyse how the different approaches have influenced the achievement of the desired goals, thus promoting reflection (Hung & Van Eck, 2010). Collaborative problem solving is also an important aspect of serious games. In games with team elements, students learn to communicate, coordinate tasks and share ideas, which leads to the development of group solutions. Such games also promote metacognitive skills as learners monitor their thought processes, become aware of their own biases and evaluate different possible outcomes of their decisions (Bernard & Bachu, 2015). Studies among adolescents playing strategy games have shown a long-term association between playing games and improved independent problem-solving skills, which contributed to their better academic performance (Adachi & Willoughby, 2013). This shows that through serious games, students not only learn the intended learning content, but also the processes of critical thinking, analysis and creative problem solving, skills that can be transferred to other situations in life.

An essential feature of serious games that significantly enhances learning outcomes is the provision of immediate feedback. Immediate feedback allows players to observe the consequences of their actions in real-time, which accelerates the learning process and boosts motivation for continuous improvement (Sales et al., 2022). Research shows that positive feedback fosters feelings of competence and intrinsic motivation, while negative feedback, although it may reduce feelings of competence initially, encourages the desire to improve. This dual effect is particularly beneficial for cultivating persistence and adaptability in learners (Burgers et al., 2015). In addition to immediate feedback, retrospective cognitive feedback plays a crucial role in the learning process within serious games. This type of feedback allows learners to monitor their progress, fostering reflection and self-regulation, which are key components of effective learning (Nadolski & Hummel, 2017). Furthermore, the impact of feedback is amplified when it is paired with mechanisms that recognize performance, such as leaderboards, scoring systems, and rewards. These features not only provide a sense of achievement but also motivate learners through elements of competition, promoting sustained engagement and progression within the game (Haruna et al., 2021). However, for feedback to be effective, its design requires careful consideration of several factors. The content of the feedback should be clear, concise, and focused on essential elements. The timing of feedback is equally critical; it should be delivered when it is most relevant to the learner's actions or decisions. Finally, the mode of delivery—whether written, visual, or auditory—should align with the learner's preferences and the context of the game (Johnson et al., 2017). By ensuring feedback is targeted, timely, and relevant, serious games can maximize their educational impact, driving both engagement and successful learning outcomes.

Research on the use of simulations and serious games in education underscores their capacity to provide students with authentic and practical experiences in a secure environment. These virtual settings allow learners to experiment with different scenarios, observe the consequences of their decisions, and develop specialized skills and knowledge that may be difficult to acquire in real-world contexts (Ney et al., 2014). Beyond skill acquisition, simulations and serious games engage learners actively, promoting reflection on their choices and actions. This reflective practice represents a significant advancement in educational methodologies, as it not only facilitates the acquisition of valuable skills but also nurtures critical thinking and personal growth, aligning with the goals of contemporary pedagogy. Moreover, serious games are an effective tool for fostering successful collaboration, particularly through their multiplayer features. These games help develop essential social skills such as teamwork, communication, constructive conflict resolution, and empathy. By creating interactive environments that encourage group dynamics and cooperation, serious games enable participants to build meaningful connections. Such environments also foster social presence and emotional bonds, which are critical for enhancing collaboration and problem-solving within teams (Chen, 2009).

Serious Games in Special Needs Education

Students with special needs are children with intellectual disabilities, deaf and hard of hearing children, blind and partially sighted children or children with visual impairment, children with speech and language impairments, children with physical disabilities, children with learning disabilities, children with long-term illnesses, children with emotional and behavioral disorders, and children with autism spectrum disorders. The educational challenges for these children are diverse and include pedagogical, organizational, social, and technical aspects. Some of them can be overcome using information and communication technology. In this chapter, we present how the characteristics of serious games presented in the previous chapter can be usefully applied to the learning process of people with disabilities. First, we present the general characteristics that apply to all serious games used in the education of students with special needs. We then focus on the specific needs selected and present the results of an extensive literature review that looked at the use of serious games for these specific needs.

The use of serious games in the education of students with special needs has been shown to enhance cognitive skill development and promote long-term retention of acquired knowledge. A meta-analysis by Wouters et al. (2013) demonstrates that serious games lead to significantly better cognitive performance compared to traditional teaching methods. This finding is particularly relevant for students with special needs, who often benefit from more structured and supportive learning environments to build foundational skills. One of the key advantages of serious games lies in their ability to boost engagement and motivation among students with special needs, who frequently encounter challenges with conventional teaching methods (Roozeboom et al., 2015). By offering playful and immersive environments, serious games transform the learning process from a potentially tedious task into an enjoyable activity, encouraging greater participation and enthusiasm for learning. Furthermore, research highlights the role of serious games in sustaining long-term interest in education, particularly for students with attention and memory difficulties. Studies by Yu et al. (2022) and Papanastasiou et al. (2022) emphasize that serious games can create dynamic and interactive experiences that not only captivate learners but also support the ongoing development of attention and memory-related skills.

The interactive nature of serious games fosters active learning and enhances student engagement. Game mechanics typically incorporate elements that require players to make decisions, solve problems, and collaborate with peers, thereby promoting greater cognitive engagement (Yu et al., 2022). The integration of advanced technologies, such as artificial intelligence, data analytics, and dynamic content adaptation, into intelligent serious games further amplifies their educational potential. These games have been shown to effectively encourage positive behaviors in students with special needs. By maintaining the focus and creating personalized learning experiences, serious games support those learners in taking greater responsibility for their education. This, in turn, boosts their motivation, confidence, and independence (Papanastasiou et al., 2022). Such features position serious games as a valuable tool for creating inclusive and empowering learning environments, particularly for students who face challenges with traditional instructional methods.

The important ability of serious games in education for students with special needs it's their possibility to personalize and adapt the learning content. By tailoring the learning environment to individual needs, preferences, and abilities, serious games help reduce the barriers associated with various forms of special needs (Santórum, 2023). For example, students with learning difficulties such as dyslexia, ADHD, or autism often require customized methods that align with their learning styles, interests, and current knowledge levels. Furthermore, adaptive capabilities of serious games can provide them the challenges that are progressively increased, sustaining attention and motivation for continued learning (Yildirim & Surer, 2021). Possibility of including dynamic content adaptation mechanisms in serious games has a potential to further improve the quality of their learning by continuously assessing a student's progress and providing real-time feedback and adjustments. Such personalization fosters a sense of achievement, encourages persistence, and supports sustained engagement. Moreover, the integration of advanced technologies such as virtual reality (VR), Kinect, and eye-tracking enables even more specific adaptations (Teoh et al., 2021).

Serious games play a crucial role in developing social skills among students with special needs by offering a safe and controlled environment for practicing social interactions without the pressures or risks of real-life consequences. Through role-play, learners can simulate real-world social scenarios, enhancing their ability to engage in social interactions and transferring these skills to real-life contexts

(Kinsell et al., 2014). This approach is particularly valuable for students with autism spectrum disorders (ASD), as serious games provide a structured and supportive space for social skills development (Tan et al., 2022). Carneiro (2024), in a systematic review of serious games for students with autism, highlights their promising role in improving social skills by offering structured opportunities for interaction. Through the provision of feedback, these games positively influence the development of essential skills such as effective communication, cooperation, and accurate interpretation of emotions, areas that are often challenging for these students. For example, the virtual escape room AScapeD allows students to collaboratively solve group tasks in a safe and enjoyable environment, fostering cooperation and peer (Terlouw et al., 2021). Jacob et al. (2022) further emphasizes that the effectiveness of serious games in promoting social skills among students with disabilities is enhanced when combined with complementary methods such as peer tutoring and video modelling. Video modelling, which involves watching videos of desired behaviors or skills, allows learners to observe, imitate, and gradually acquire new behaviors at their own pace. This approach significantly improves the social skills of individuals with cognitive disabilities by facilitating the transfer of learned behaviors to real-world situations. In addition to promoting individual social skills, serious games are effective in fostering teamwork and collaboration. Multiplayer or cooperative games require students to communicate effectively, share responsibilities, and work together to achieve common goals. These cooperative elements are particularly beneficial for students with disabilities, as they allow for the practice of social skills in a supportive and stress-free learning environment (Papanastasiou et al., 2022). The playful nature of serious games, combined with immediate feedback and incentives such as rewards or recognition, reinforces the learning process and ensures the sustainability of acquired skills.

Serious games play a significant role in promoting physical activity and developing psychomotor skills in students with special needs. By integrating educational objectives with game mechanics that encourage movement, coordination, and motor skills, these games provide a unique platform for skill development. Unlike traditional methods of promoting physical activity, serious games create highly engaging environments that motivate students to participate actively in physical exercises (Bonnechère et al., 2017). The integration of advanced technologies, such as virtual reality (VR), enhances the potential of serious games by simulating realistic scenarios that require physical activity. These simulations provide students with disabilities the opportunity to engage in movement, thereby improving their psychomotor skills. Moreover, the multi-sensory nature of such activities makes learning more engaging and encourages active participation (Cai & Cao, 2021). Modern interaction technologies further expand the capabilities of serious games. Features such as body movement tracking, posture and joint position analysis, real-time feedback, and data recording enable precise monitoring and adaptation of the learning process. These functionalities are particularly beneficial for developing motor skills and enhancing overall physical coordination in students with disabilities (Zhang et al., 2018). There are many serious games that have used Microsoft Kinect to implement these features. Although Kinect was discontinued in 2017, alternatives such as Azure Kinect offer similar functionalities, ensuring continued innovation in this domain. For instance, Kusumaningsih et al. (2022) developed a serious game using Kinect's 3D camera to help students with disabilities improve motor skills, balance, and coordination in a virtual learning environment, demonstrating its effectiveness. Similarly, Kourakli et al. (2017) reported that Kinect-based games incorporating movement activities not only enhanced cognitive and motor skills but also positively influenced the academic performance of students with disabilities. The flexibility of serious games also allows for the inclusion of physical challenges tailored to individual learners' needs. De Greef et al. (2013) describe how customized Kinect-based games effectively address the needs of students with motor difficulties, such as developmental coordination disorder and cerebral palsy, by providing targeted physical activities. This adaptability ensures inclusivity, enabling students with different psychomotor challenges to engage in activities that foster its development. Based on the presented literature review on the use of serious games in the education of students with special needs, it can be concluded that serious games provide a versatile and inclusive educational approach. They enhance cognitive, social, and psychomotor skills, sustain engagement and motivation through adaptive and personalized learning experiences, and leverage advanced technologies to create immersive, safe, and supportive environments tailored to the unique needs of individual learners.

Game-Based Learning, Gamification, and Inclusion

In its "Guidelines for Inclusion," UNESCO (2009) defines inclusion as a process that recognizes and addresses the diverse needs of all learners by increasing participation in learning and reducing exclusion in education. In this section, we will outline how the features of gamification and game-based learning can be used to achieve the goals of inclusive education.

Educational games allow us to create accessible and flexible learning environments where differentiation of learning is possible so that it can be adapted to the learner's individual needs, abilities and ultimately interests (Streicher & Smeddinck, 2016). For example, a dyslexic learner can use audio instructions in a game, ensuring that the deficit does not hinder knowledge acquisition. An important feature of games is that they can be used to implement a personalized learning pace in a meaningful way and provide relevant and immediate feedback (Ke & Abras, 2013). This allows learners who need more time to understand to learn without time pressure, progress at their own pace and continuously learn from their mistakes. To provide an inclusive learning experience for learners with disabilities, an important feature of educational games is that different modes of interaction can be implemented in them with relatively simple adaptations, which increases the accessibility of such materials. Various controllers, sensors, and other input devices can be used to implement visual, auditory, tactile or kinesthetic ways of interacting with the material (Korozi et al., 2018). For example, a child with ADHD may find it easier to concentrate in this way when learning math and solving tasks through movement or touch. People with disabilities often face challenges in learning motivation, especially when they are involved in an educational process based on traditional teaching methods. For them, it is particularly important that learning experiences are actively designed and include approaches that influence situational interest and motivation (Bishara, 2018). The use of gamification, i.e., earning points, achieving levels, collecting badges and other rewards, or comparing learning successes on a leaderboard, has a positive effect on situational interest in the learning material, which can lead to higher motivation to learn. This, in turn, can positively contribute to reducing disengagement and achieving better learning outcomes (García-López et al., 2023). Many games also have a multiplayer mode, which can help students with disabilities to build interpersonal relationships and strengthen social skills. By participating in a virtual environment, learners can practice social interactions in a safe, controlled and stimulating environment. Various adaptations can help to reduce the limitations that different special needs bring and create an inclusive environment where their strengths can come to the fore. This in turn can have a positive impact on their social integration and self-esteem (Reprintceva, 2016).

We therefore believe that the use of games and gamification elements in the educational process is a meaningful and effective way to put the principles of inclusive education into practice, as it directly supports the central goals of inclusion such as equality, accessibility, active participation, and acceptance of diversity. These approaches are also in line with the principles of Universal Design for Learning (UDL), which emphasizes diverse opportunities for representation, interaction and expression as key to the successful inclusion of all learners in the learning process (Rogers-Shaw et al., 2018). We argue that the use of games and gamification elements in the educational process is not only a complement to traditional practices, but also an effective strategy for implementing the principles of inclusion in education.

Using Serious Games for Specific Special Needs

Using Serious Games with Students with Intellectual Disabilities

An intellectual disability is a neurodevelopmental disorder that begins before the age of 18 and leads to significantly reduced intellectual abilities and considerable deviations in adaptive skills. Students with this disorder have significantly diminished general intellectual level/functioning, including diminished learning, thinking, and problem-solving abilities and diminished abstract reasoning and judgment skills. Deficits in adaptive skills are evident in the areas of language and communication, self-care, independence, social skills, learning and work skills, functional learning skills, practical skills, and self-care.

Several studies (Cano et al., 2015; Koh, 2020) investigating the use of serious games with students with intellectual disabilities demonstrate their potential to enhance various aspects of learning process. Compared to traditional learning methods, serious games have been shown to foster greater focus on learning materials, encourage active participation in learning, promote adherence to rules and goals set by the game, and increase willingness to interact with peers and teachers (Saridaki & Mourlas, 2014). These factors collectively contribute to enhanced engagement and motivation to learn. Serious games also play a significant role in improving the social skills of students with intellectual disabilities, particularly in recognizing and interpreting emotions and emotional expressions, enhancing communication, and understanding social situations. Simulations of real-life scenarios within serious games have been shown to improve independence and adaptability in practical tasks, such as handling money, navigating routes, using public transportation, and orienting themselves in unfamiliar environments (Cano et al., 2015). In addition to social skills, serious games effectively support the development of cognitive skills in students with intellectual disabilities, including rule comprehension, attention enhancement, and problem-solving abilities (Moreno et al., 2021; Stancin et al., 2020). Furthermore, serious games have demonstrated benefits in improving physical skills of this target group. For example, Hsu (2016) conducted a study with the Nintendo Wii game Wii Fit, which integrates gamification elements, progress monitoring, and personalization. The study found that using this game positively impacted the physical abilities of participating students with intellectual disabilities by providing an engaging and enjoyable way to perform exercises.

Using Serious Games with Deaf and Hearing-Impaired Students

A hearing-impaired child is typically characterized by an average hearing loss in the speech frequency range (500, 1000, 2000, and 4000 Hz) of less than 110 dB, whereas a deaf child has a hearing loss exceeding 110 dB.

Serious games provide deaf and hard-of-hearing children with innovative opportunities to acquire specific skills in areas such as reading, mathematics, sound recognition, and basic language development. Interactive elements, including voice commands and character control in games, can be incorporated into engaging language exercises that are often preferred by deaf and hard-of-hearing children over traditional therapy methods (Nasiri et al., 2017).

In addition to language skills, serious games can support the development of reading proficiency, particularly in learning letters, words, and grammatical structures. For example, the game Literacy with Fitzgerald employs the Fitzgerald Key method—a visual approach that uses colour codes to represent different parts of a sentence—to help children understand sentence structure and formation (Cano et al., 2015).

Serious games are also effective in fostering mathematical (Salsabila et al., 2020) and computational thinking skills (Cano et al., 2020), often yielding better results than traditional teaching approaches. Furthermore, serious games have proven beneficial for children with cochlear implants, providing sound recognition and discrimination training. These activities are critical for enhancing the ability of these children to engage in social interactions and interpret their surroundings more effectively (Manresa-Yee et al., 2017).

Using Serious Games with Blind, Partially Sighted, and Low Vision Children

Blind, partially sighted, and low-vision children experience reduced visual acuity, restricted visual fields, or other forms of visual impairment.

Research on the application of serious games for this population highlights several educational benefits, particularly in enhancing spatial orientation, memory, mathematics, and social integration. Serious games have proven effective in developing spatial orientation skills by enabling the use of mental maps—mental representations of space created through experiences, perceptions, and ideas. For example, Hungry Cat (Chai et al., 2019) allows children to improve spatial navigation and understanding of objects in space through gameplay. The game employs audio cues to construct mental maps of virtual spaces, helping children learn to navigate a room more efficiently.

Tactile serious games have also been shown to enhance memory by leveraging tactile information. These games present patterns and interactive content through vibrations and other tactile feedback, enabling students to engage in environments tailored to their sensory needs (Raisamo et al., 2007).

Additionally, serious games can facilitate the learning of mathematical skills. For instance, games designed for blind and partially sighted students often replace graphics with auditory information, such as sounds representing mathematical elements in a 2D spatial audio environment. This approach not only aids in problem-solving but also fosters inclusive learning environments where visually impaired and sighted students can play together, enhancing interest and motivation in mathematics for both groups (Ferreira & Cavaco, 2014).

Serious games can also contribute to improving learning confidence and social integration. The game See (Lievense et al., 2021), developed based on rational-emotive behavior theory, helps children recognize and overcome negative thought patterns. By offering tasks tailored to their abilities yet challenging enough to provide a sense of achievement, the game boosts self-esteem and learning confidence. Furthermore, its cooperative elements encourage collaboration, fostering social cohesion and reducing feelings of isolation.

Using Serious Games with Children with Deficits in Specific Areas of Learning

Children with a more severe form of specific learning difficulties who, despite average or above average intellectual ability, have significant difficulties due to known or unknown disorders or differences in the functioning of the central nervous system are referred to as children with deficits in specific areas of learning.

Research indicates that serious games can effectively address deficits in specific learning areas, offering targeted interventions for children with various learning challenges. García-Redondo et al. (2019) demonstrated that games designed to enhance different types of intelligence—such as visual-spatial, verbal-linguistic, logical-mathematical, bodily-kinesthetics, and interpersonal intelligence—significantly improve attention in children with attention deficits. Specifically, these games help children focus on learning materials, sustain attention to visual stimuli, recognize information, follow instructions, and monitor their progress, leading to more effective learning outcomes.

Systematic literature reviews further confirm the positive impact of serious games on literacy skill development (Lämsä et al., 2018; Yildirim & Surer, 2021; Marinelli et al., 2023). Games incorporating motivational elements, meaningful feedback (e.g., immediate success feedback, improvement suggestions, praise, and encouragement), and adaptive adjustments based on performance have been shown to enhance reading and phonological skills in children with learning deficits (Marinelli et al., 2023). The efficacy of serious games in addressing dyslexia has also been widely studied. For example, Jaramillo-Alcázar et al. (2021) developed Puzzle Pieces, a game designed to enhance attention, visual recognition, phonological, and semantic awareness in children with dyslexia. The game not only supports learning and therapy but also collects performance data, enabling therapists to analyze individual progress and tailor interventions accordingly. Similarly, Prosodiya focuses on improving language skills by helping children practice syllable stress, a critical component for developing reading and writing abilities (Holz et al., 2017). Other serious games, such as Cosmic Sounds, target phonological awareness by improving sound and syllable recognition. The game incorporates co-construction elements, which positively influence children's willingness to learn, with research showing significant improvements in phonological awareness, including consonant and vowel recognition and syllable formation (Brennan et al., 2022). Meanwhile, MILA-Learn focuses on rhythm training to enhance phonological awareness and reading skills, addressing a crucial cognitive component associated with dyslexia (Vonthron et al., 2022). Additionally, Words Matter approaches dyslexia from a social perspective. Rooted in a social constructivist framework, the game promotes peer interaction and collaboration, fostering social skills and a sense of belonging. This, in turn, positively impacts the social integration and self-esteem of children with dyslexia (Vasalou et al., 2017).

Using Serious Games with Children with Autism

Serious games have demonstrated significant effectiveness in the educational process for children with autism by providing structured, interactive, and flexible learning environments. Structured settings are particularly beneficial for children with autism, as they often thrive in predictable and stable contexts. Serious games offer the advantage of allowing tasks to be repeated as needed, which can reduce anxiety and foster a sense of safety (Carlier et al., 2019). One of the primary applications of serious games for children with autism is the development of social and communication skills. These games can simulate social scenarios, enabling children to practice interactions such as greetings, maintaining eye contact, and conversational skills in a controlled and safe environment (Bernardini et al., 2014; Uzuegbunam et al., 2018). Serious games have also been shown to enhance functional communication by improving skills such as visual scanning, discrimination, and sentence formation (Nawahdah & Ihmouda, 2019).

Emotion recognition, a common challenge for students with autism, is another area where serious games are particularly effective. Games employing characters with diverse facial expressions and body language help students learn to identify and interpret emotions, including subtle differences in expressions and gestures (Elhaddadi et al., 2021). For example, the game Emotiplay has been shown to significantly improve social interaction skills after 8–12 weeks of practice with recognizing facial expressions and body language (Fridenson-Hayo et al., 2017).

Serious games also support the development of practical everyday skills. For instance, games designed to simulate shopping tasks (Vallefuoco et al., 2022) or route planning for shopping trips (Taib et al., 2018) allow students with autism to practice organizational skills, spatial orientation, attention management, and problem-solving. These activities not only improve their ability to navigate real-life situations, but also contribute to a greater sense of independence.

Using Serious Games with Students with ADHD

ADHD, a neurodevelopmental disorder affecting approximately 7% of children in the general population, is characterized by attention deficits, impulsivity, and hyperactivity. Serious games have emerged as an effective ICT-based intervention for addressing the challenges faced by students with ADHD, with applications in both therapeutic and diagnostic contexts (Kato & de Klerk, 2017). Serious games designed for students with ADHD games create engaging environments that enhance situational interest, while their high interactivity encourages active participation in the learning process. The integration of gamification elements—such as points, rewards, and levels—further supports improvements in selective and sustained attention (Zheng et al., 2021). These games address various aspects of the disorder, often targeting cognitive and executive functions. For example, *Braingame Brian* engages players in tasks that require overcoming obstacles, planning steps, and avoiding impulsive actions, while *Plan-It Commander* places students in the role of a spaceship captain completing missions through strategic organization and time management. Both games have been shown to enhance cognitive skills, including working memory, planning, organization, problem-solving, time management, and inhibitory control in ADHD students (Prins et al., 2013; Bul et al., 2015; Zheng et al., 2021).

A second category of games focuses on improving impulse control and fostering self-regulation. For instance, *Antonyms* challenges players to choose correct opposite terms while discouraging impulsive responses. By requiring students to think before answering, such games help develop inhibition skills and improve self-regulation, reducing inappropriate or unwanted behaviors (Crepaldi et al., 2020).

Serious games for students with ADHD also facilitate the transfer of skills to real-life contexts by simulating everyday scenarios in a safe and predictable environment. These games often involve tasks designed to develop problem-solving abilities, such as breaking complex tasks into manageable parts, and time estimation skills, which are crucial for managing real-world challenges these students often face.

Another important application of serious games for ADHD is in supporting emotional regulation and social skill development. For example, *The Secret Trail of the Moon* immerses players in a fantasy world where they take on the role of a hero tasked with restoring balance to the forest. By incorporating virtual reality elements, the game motivates students to participate actively while teaching emotional regulation and fostering social skills such as cooperation and teamwork (Rodrigo-Yanguas, 2021).

In addition to therapeutic applications, serious games are increasingly used in diagnostic contexts. Their objectivity offers advantages over traditional diagnostic methods, as they are less influenced by assessor bias or external circumstances that might affect accuracy. Furthermore, serious games can minimize early termination of assessments by maintaining the child's engagement, ensuring more reliable diagnostic outcomes (Zheng et al., 2021).

Overall, serious games offer a versatile tool for addressing the multifaceted challenges associated with ADHD. They not only support cognitive, emotional, and social development but also provide innovative solutions for diagnostic and therapeutic processes, making them a valuable resource in managing ADHD.

Guidelines for Designing Serious Games for Students with Specific Special Needs

The SADDIE method, developed through over a decade of research in serious game design, represents a structured learning approach grounded in the principles of constructivism, problem-based learning, and computer-assisted learning. This method outlines a systematic process for designing serious games intended for educational purposes, with its name serving as an acronym for its six distinct phases.

- Specification: Didactic elements of the game are defined.
- Analysis: Relevant information and learner needs are thoroughly examined.
- Design: Game objectives are aligned with educational goals.
- Development: The game is created based on the design specifications.
- Implementation: Integration into the learning process is considered.
- Evaluation: The game is assessed, and iterative improvements are made.

A comprehensive description of each phase can be found in Zapušek and Rugelj (2023). This method holds significant potential for the development of serious games tailored to learners with special needs. Adapting the SADDIE method requires consideration of the specific characteristics and requirements of various special needs during each phase of the process.

In this chapter, we synthesize findings from a systematic literature review of diverse applications, methodologies, and theoretical frameworks related to designing serious games for students with special needs. These findings provide valuable insights for effectively applying the SADDIE method to develop serious games that cater to the unique challenges and requirements of learners with special needs, ensuring inclusive and impactful educational outcomes.

General Guidelines for Designing Serious Games for Students with Special Needs

This section outlines general recommendations for designing and producing serious games for students with special needs. These recommendations are derived from our experience using the SADDIE method, collaborating with experts in special education, analysing a large body of literature on serious games for students with special needs, and synthesizing key findings. The guidelines presented here are applicable to the development of serious games across various types of special needs.

We stress that the development process should be *participatory*, involving experts in the specific area of the special need being addressed, such as therapists, special educators, teachers, and parents. Their input ensures that the game aligns with both educational and therapeutic goals. The process should follow an *iterative cycle* of testing and refinement. Each game version should be tested, feedback analysed, and improvements implemented before further testing. This iterative approach ensures the game evolves to meet the needs of its target audience effectively.

Accessibility is a critical consideration when developing serious games for students with special needs. As noted by Tlili et al. (2022), many educational games are restricted to specific platforms, limiting their usability. We recommend using development tools that support multi-platform export, including PCs (Windows, macOS), mobile devices (Android, iOS), and gaming consoles (Xbox, PlayStation,

Nintendo Switch). Popular tools like Unity, Unreal Engine, and Godot enable developers to create serious games that can be adapted for various platforms with minimal customization, ensuring broader accessibility.

Creating a *safe and supportive environment* in the game is essential to reduce stress, anxiety, and frustration, which are common among students with disabilities. Based on the synthesis of the findings from the literature review (Self et al., 2007; Durkin et al., 2013; Wijnhoven et al., 2015; Kokol et al., 2020), we propose the following recommendations:

- Clear and Positive Feedback: Feedback should encourage persistence and combine visual and auditory elements.
- Adaptive Content: Implement systems to detect a child's skill level and dynamically adjust the difficulty to ensure tasks are challenging yet achievable.
- Learning Through Mistakes: Feedback should frame mistakes as learning opportunities rather than failures, fostering resilience and a growth mindset.
- Gradual Assistance: Offer hints or cues that progress from general to specific, helping students succeed while promoting independent learning.
- Exploration Without Time Pressure: Allow students to explore at their own pace without expectations of rapid progression.

One of the most impactful ways to create *inclusive environments*. We suggest including cooperative activities that facilitates meaningful interactions between students with special needs and their peers in the general population that require students to collaborate and achieve common goals. This approach strengthens social skills, empathy, and emotional regulation while promoting teamwork and respect for diversity (Kirst et al., 2020; Ugalde et al., 2021; Gurbuz & Celik, 2022). Such interactions build self-confidence, competence, and a sense of belonging while fostering positive values and inclusion (Lievense et al., 2021).

Guidelines for Designing Serious Games for Students with Intellectual Disabilities

Based on the literature review (Lanyi & Brown, 2010; El-Din & Alja'Am, 2011; Wajihullah et al., 2020), the following guidelines have been developed for the design and production of serious games for students with intellectual disabilities:

- Intuitive and Simple User Interface: Games should feature a user interface that minimizes cognitive load and facilitates easy navigation, ensuring accessibility and usability for students with intellectual disabilities.
- Use of Multimedia Elements: To sustain attention and motivation, games should incorporate visual elements such as images and animations, as well as auditory features like sounds, to serve as alternatives to textual information, making the content more engaging and accessible.

- Incorporation of Sensory Interaction Technologies: Serious games should leverage technologies that enable physical activity and other sensory interactions. These features not only make gameplay more engaging but also stimulate motor, cognitive, and socio-emotional development.
- Positive Reinforcement in Feedback Mechanisms: Feedback systems should emphasize positive reinforcement, regardless of the game's outcome, to avoid frustration and encourage continued participation.
- Adjustable Difficulty and Pace: Games should allow for dynamic adjustments to difficulty levels and pacing, giving students sufficient time to think and interact. This adaptability reduces the likelihood of frustration and creates a supportive learning environment.

These guidelines emphasize the importance of creating accessible, engaging, and adaptive serious games that cater to the unique needs of students with intellectual disabilities, ensuring both their educational and developmental benefits.

Guidelines for Designing Serious Games for Deaf and Hearing-Impaired Students

A synthesis of research on the design of serious games for deaf and hard-of-hearing students (Adamo-Villani & Wright, 2007; Henderson et al., 2005; Winarsih & Sarris, 2018; Cano et al., 2020) highlights several key recommendations to consider during the development process:

- Integration of Intense Visual Elements and Physical Interactions: Games should incorporate engaging visual elements such as animations and 3D models, combined with physical interactions like touch or movement. These features can create immersive virtual environments where students solve tasks using interactive objects that respond to their actions.
- Inclusion of Sign Language Features: Games should feature avatars, videos, or animations that demonstrate sign language. These elements can enable students to practice sign language through interactive tasks and repetition, supporting the development of communication skills.
- Support for Literacy Development: Tasks designed to promote early literacy and language skills, such as matching pictures to words, should be included in the games. These activities are particularly effective in fostering reading and writing abilities.
- Tailored Feedback Systems: Feedback mechanisms should be tailored to the cognitive and language needs of deaf students. Visual feedback, including responses in sign language, should adapt to the child's progress to ensure a supportive and effective learning experience.

These recommendations emphasize the importance of integrating visual, interactive, and adaptive elements into serious games to enhance their educational value for deaf and hard-of-hearing students. By addressing their unique needs, these games can support cognitive, linguistic, and literacy development while fostering an engaging and inclusive learning environment.

Guidelines for Designing Serious Games for Blind, Partially Sighted, and Low Vision Students

Based on the findings from the literature review (Raisamo et al., 2007; Simões & Cavaco, 2014; Radecki et al., 2020; Othman et al., 2020), we propose the following guidelines for designing and developing serious games for blind and visually impaired students:

- Effective Use of Sound: Sound should be utilized as a primary substitute for visual information. The use of 3D spatial sound is recommended to help students navigate virtual spaces and distinguish the direction and distance of objects.
- Integration of Haptic Feedback: Games should incorporate interfaces that use vibrations of varying intensities and haptic feedback to provide sensory input. For example, feedback in the form of texture perception through touch can enhance the interactivity and accessibility of the game.
- Interactive Sonification: Implementing interactive sonification allows students to explore shapes and colors through sound. By touching objects on a screen, students can generate sounds to recognize shapes, lines, or spatial arrangements.
- Adaptation of Interfaces: Game interfaces should be designed to accommodate the specific needs of blind and visually impaired students. Features such as voice-activated commands can enable hands-free navigation, while alternatives to visual supervision—such as Braille displays, keyboards, or text-to-Braille software—can ensure inclusivity.

These guidelines emphasize the importance of leveraging multisensory interactions, adaptive interfaces, and inclusive design to create games that are not only accessible to blind and visually impaired students but also promote their social and cognitive development in engaging and meaningful ways.

Guidelines for Designing Serious Games for Students with Deficits in Specific Areas of Learning

Based on an analysis of resources on serious games for students with deficits in specific areas of learning with focus on dyslexia (Ohene-Djan & Begum, 2008; Zorzi et al., 2012; Bachmann & Mengheri, 2018; Jaramillo-Alcázar et al., 2021; Brennan et al., 2022), the following recommendations have been developed:

- Phonological Awareness Activities: Incorporate elements that stimulate and strengthen phonological processing skills. These activities should focus on since they are fundamental for improving phonological awareness, a critical foundation for reading and language development: recognizing individual sounds (phonemes): helping students distinguish specific sounds within a word; identifying syllables: supporting the ability to segment words into syllables; developing a sense of rhyme: encouraging the recognition of words with similar endings; identifying initial sounds in words: Enhancing early phoneme recognition.
- Multisensory Experiences: Serious games should integrate visual, auditory, and kinesthetics stimuli to support learning. For example: letters could have distinct shapes (visual); the pronunciation of a word can be played when its letters are displayed (auditory); students could trace the shape of a letter with their finger or replicate it through body movements (kinesthetics).
- Simplified and Intuitive Game Design: The game structure should be simple and intuitive, reducing cognitive load and enabling students to focus on learning tasks. Interfaces should prioritize clarity, and tasks should be straightforward to maintain attention and reduce frustration.
- Adapted Typography and Visual Elements: Use fonts and design elements that facilitate reading and comprehension. Recommendations include high-contrast, large fonts and clear, uncluttered interfaces to aid readability; special fonts such as EasyReading, which have been shown to improve reading speed and accuracy in students with dyslexia; wider letter and word spacing, which positively impacts reading fluency and comprehension.

These recommendations emphasize the importance of phonological awareness, multisensory engagement, accessible design, and social interaction in creating effective serious games for students with deficits in specific areas of learning with focus on dyslexia, enhancing both educational and social outcomes.

Guidelines for Designing Serious Games for Students with Autism

Based on a comprehensive review of the scientific literature and synthesis of findings, we propose the following guidelines for the design of serious games tailored to students with autism spectrum disorder (Oppenheim-Leaf et al., 2012; Zakari et al., 2014; Satsangi & Bofferding, 2017; Grossard et al., 2017; Tan et al., 2019; Kellidou et al., 2020; Daud et al., 2023):

- Clear and Simple Structure: Serious games should have a straightforward and predictable structure, including simple and well-defined goals that help students understand what is expected of them. Predictable sequences of events introduce routine, consistency, and predictability, which are essential for students with ASD.

- Clear and Accessible Instructions: Instructions should be concise and easy to understand. For better comprehension, textual instructions should be complemented with visual aids such as pictures, icons, or symbols. These graphic elements should be clean and devoid of unnecessary complexity to avoid confusion.
- Avoiding Sensory Overload: The design should minimize the use of distracting elements and intense visual or auditory stimuli to prevent sensory overload, which can hinder engagement.
- Customization and Individualization: Games should allow for manual or dynamic adjustment of difficulty and pacing to match the child's abilities. The option to complete tasks without time constraints is crucial for reducing stress and fostering a more stimulating learning environment. Additionally, personalization features—such as letting the child select game themes or customize a character to reflect their preferences—enhance engagement and enjoyment of students with ASD.
- Immediate and Positive Feedback: Incorporate immediate, positive reinforcement to reward successful actions. Visual indicators of progress, such as progress bars or achievement markers, should also be included to help students track their advancement and maintain motivation.
- Safe and Supportive Environment: The game environment should be designed to ensure safety and support, avoiding violent or inappropriate content. A safe space encourages students to explore and learn without fear, reducing stress and enhancing engagement.
- Development of Social and Emotional Skills: Given the challenges students with ASD face in developing social skills, games should include scenarios that promote the recognition and expression of emotions, as well as the understanding of social situations. These features can help improve social interaction.

By adhering to these guidelines, serious games can effectively support the cognitive, social, and emotional development of students with ASD, creating inclusive and enriching educational experiences.

Guidelines for Designing Serious Games for Students with ADHD

A synthesis of research on the design of serious games for students with ADHD (Bul et al., 2015; Crepaldi et al., 2020; Rodrigo-Yanguas, 2021; Zheng et al., 2021; Penuelas-Calvo et al., 2022; Gallardo Vergara & Gallardo, 2023), we propose these design guidelines:

- Adapted Complexity: Design intuitive and simple interfaces to match the child's cognitive abilities and prevent frustration.
- Gradual Difficulty Progression: Implement adjustable difficulty levels that adapt to the child's performance, ensuring personalized and manageable challenges.

- Immediate Feedback: Provide visual and auditory feedback to help the child understand and adjust actions in real time.
- Positive Reinforcement: Use frequent rewards and recognition to sustain motivation and attention.
- Engaging Content: Create relatable characters and narratives while avoiding overstimulation to maintain focus and motivation.
- Controlled Environment: Minimize distractions with simple visuals and a focused game environment to enhance attention and impulse control.

Discussions and Conclusions

Serious games offer a great opportunity to improve the educational process for students with special needs. Their characteristics make it possible to create safe, stimulating and interactive learning environments that meet the various challenges and limitations of these students. By incorporating elements such as adaptive content, immediate feedback, multi-sensory approaches and the ability to repeat tasks, serious games encourage students to actively engage in the learning process. In addition, they contribute to the development of cognitive, social, and motor skills while boosting students' self-confidence and sense of competence, thereby promoting their academic and personal development.

To adapt the SADDIE methodology for the developing of serious games tailored to students with special needs, the following improvements are suggested.

The development process must be participatory and iterative, involving special educators, therapists, parents and students. This will ensure that the games are not only educationally sound, but also effectively address the specific needs of the target group. Accessibility should be prioritized, using tools that support multi-platform use and include features such as adjustable difficulty levels and real-time content customization. Games should create a safe environment through clear, positive and multimodal feedback that reduces frustration and encourages persistence. Mistakes should be seen as learning opportunities and exploration tasks should be free from time constraints to enable stress-free learning. In addition, collaborative activities in serious games, where students with and without special needs work together, can improve social skills, empathy and respect for diversity, contributing significantly to a more inclusive learning environment.

The analysis results show that it is crucial for students with intellectual disabilities to develop simple and intuitive user interfaces supported by visual and auditory elements to reduce cognitive load. For deaf and hard of hearing students, the use of rich visual content, animations and sign language support is essential, as are tasks that promote early literacy and language development through interactive and repetitive activities. Blind and visually impaired students especially need auditory and haptic signals and interfaces that are compatible with Braille. Games for this group should facilitate spatial exploration through spatial sounds and tactile feedback and promote spatial orientation. For students with dyslexia and learning difficulties, the focus is on integrating activities that promote phonological awareness, multisensory tasks, and accessible typography, including special fonts and clear interfaces. Collaborative games can add value by promoting social interactions and facilitating group learning. For students with autism spectrum disorders, structured and predictable environments with clearly defined goals and scenarios for practicing social interactions and recognizing emotions are important. Such games promote the development of social skills in a safe and supportive environment. Students with ADHD benefit most from controlled environments with minimal distractions, immediate feedback, and gradually increasing task complexity to maintain focus and motivation.

Future advances in the development of serious games should emphasize the integration of advanced technologies such as virtual reality and adaptive artificial intelligence. In this way, serious games can become indispensable tools for inclusive education, enabling students with special needs to reach their full potential in both academic and social contexts.

References

Adachi, P., & Willoughby, T. (2013). More than just fun and games: The longitudinal relationships between strategic video games, self-reported problem solving skills, and Academic grades. *Journal of Youth and Adolescence, 42*, 1041–1052. https://doi.org/10.1007/s10964-013-9913-9

Adamo-Villani, N., & Wright, K. (2007). *SMILE: An immersive learning game for deaf and hearing children*. 17. https://doi.org/10.1145/1282040.1282058.

Aldrich, C. (2009). *Learning online with games, simulations, and virtual worlds: Strategies for online instruction* (Vol. 11). John Wiley & Sons.

Bachmann, C., & Mengheri, L. (2018). Dyslexia and fonts: Is a specific font useful? *Brain Sciences, 8*(5), 89. https://doi.org/10.3390/brainsci8050089

Bernard, M., & Bachu, E. (2015). Enhancing the metacognitive skill of novice programmers through collaborative learning. In A. Pena-Ayala (Ed.), *Metacognition: Fundaments, applications, and trends* (pp. 277–298). Springer. https://doi.org/10.1007/978-3-319-11062-2_11

Bernardini, S., Porayska-Pomsta, K., & Smith, T. (2014). ECHOES: An intelligent serious game for fostering social communication in children with autism. *Information Science, 264*, 41–60. https://doi.org/10.1016/j.ins.2013.10.027

Bishara, S. (2018). Active and traditional teaching, self-image, and motivation in learning math among pupils with learning disabilities. *Cogent Education, 5*(1), 1436123.

Bonnechère, B., Omelina, L., Jansen, B., & Van Sint Jan, S. (2017). Balance improvement after physical therapy training using specially developed serious games for cerebral palsy children: preliminary results. *Disability and Rehabilitation, 39*(4), 403–406.

Brennan, A., Mcdonagh, T., Dempsey, M., & McAvoy, J. (2022). Cosmic sounds: A game to support phonological awareness skills for children with dyslexia. *IEEE Transactions on Learning Technologies, 15*(3), 301–310. https://doi.org/10.1109/tlt.2022.3170231

Bul, K. C., Franken, I. H., Van der Oord, S., Kato, P. M., Danckaerts, M., Vreeke, L. J., et al. (2015). Development and user satisfaction of "Plan-It Commander," a serious game for children with ADHD. *Games for Health Journal, 4*(6), 502–512.

Burgers, C., Eden, A., Engelenburg, M., & Buningh, S. (2015). How feedback boosts motivation and play in a brain-training game. *Computers in Human Behavior, 48*, 94–103. https://doi.org/10.1016/j.chb.2015.01.038

Cai, Y., & Cao, Q. (2021). VR serious games for special needs education on living skills training. *EDULEARN21 Proceedings*. https://doi.org/10.21125/EDULEARN.2021.1551
Cano, A. R., García-Tejedor, Á. J., & Fernández-Manjón, B. (2015). *A literature review of serious games for intellectual disabilities*. Lecture Notes in Computer Science (Vol. 9307). Springer. https://doi.org/10.1007/978-3-319-24258-3_59
Cano, S., Naranjo, J., Henao, C., Rusu, C., & Albiol-Pérez, S. (2020). Serious game as support for the development of computational thinking for children with hearing impairment. *Applied Sciences*. https://doi.org/10.3390/app11010115
Carlier, S., Paelt, S., Ongenae, F., Backere, F., & Turck, F. (2019). Using a serious game to reduce stress and anxiety in children with autism spectrum disorder. In *Proceedings of the 13th EAI International Conference on Pervasive Computing Technologies for Healthcare*. https://doi.org/10.1145/3329189.3329237
Carneiro, T., Carvalho, A., Frota, S., & Filipe, M. G. (2024). Serious games for developing social skills in children and adolescents with autism spectrum disorder: A systematic review. *Healthcare, 12*(5), 508. https://doi.org/10.3390/healthcare12050508
Chai, C., Lau, B., & Zheng, P. (2019). Hungry Cat - A serious game for conveying spatial information to the visually impaired. *Multimodal Technologies and Interaction, 3*, 12. https://doi.org/10.3390/MTI3010012
Chen, M. (2009). Communication, coordination, and camaraderie in world of warcraft. *Games and Culture, 4*, 47–73. https://doi.org/10.1177/1555412008325478
Crepaldi, M., Colombo, V., Mottura, S., Baldassini, D., Sacco, M., Cancer, A., & Antonietti, A. (2020). Antonyms: a computer game to improve inhibitory control of impulsivity in children with attention deficit/hyperactivity disorder (ADHD). *Information, 11*(4), 230.
Csikszentmihalyi, M. (1990). *The domain of creativity. Theories of creativity*. Sage.
Daud, N., Abdullah, M., & Zakaria, M. (2023). Serious game design principles for children with autism to facilitate the development of emotion regulation. *International Journal of Advanced Computer Science and Applications*. https://doi.org/10.14569/ijacsa.2023.01405100
Durkin, K., Boyle, J., Hunter, S., & Conti-Ramsden, G. (2013). Video games for children and adolescents with special educational needs. *Zeitschrift Fur Psychologie-Journal of Psychology, 221*, 79–89. https://doi.org/10.1027/2151-2604/A000138
El-Din, A., & Alja'Am, J. (2011). On the design of learning games and puzzles for children with intellectual disability. 2011. https://doi.org/10.5339/QFARF.2011.CSP7
Elhaddadi, M., Maazouz, H., Alami, N., Drissi, M., Mènon, C., Latifi, M., & Ahami, A. (2021). Serious games to teach emotion recognition to children with autism spectrum disorders (ASD). *Acta Neuropsychologica, 19*, 81–92. https://doi.org/10.5604/01.3001.0014.7569
Ferreira, F., & Cavaco, S. (2014). Mathematics for all: A game-based learning environment for visually impaired students. In *2014 IEEE Frontiers in Education Conference (FIE) Proceedings* (pp. 1–8). https://doi.org/10.1109/FIE.2014.7044493
Fridenson-Hayo, S., Berggren, S., Lassalle, A., Tal, S., Pigat, D., Meir-Goren, N., O'Reilly, H., Ben-Zur, S., Bölte, S., Baron-Cohen, S., & Golan, O. (2017). 'Emotiplay': A serious game for learning about emotions in children with autism: results of a cross-cultural evaluation. *European Child & Adolescent Psychiatry, 26*, 979–992. https://doi.org/10.1007/s00787-017-0968-0
Gallardo Vergara, R., & Gallardo, M. M. (2023). Serious games to improve attention in boys and girls with attention deficit hyperactivity disorder (ADHD): A pilot study. *Acta Colombiana de Psicología, 26*(2), 33–49.
García-López, I. M., Acosta-Gonzaga, E., & Ruiz-Ledesma, E. F. (2023). Investigating the impact of gamification on student motivation, engagement, and performance. *Education Sciences, 13*(8), 813.
García-Redondo, P., García, T., Areces, D., Núñez, J. C., & Rodríguez, C. (2019). Serious games and their effect improving attention in students with learning disabilities. *International Journal of Environmental Research and Public Health, 16*(14), 2480.
Gee, J. P. (2003). What video games have to teach us about learning and literacy. *Computers in Entertainment (CIE), 1*(1), 20–20.

Goh, Z., Cao, Q., Chen, J., & Cai, Y. (2021). *iPad Serious game to aid children with special needs in emotional learning*. When VR Serious Games Meet Special Needs Education. https://doi.org/10.1007/978-981-33-6942-9_10

Greef, K., Spek, E., & Bekker, M. (2013). Designing Kinect games to train motor skills for mixed ability players. 197–205. https://doi.org/10.1007/978-3-658-02897-8_15.

Grossard, C., Grynszpan, O., Serret, S., Jouen, A., Bailly, K., & Cohen, D. (2017). Serious games to teach social interactions and emotions to individuals with autism spectrum disorders (ASD). *Computers & Education, 113*, 195–211. https://doi.org/10.1016/j.compedu.2017.05.002

Gurbuz, S., & Celik, M. (2022). Serious games in future skills development: A systematic review of the design approaches. *Computer Applications in Engineering Education, 30*, 1591–1612. https://doi.org/10.1002/cae.22557

Hare, R., & Tang, Y. (2022). Petri nets and hierarchical reinforcement learning for personalized student assistance in serious games. In *2022 International Conference on Cyber-Physical Social Intelligence (ICCSI)* (pp. 733–737). https://doi.org/10.1109/ICCSI55536.2022.9970680

Haruna, H., Zainuddin, Z., Okoye, K., Mellecker, R., Hu, X., Chu, S., & Hosseini, S. (2021). Improving instruction and sexual health literacy with serious games and gamification interventions: An outlook to students' learning outcomes and gender differences. *Interactive Learning Environments, 31*, 2392–2410. https://doi.org/10.1080/10494820.2021.1888754

Henderson, V., Lee, S., Brashear, H., Hamilton, H., Starner, T., & Hamilton, S. (2005). *Development of an American sign language game for deaf children*. 70–79. https://doi.org/10.1145/1109540.1109550

Holz, H., Brandelik, K., Brandelik, J., Beuttler, B., Kirsch, A., Heller, J., et al. (2017). Prosodiya – a mobile game for german dyslexic children. Lecture Notes in Computer Science, 73–82. https://doi.org/10.1007/978-3-319-71940-5_7

Hsu, T. (2016). Effects of Wii Fit® balance game training on the balance ability of students with intellectual disabilities. *Journal of Physical Therapy Science, 28*(5), 1422–1426. https://doi.org/10.1589/jpts.28.1422

Hung, W., & Van Eck, R. (2010). Aligning problem solving and gameplay: A model for future research and design. In *Interdisciplinary models and tools for serious games: Emerging concepts and future directions* (pp. 227–263). IGI Global.

Jacob, U. S., Edozie, I. S., & Pillay, J. (2022). Strategies for enhancing social skills of individuals with intellectual disability: A systematic review. *Frontiers in Rehabilitation Sciences, 3*. https://doi.org/10.3389/fresc.2022.968314

Jaramillo-Alcázar, A., Venegas, E., Criollo-C, S., & Luján-Mora, S. (2021). An approach to accessible serious games for people with dyslexia. *Sustainability, 13*(5), 2507.

Johnson, C., Bailey, S., & Buskirk, W. (2017). Designing effective feedback messages in serious games and simulations: A research Review. 119–140. https://doi.org/10.1007/978-3-319-39298-1_7

Kato, P. M., & de Klerk, S. (2017). Serious games for assessment: Welcome to the jungle. *Journal of Applied Testing Technology*, 1–6.

Ke, F., & Abras, T. (2013). Games for engaged learning of middle school children with special learning needs. *British Journal of Educational Technology, 44*(2), 225–242.

Kellidou, P., Kotzageorgiou, M., Voulgari, I., & Nterou, E. (2020). A review of digital games for children with autism spectrum disorder. In *Proceedings of the 9th International Conference on Software Development and Technologies for Enhancing Accessibility and Fighting Info-exclusion*. https://doi.org/10.1145/3439231.3439270

Kickmeier-Rust, M., & Albert, D. (2012). Educationally adaptive: Balancing serious games. *International Journal of Computer Science*, 11.

Kiili, K. (2005). Digital game-based learning: Towards an experiential gaming model. *The Internet and Higher Education, 8*(1), 13–24.

Kinsell, C., DaCosta, B., & Nasah, A. (2014). Simulation games as interventions in the promotion of social skills development among children with autism spectrum disorders. 1788–1808. https://doi.org/10.4018/978-1-4666-5015-2.CH011

Kirst, S., Diehm, R., Bögl, K., Wilde-Etzold, S., Bach, C., Noterdaeme, M., Poustka, L., Ziegler, M., & Dziobek, I. (2020). Fostering socio-emotional competencies in children with autism using a parent-assisted serious game: A multicenter randomized controlled trial (Preprint). https://doi.org/10.31219/osf.io/pgc7m

Koh, C. (2020). A qualitative meta-analysis on the use of serious games to support learners with intellectual and developmental disabilities: What we know, what we need to know and what we can do. *International Journal of Disability, Development and Education, 69*, 919–950. https://doi.org/10.1080/1034912X.2020.1746245

Kokol, P., Vošner, H., Završnik, J., Vermeulen, J., Shohieb, S., & Peinemann, F. (2020). Serious game-based intervention for children with developmental disabilities. *Current Pediatric Reviews*. https://doi.org/10.2174/1573396315666190808115238

Korozi, M., Leonidis, A., Ntoa, S., Arampatzis, D., Adami, I., Antona, M., & Stephanidis, C. (2018). Designing an augmented tabletop game for children with cognitive disabilities: The "Home game" case. *British Journal of Educational Technology, 49*(4), 701–716.

Kourakli, M., Altanis, I., Retalis, S., Boloudakis, M., Zbainos, D., & Antonopoulou, K. (2017). Towards the improvement of the cognitive, motoric and academic skills of students with special educational needs using Kinect learning games. *International Journal of Child-Computer Interaction, 11*, 28–39. https://doi.org/10.1016/J.IJCCI.2016.10.009

Kusumaningsih, A., Kurniawati, A., Wahyuningrum, R., Khozaimi, A., & Pratama, R. (2022). Serious Exergame for special education needs using 3d-depth camera. In *2022 10th International Conference on Information and Communication Technology (ICoICT)*, 59–63. https://doi.org/10.1109/ICoICT55009.2022.9914903

Lämsä, J., Hämäläinen, R., Aro, M., Koskimaa, R., & Äyrämö, S. M. (2018). Games for enhancing basic reading and maths skills: A systematic review of educational game design in supporting learning by people with learning disabilities. *British Journal of Educational Technology, 49*(4), 596–607.

Lanyi, C. S., & Brown, D. J. (2010). Design of serious games for students with intellectual disability. In *India HCI 2010/Interaction Design & International Development 2010*. BCS Learning & Development.

Lievense, P., Vacaru, V. S., Kruithof, Y., Bronzewijker, N., Doeve, M., & Sterkenburg, P. S. (2021). Effectiveness of a serious game on the self-concept of children with visual impairments: A randomized controlled trial. *Disability and Health Journal, 14*(2), 101017.

Manresa-Yee, C., Mas, R., & Cano, S. (2017). Serious game to train auditory discrimination and identification in children with hearing impairments. In *Proceedings of the XVIII International Conference on Human Computer Interaction*. https://doi.org/10.1145/3123818.3123847

Marinelli, C., Nardacchione, G., Trotta, E., Fuccio, R., Palladino, P., Traetta, L., & Limone, P. (2023). The effectiveness of serious games for enhancing literacy skills in children with learning disabilities or difficulties: A systematic review. *Applied Sciences*. https://doi.org/10.3390/app13074512

Melero, J., El-Kechaï, N., Yessad, A., & Labat, J. (2015). Adapting learning paths in serious games: An approach based on teachers' requirements, 376–394. https://doi.org/10.1007/978-3-319-29585-5_22

Michael, D. R., & Chen, S. L. (2005). *Serious games: Games that educate, train, and inform*. Muska & Lipman/Premier-Trade.

Moreno, M. T., Canals, J., & Fosch, M. T. C. (2021). Behavioral and cognitive interventions with digital devices in subjects with intellectual disability: A systematic review. *Frontiers in Psychiatry, 12*. https://doi.org/10.3389/fpsyt.2021.647399

Nadolski, R., & Hummel, H. (2017). Retrospective cognitive feedback for progress monitoring in serious games. *British Journal of Educational Technology, 48*, 1368–1379. https://doi.org/10.1111/bjet.12503

Nasiri, N., Shirmohammadi, S., & Rashed, A. (2017). A serious game for children with speech disorders and hearing problems. In *2017 IEEE 5th International Conference on Serious Games and Applications for Health (SeGAH)*, 1–7. https://doi.org/10.1109/SeGAH.2017.7939296

Nawahdah, M., & Ihmouda, W. (2019). Implementing a serious game to improve communication and social skills for children with autism. 202–211. https://doi.org/10.1007/978-3-030-28011-6_14

Ney, M., Gonçalves, C., & Balacheff, N. (2014). Design heuristics for authentic simulation-based learning games. *IEEE Transactions on Learning Technologies, 7*, 132–141. https://doi.org/10.1109/TLT.2014.2316161

Ohene-Djan, J., & Begum, R. (2008). Multisensory games for dyslexic children. In 2008 *Eighth IEEE International Conference on Advanced Learning Technologies* (pp. 1040–1041). https://doi.org/10.1109/ICALT.2008.98

Oppenheim-Leaf, M., Leaf, J., & Call, N. (2012). Teaching board games to two children with an autism spectrum disorder. *Journal of Developmental and Physical Disabilities, 24*, 347–358. https://doi.org/10.1007/S10882-012-9274-4

Othman, N. I., Zin, N. A. M., & Mohamed, H. (2020). Play-centric designing of a serious game prototype for low vision children. *International Journal of Advanced Computer Science and Applications, 11*(5).

Papanastasiou, G., Drigas, A., & Skianis, C. (2022). Serious games: How do they impact special education needs children. *Technium Education and Humanities, 2*(3), 41–58. https://doi.org/10.47577/teh.v2i3.7407

Penuelas-Calvo, I., Jiang-Lin, L. K., Girela-Serrano, B., Delgado-Gomez, D., Navarro-Jimenez, R., Baca-Garcia, E., & Porras-Segovia, A. (2022). Video games for the assessment and treatment of attention-deficit/hyperactivity disorder: A systematic review. *European Child & Adolescent Psychiatry*, 1–16.

Pintrich, P. R. (2003). A motivational science perspective on the role of student motivation in learning and teaching contexts. *Journal of educational Psychology, 95*(4), 667.

Plass, J. L., Mayer, R. E., & Homer, B. D. (2020). *Handbook of game-based learning*. MIT Press.

Prensky, M. (2001). Digital natives, digital immigrants part 2: Do they really think differently? *On the Horizon, 9*(6), 1–6.

Prins, P. J., Brink, E. T., Dovis, S., Ponsioen, A., Geurts, H. M., De Vries, M., & Van Der Oord, S. (2013). "Braingame Brian": Toward an executive function training program with game elements for children with ADHD and cognitive control problems. *GAMES FOR HEALTH: Research, Development, and Clinical Applications, 2*(1), 44–49.

Radecki, A., Bujacz, M., Skulimowski, P., & Strumiłło, P. (2020). Interactive sonification of images in serious games as an education aid for visually impaired children. *British Journal of Educational Technology, 51*, 473–497. https://doi.org/10.1111/BJET.12852

Raisamo, R., Patomäki, S., Hasu, M., & Pasto, V. (2007). Design and evaluation of a tactile memory game for visually impaired children. *Interaction Computer, 19*, 196–205. https://doi.org/10.1016/j.intcom.2006.08.011

Reprintceva, E. (2016). The use of games and ICT in education of children with special needs. *Edutainment, 1*(1).

Rodrigo-Yanguas, M., Martin-Moratinos, M., Menendez-Garcia, A., Gonzalez-Tardon, C., Royuela, A., & Blasco-Fontecilla, H. (2021). A Virtual Reality Game (The Secret Trail of Moon) for Treating Attention-Deficit/Hyperactivity Disorder: Development and Usability Study. *JMIR Serious Games, 9*(3), e26824. https://doi.org/10.2196/26824

Rogers-Shaw, C., Carr-Chellman, D. J., & Choi, J. (2018). Universal design for learning: Guidelines for accessible online instruction. *Adult Learning, 29*(1), 20–31.

Roozeboom, M. B., Visschedijk, G., & Oprins, E. (2015). The effectiveness of three serious games measuring generic learning features. *British Journal of Educational Technology, 48*(1), 83–100. https://doi.org/10.1111/bjet.12342

Sales, A., Santos, B., & Palmeira, E. (2022). Feedback Mechanisms in Human-Computer Interaction Serious Games. in*2022 17th Iberian Conference on Information Systems and Technologies (CISTI)*, 1–6. https://doi.org/10.23919/cisti54924.2022.9820368

Salsabila, F., Yuhana, U., Yuniarno, E., & Purnomo, M. (2020). Sifte-Math, A Sifteo based mathematics assessment serious game for deaf children. In *2020 International Electronics Symposium (IES)*, 620–625. https://doi.org/10.1109/IES50839.2020.9231578

Santórum, M. (2023). An accessible serious game-based platform for process learning of people with intellectual disabilities. *Applied Sciences, 13*(13), 7748. https://doi.org/10.3390/app13137748

Saridaki, M., & Mourlas, C. (2014). Flow, fun and frame in the classroom: Redefining the engagement and self-determination of students with intellectual disability through games. *International Conference on Interactive Technologies and Games, 2014*, 44–50. https://doi.org/10.1109/iTAG.2014.19

Satsangi, R., & Bofferding, L. (2017). Improving the numerical knowledge of children with autism spectrum disorder: The benefits of linear board games. *Journal of Research in Special Educational Needs, 17*, 218–226. https://doi.org/10.1111/1471-3802.12380

Self, T., Scudder, R., Weheba, G., & Crumrine, D. (2007). A virtual approach to teaching safety skills to children with autism spectrum disorder. *Topics in Language Disorders, 27*, 242–253. https://doi.org/10.1097/01.TLD.0000285358.33545.79

Shin, S., Lim, C., Moon, H., Chung, J., Cho, H., & Chung, S. (2018). Development of serious game and integrated management service model for the cognitive rehabilitation. 81–88. https://doi.org/10.1007/978-3-319-92279-9_11

Simões, D., & Cavaco, S. (2014, November). An orientation game with 3D spatialized audio for visually impaired children. In *Proceedings of the 11th Conference on Advances in Computer Entertainment Technology* (pp 1–4).

Squire, K. (2011). Video games and learning: Teaching and participatory culture in the digital age. In *Technology, Education--Connections (the TEC Series)*. Teachers College Press.

Stancin, K., Hoić-Božić, N., & Mihić, S. (2020). Using digital game-based learning for students with intellectual disabilities - A systematic literature review. *Informatics Education, 19*, 323–341. https://doi.org/10.15388/INFEDU.2020.15

Streicher, A., & Smeddinck, J. D. (2016). Personalized and adaptive serious games. In *Entertainment Computing and Serious Games: International GI-Dagstuhl Seminar 15283, Dagstuhl Castle, Germany, July 5–10, 2015*, Revised Selected Papers (pp. 332–377). Springer International Publishing.

Taib, S., Zhang, Y., Cai, Y., & Goh, T. (2018). *Supermarket route-planning game: A serious game for the rehabilitation of planning executive function of children with ASD*. VR, Simulations and Serious Games for Education. https://doi.org/10.1007/978-981-13-2844-2_10

Tan, Q., Huang, L., Xu, D., Cen, Y., & Cao, Q. (2022). Serious game for VR road crossing in special needs education. *Electronics, 11*(16), 2568. https://doi.org/10.3390/electronics11162568

Tan, S., Abdullah, M., & Daud, N. (2019). Mobile games for children with autism spectrum disorder to support positive behavioural skills. *Intelligent and Interactive Computing*. https://doi.org/10.1007/978-981-13-6031-2_43

Teoh, S. E. M., Cao, Q., & Cai, Y. (2021). Learning to Take a Shower Through VR Serious Gaming. *When VR Serious Games Meet Special Needs Education*, 3–29. https://doi.org/10.1007/978-981-33-6942-9_2

Terlouw, G., Kuipers, D., van't Veer, J., Prins, J. T., & Pierie, J. P. E. (2021). The development of an escape room-based serious game to trigger social interaction and communication between high-functioning children with autism and their peers: An iterative design approach. *JMIR Serious Games, 9*(1), e19765.

Tlili, A., Denden, M., Duan, A., Padilla-Zea, N., Huang, R., Sun, T., & Burgos, D. (2022). Game-based learning for learners with disabilities—what is next? A systematic literature review from the activity theory perspective. *Frontiers in Psychology, 12*, 814691.

Toukiloglou, P., & Xinogalos, S. (2022). NanoDoc: Designing an adaptive serious game for programming with working examples support. *European Conference on Games Based Learning*. https://doi.org/10.34190/ecgbl.16.1.463

Ugalde, L., Santiago-Garabieta, M., Villarejo-Carballido, B., & Puigvert, L. (2021). Impact of interactive learning environments on learning and cognitive development of children with special educational needs: A literature review. *Frontiers in Psychology, 12*. https://doi.org/10.3389/fpsyg.2021.674033

UNESCO. (2009). Policy guidelines on inclusion in education.

Uzuegbunam, N., Wong, W., Cheung, S., & Ruble, L. (2018). MEBook: Multimedia social greetings intervention for children with autism spectrum disorders. *IEEE Transactions on Learning Technologies, 11*, 520–535. https://doi.org/10.1109/TLT.2017.2772255

Vallefuoco, E., Bravaccio, C., Gison, G., Pecchia, L., & Pepino, A. (2022). Personalized training via serious game to improve daily living skills in pediatric patients with autism spectrum disorder. *IEEE Journal of Biomedical and Health Informatics, 26*, 3312–3322. https://doi.org/10.1109/JBHI.2022.3155367

Vasalou, A., Khaled, R., Holmes, W., & Gooch, D. (2017). Digital games-based learning for children with dyslexia: A social constructivist perspective on engagement and learning during group game-play. *Computers & Education, 114*, 175–192. https://doi.org/10.1016/j.compedu.2017.06.009

Vonthron, F., Bégel, V., Yuen, A., Pellerin, H., Cohen, D., & Grossard, C. (2022). MILA-Learn, a serious game to train rhythmic abilities in children with dyslexia: Feasibility and Usability Study. *JMIR Serious Games*. https://doi.org/10.2196/42733

Wajihullah, A., Ashraf, S., & Majid, S. (2020). Teaching time concepts to children with intellectual disability through computer game based learning. *3*, 265–274. https://doi.org/10.47067/real.v3i2.59

Wijnhoven, L., Creemers, D., Engels, R., & Granic, I. (2015). The effect of the video game Mindlight on anxiety symptoms in children with an Autism Spectrum Disorder. *BMC Psychiatry, 15*. https://doi.org/10.1186/s12888-015-0522-x

Winarsih, M., & Sarris, A. (2018). Educative Video Game based android system for learning early reading for children with hearing impairment. *American Journal of Educational Research*. https://doi.org/10.12691/EDUCATION-6-8-8

Wouters, P., Nimwegen, C., Oostendorp, H., & Spek, E. (2013). A meta-analysis of the cognitive and motivational effects of serious games. *Journal of Educational Psychology, 105*(2), 249–265. https://doi.org/10.1037/a0031311

Yildirim, O., & Surer, E. (2021). Developing adaptive serious games for children with specific learning difficulties: A two-phase usability and technology acceptance study. *JMIR Serious Games, 9*. https://doi.org/10.2196/25997

Yu, Z., Sukjairungwattana, P., & Xu, W. (2022). Effects of serious games on student engagement, motivation, learning strategies, cognition, and enjoyment. *International Journal of Adult Education and Technology, 13*(1), 1–15. https://doi.org/10.4018/ijaet.314607

Zakari, H., Ma, M., & Simmons, D. (2014). A review of serious games for children with autism spectrum disorders (ASD). 93–106. https://doi.org/10.1007/978-3-319-11623-5_9

Zapušek, M., & Rugelj, J. (2023). Developing educator-specific digital competences with serious game design. In *Handbook of research on decision-making capabilities improvement with serious games* (pp. 50–69). IGI Global.

Zhang, M., Zhang, Z., Chang, Y., Aziz, E., Esche, S., & Chassapis, C. (2018). Recent developments in game-based virtual reality educational laboratories using the Microsoft Kinect. *International Journal of Emerging Technologies in Learning (Ijet), 13*(01), 138. https://doi.org/10.3991/ijet.v13i01.7773

Zheng, Y., Li, R., Li, S., Zhang, Y., Yang, S., & Ning, H. (2021). *A review on serious games for ADHD*. arXiv preprint arXiv:2105.02970.

Zorzi, M., Barbiero, C., Facoetti, A., Lonciari, I., Carrozzi, M., Montico, M., et al. (2012). Extra-large letter spacing improves reading in dyslexia. *Proceedings of the National Academy of Sciences, 109*(28), 11455–11459. https://doi.org/10.1073/pnas.1205566109

Chapter 9
Empowering Learners with Autism Spectrum Disorder (ASD) Through Gamification

Munir Moosa Sadruddin

Abstract This chapter examines the potential of gamification to promote the skills development of learners with disabilities. Using a desk review approach, this chapter has collected gamification practices that have supported the development of different skills in people with ASD and explored some barriers to effective use in different settings. It also provides some concrete, actionable strategies for educators and administrators to use gamification effectively for inclusion. By providing personalized learning experiences, gamification improves the motivation and social-communicative, motor, and cognitive skills of autistic learners. It also improves academic skills such as vocabulary, pronunciation, and math skills. Challenges such as accessibility of game design, sensory sensitivity, information overload, limited availability of contextualized games, and lack of collaboration to understand the complexity of conditions, learner interests, and game design need to be addressed.

Introduction

Gamification is an integrative technique for improving the quality of the learning process. It is used in various disciplines and in different environments, such as healthcare, psychology, human resources, wellness, environmental sustainability, and marketing. In education, it has been used primarily to increase learner motivation and academic achievement (Linehan et al., 2011; Smiderle et al., 2020). Nevertheless, it has not attracted much attention to support learners with disabilities as they are underrepresented in the development of gamified solutions.

M. M. Sadruddin (✉)
Sindh Madressatul Islam University, Karachi, Pakistan
e-mail: mmsadruddin@smiu.edu.pk

I. Boghian, G. Mareş (eds.), *Gamification and Inclusion*, Inclusive Learning and Educational Equity 12, https://doi.org/10.1007/978-3-031-98390-0_9

The foundation of gamification in education is rich and varied and spans several decades. The Sumerian Game, developed by Mabel Addis, a school teacher, in 1964, is the earliest available example of digital gamification in education. This text-based educational game focused on teaching concepts of Sumerian culture, economics, and governance (The New York Times, 2024). After that, LOGO - a programming language was used to teach math and the first computer programs. In the 1970s, various educational games were invented, such as Oregon Trail, which is used to teach history. In the 1980s, at the height of the video game industry, Tom Malone from MIT developed the first video game that showed that children can learn well through games (Khaitova, 2021). With the invention of IBM DOS, hundreds more educational games were introduced. In the 2000s, educators began to incorporate points, badges, and leaderboards into educational games to increase learner motivation and engagement. The term "gamification" was coined in 2002. Over time, the concept of artificial intelligence was integrated into gamification and brought innovative solutions to the field.

Gamification has been used in academia in various ways to improve scientific knowledge (Kalogiannakis et al., 2021); to improve problem solving in mathematics (Smith, 2018); to improve critical thinking in programming education (Zhan et al., 2022); to improve English language (Zhang & Hasim, 2023); in statistics education (Legaki et al., 2020), to enrich vocabulary (Chowdhury et al., 2024), to improve teacher training (Liu et al., 2023; Yildiz et al., 2021) and to improve the learning performance of students at universities (Aguiar-Castillo et al., 2020, 2021; Sánchez-Martín et al., 2017; Zhang et al., 2024). Nevertheless, many disciplines have not yet adapted gamification for learning purposes, especially in underdeveloped countries.

Gamification increases motivation (Mohammed et al., 2024); improves student engagement (Bai et al., 2020; Chen & Liang, 2022; Núñez-Naranjo et al., 2024; Putz et al., 2020; Zeng et al., 2024), promotes social connectedness (Ratinho & Martins, 2023; Rodriguez-Calzada et al., 2024; Zainuddin et al., 2020); and improves critical thinking skills (Angelelli et al., 2023; Oliveira et al., 2022; Metwally et al., 2020). Some studies point to negative effects. For example, it increases frustration (Dichev & Dicheva, 2017; Toda et al., 2018) and worsens academic performance (Almeida et al., 2021). Game design elements can worsen performance and raise ethical issues, such as cheating (Almeida et al., 2023), problems with cognitive manipulation (Klock et al., 2023), and exploitation of learners (Thorpe & Roper, 2019). In addition, the gamification industry raises ethical issues such as the violation of privacy (Kröger et al., 2023; Trang & Weiger, 2021).

An experimental study investigated how gamification motivates and satisfies the psychological needs of learners. This showed that gamification alone may not be sufficient; rather, it is specific design elements that trigger the desired results (Sailer et al., 2017). Certain game elements can even hinder the satisfaction of psychological needs (Van Roy & Zaman, 2019). This raises the question of whether the elements used in educational games really motivate learners. Does gamification improve educational outcomes? Does it support the different needs of learners? While this concept continues to gain traction in the academic environment, its integration into educational systems at different levels, in different disciplines and in different countries remains inconsistent due to cultural differences in teaching, different educational priorities and different levels of technological infrastructure.

The gamification market in education is a billion-dollar industry that is growing with time. It is crucial to understand whether it supports learners' social and educational needs or aims to generate profit and increase revenue.

Gamification and Disability

Around 1.3 billion people worldwide live with disabilities, including over 650 million in Asia and the Pacific (UNFPA, 2022). Despite policy progress, people with disabilities still face barriers to education. Especially in low-income countries, access to education remains a major challenge for learners with disabilities (UNICEF, 2022). Even where education is accessible, there are still challenges in providing quality, inclusive education (Hayes & Bulat, 2017). Disability-inclusive education practices are minimal. Where support is available, learners often lack help as teachers are not adequately equipped to address diverse learning needs. One of the reports states "As it stands, the world will not achieve the SDGs by, for and with persons with disabilities by 2030. Accelerations are needed to make physical and virtual environments accessible to persons with disabilities, adopt anti-discrimination laws, expand social protection and implement measures to ensure the safety and protection of all persons with disabilities in disasters and emergencies" (United Nations, 2024).

Technology provides a gateway to educational accessibility for many learners with disabilities. The use of assistive technology is increasing, but it is unclear how learners with disabilities are using it for educational purposes. One of the reports states "Technologies developed for other purposes cannot necessarily be expected to be suitable for all learners in all educational settings. When considering the adoption of digital technologies, education systems should always ensure that the interests of learners are placed at the center of a rights-based framework. The focus should be on learning outcomes and not on digital input" (UNESCO, 2024).

Learners with disabilities have unique learning styles. Their emotions, motivation, information intake and engagement are different from those of other learners. They require individualized learning experiences and additional academic support. This brings gamification to the fore as a potential tool for inclusion. This learning approach has been used for the development of various skills, such as analytical thinking, problem-solving skills, cooperative learning skills, motivation, and collaboration in learners with different types of disabilities (Alkhawaldeh & Khasawneh, 2024; Dziorny, 2007; Ghasemi et al., 2021; Jadán-Guerrero et al., 2023; Khaleghi et al., 2022; Martín-Gutiérrez et al., 2022; Stančin et al., 2020; Tlili et al., 2022; Zlotnik et al., 2024). It is important to emphasize that not all games are suitable for all learners with disabilities, as they have different learning styles. The effectiveness of the game in developing skills for a wider group of people with disabilities depends on the learning design framework, the strategies and game elements used and, most importantly, the interest of those involved.

Gamification, Skills Development, and Autism Spectrum Disorder (ASD)

ASD "is a neurodevelopmental disorder characterized by deficits in social communication and the presence of restricted interests and repetitive behaviors" (American Psychiatric Association, 2013). One in 100 children has ASD (World Health Organization, 2023). Learners with ASD lack social interaction. However, they have unique perspectives and exceptional memory. Some children with autism are extremely good at reading and math compared to their peers. They perceive visual information better than other children (Cañete et al., 2023; Chung & Son, 2020; Zhou et al., 2023). However, learners with ASD face challenges in learning. They have special learning needs and require an individualized learning environment. Their limited social skills sometimes hinder their academic performance. They may be able to participate in mainstream classes, but social stigma and prejudice often prevent parents from sending them to school. These learners are less expressive and need time to adapt to new environments. They may also face health problems that affect their learning in various ways.

Gamification is a tool for inclusion. It provides learners with ASD with immersive learning experiences, supports their social, emotional and cognitive development and improves their academic performance in different settings, such as rehabilitation and work. However, their performance and interest in gamification varies. For example, even learners who are categorized as easy will not achieve at the same pace due to their unique learning characteristics.

Learners with ASD can learn a variety of academic skills through gamification. For example, El Shemy et al. (2025) developed two augmented reality games for vocabulary learning for autistic learners and their parents. The games supported the learning of new vocabulary about brushing teeth and hygiene practices. Teaching strategies such as repetition, personal experience, and classification were successful. In addition, collaboration with parents was beneficial in developing educational interventions. Another game-based intervention was developed and used with children with autism and dyscalculia to learn math. The games motivated the participants and gave them confidence in learning math (Pradiante, 2022). Similarly, gamification has been used to help learners acquire English vocabulary. In one study, an enhanced app was developed and tested with six mildly autistic learners. The games helped them to expand their vocabulary, pronunciation skills, and language articulation. It also encouraged their interest in the language learning process (Hashim et al., 2022). These studies emphasize the role of games in skill development. However, in the current contexts, it cannot be readily determined whether the use of gamification is effective for teaching in different subjects and at different levels. Further studies are needed to confirm these claims.

Learners with ASD lack social interaction and cooperation. They have limited interests and limited skills, especially social skills. Gamification offers opportunities to teach them social skills through positive reinforcement in different environments (Azadboni et al., 2024; Tezcan & Sadık, 2018; Walsh et al., 2024). For example, a game was developed and tested to teach self-care and personal hygiene skills to learners with autism in Brazilian public schools. The game helps to recognize pictures and improve vocabulary and reading skills (Gobbo et al., 2021). Lopez-Bouzas et al (2024) experimented with extended games with ASD learners that improved their socioemotional skills. Wang and Xing (2021) found that 3D games improved social skills and social interaction behavior in adolescents with autism. Wainer et al. (2014) also developed a social robot (KASPAR) and evaluated it with autistic learners aged 8–9 years. It helped them to improve their social behavior and cooperation skills. These studies show that gamification can promote the social skills of learners with autism. However, many other skills, such as initiating friendships, engaging in conversations, collaborating and expressing emotions, have not yet been extensively studied to determine whether gamification can help with these skills.

There is a growing trend towards the use of cell phones and tablets by autistic learners. Many mobile apps offer real-time learning experiences, but not all gamification apps are designed for educational purposes. Thirty-two gamified mobile apps demonstrating communication and self-management skills were identified in a scoping review (Mahmoudi et al., 2024). Boyd et al. (2014) experimented with the iPad game "Zody" and found that learners with ASD improved their collaboration and communication skills through gamification. Similarly, Penev et al. (2021) developed a mobile application for children with autism aged 3–12 years that showed a significant improvement in their socialization. These results confirm the development of skills, especially social skills, in learners with ASD. However, it is important to investigate the patterns of technology use in autistic learners as this area is not well documented. In addition, learners with autism often require the support of others, so assuming that gamification alone can lead to improvements without external support would be a misconception.

The trend of using serious games with learners with ASD for academic and therapeutic purposes is increasing (Azadboni et al., 2024; Barajas et al., 2017; Carneiro et al., 2024; Hassan et al., 2021; Kousar et al., 2019; Khabbaz et al., 2023; López-Bouzas et al., 2024; Zakari et al., 2014). For example, Elshahawy et al. (2022) prepared serious games and block-based programming platforms that improved the problem-solving skills of learners with autism. Similarly, a systematic review showed that cognitive computer games improved social cognition and emotional understanding in autistic learners (Rezayi et al., 2023). While limited studies confirm the effective use of serious games and cognitive games, their impact can vary significantly depending on age, specific learning goals and learning style, which calls for more nuanced research on adapting games to maximize their engagement and learning outcomes.

Learners with autism need motivation and support that gamification can bridge. Che Ku Mohd et al. (2019) developed and tested a game application with autistic students, teachers, and parents. It improved their grades and increased their motivation. Similarly, Silva-Calpa et al. (2018) developed a collaborative game "CoASD" and experimented with seven children with autism aged 5–14 years. The game improved motivation and encouraged them to engage in collaborative tasks. It is important to emphasize that motivating learners with ASD does not come from gamification alone; it also requires patience and a support system. Furthermore, these learners often lack intrinsic motivation, making it difficult to use gamification effectively. Further studies are needed to understand how gamification can help improve their intrinsic motivation.

Learners with ASD generally have a shorter attention span than other children. Gamification has the potential to increase their attention span. Mercado et al. (2019) developed a neurofeedback brain training game and experimented with sixty autistic children aged 4–11 years. The game improved attention span. Similarly, Cruz et al. (2011) experimented with games with ten autistic children aged 5-10 years. The results suggest that video games have a positive effect on attention span compared to traditional toy games. In another study, Wagle et al. (2021) designed and tested smartphone-based games and showed a strong correlation between game performance and improvement in working memory. The use of games enables the development of attention skills, but with limitations. Previous studies do not indicate whether attention span was considered as a critical factor in game design when developing games for learners with autism. It is also unclear what features have been successfully used in previous games to improve attention span.

There is limited participation of learners with autism in physical activities. Gamified mobile technology is a promising way to develop their motor skills (Lee & Gutierrez, 2023). Hassani et al. (2020) experimented with exercise programs using gamified technologies that reduced unwanted behaviors, supported positive interactions, and improved motor skills. Similarly, Kim et al. (2020) experimented with a mobile game that increased physical activity in 229 autistic adults aged 18 to 55 years and motivated them to continue participating in activities through the leaderboard. While gamified approaches may improve some aspects of physical activity, they may unintentionally limit opportunities for socialization and collaboration with peers. There is insufficient empirical evidence that gamification consistently leads to meaningful improvements in motor skills for different groups of learners with autism. Increasing physical activity through gamification also does not take into account the sustainability of such engagement.

Challenging behavior and emotional distress are often associated with learners with ASD (Boonen et al., 2014; Hastings et al., 2021). Gamification can improve behavioral skills (Mota et al., 2020) and increase emotional understanding skills (Wang et al., 2023). Navan and Khaleghi (2020) developed an intervention game and tested it on children with autism. Although the study did not reduce behavioral problems, it helped them learn about facial expressions. In contrast, Wan and Li (2023) studied the effects of interactive games and behavioral skills on eight children with autism in a special kindergarten. They promoted their physical and mental health to a greater extent, highlighting that gamification could potentially support learners' well-being, albeit not for behavioral or emotional challenges. There are few studies demonstrating whether gamification supports behavioral and emotional challenges in learners with ASD.

With technological advances, virtual reality and artificial intelligence in gamification have opened up promising avenues for promoting various skills such as communication (Suparjoh et al., 2020; Valencia et al., 2019). Soltiyeva et al. (2023) proposed a virtual reality training system and conducted initial observations that improved communication and social interaction among learners with ASD in Kazakhstan. Although the study cannot be generalized and was not used in an educational setting, it provides a perspective on technological advancement for skill development.

Potential Barriers

Gamification has some potential barriers that could hinder its effective use in developing skills in learners with ASD. Accessibility of game design remains a challenge in gamification due to the lack of research and development focused on developing customized games for learners with autism. Accessibility here refers to user interface design, sensory adaptation, social interaction, and visual and auditory accessibility.

Gamifications are not primarily designed to take into account the sensory limitations of learners with ASD. It is also difficult for them to understand complex information. The available games are usually filled with overloaded information, which can lead to stressful situations (Elcik, 2021). Costello and Donovan (2019) developed a prototype video game, investigated its accessibility features and found that it is difficult for autistic users to read or understand non-verbal cues. They also struggle with sensory problems when playing the game. Furthermore, their ability to absorb information is limited (Marco et al., 2011).

Not all children with autism respond positively to gamification, as individual preferences and sensitivities significantly affect their engagement. Although the color combination and visual appearance of the game appeals to learners with ASD, they are overwhelmed by the gamified environments available, which often include bright colors and loud sounds.

Many gamified activities have complex or multi-step instructions that are difficult for learners with ASD to follow. In addition, some learners may find the competitive aspects of gamification applications overwhelming or stressful, potentially leading to increased anxiety rather than motivating them to participate in physical activities.

Learners with ASD may exhibit restricted behaviors or become overly dependent on gamification. Excessive game use can lead to aggression and have a negative impact on academic performance (Kuo et al., 2024; Murray et al., 2022; Paulus et al., 2020). Certain game designs, even those not specifically tailored to educational contexts, can exacerbate problem behaviors in learners with ASD. Research shows that attention, social dynamics, access to games, and time spent predict problematic video game use (Craig et al., 2021). Games to address behavioral challenges in learners with ASD are still lacking.

The design of games, particularly the lack of customization, is a gap in providing unique learning experiences for all learners with ASD (Smith & Abrams, 2019). There is a lack of awareness among game designers about ASD, its complexity and the needs and interests of learners. Parents, teachers, and health professionals are not involved in game development (Camargo et al., 2019; Malinverni et al., 2017). Ribeiro Silva et al. (2024), in collaboration with autism experts, developed a gamified prototype that reduced unwanted behaviors in learners with ASD. This example lays the foundation for the importance of involving a wide range of stakeholders in the development of games for learning purposes. However, there is a significant research gap in the gamification industry to provide meaningful gamification experiences for all learners with ASD.

Conclusions and Recommendations

Gamification holds great promise for supporting the social, emotional, cognitive, and academic development of learners with ASD. Its engaging, customizable, and interactive features allow learning pathways to be tailored to individual learner needs. With advances in technology, gamification design is expected to improve and accelerate the quality of the learning experience with potential opportunities for collaboration.

The available studies do not explicitly target gamification for learners with ASD. However, they offer a promising perspective on how gamification can support skill development. Educating learners with ASD poses significant challenges for the gaming industry, which emphasizes the need to understand different approaches to gamification in education.

Below are some actionable strategies for educators and administrators to effectively implement gamification for inclusion.

For Educational Policymakers

An inclusive gamification policy should be introduced that supports research and evidence-based sustainable gamification initiatives for learners with ASD. The policy should encourage collaboration between educational institutions, game designers, and industry to develop innovative gamified learning solutions that meet the diverse learning needs of learners with ASD.

For Curricula Developers

Understanding the characteristics of learners with ASD is important in order to understand their strengths, preferences, and sensitivities. In this context, curricula for both ASD and gamification should be introduced, especially for learners interested in pursuing higher education in the fields of technology, game design or AI.

For School Management and Administrators

The availability of various educational games to support the social, communicative, and behavioral learning of learners with ASD is limited due to a lack of awareness and understanding of their educational needs. Free online training, workshops, and curriculum integration across disciplines on ASD would help game designers and the research community to understand the educational needs of learners and ultimately facilitate their learning experience in a gamification environment. In addition, this will also help to review existing educational games and modify them according to learners' needs.

Evidence-based studies on how gamification supports the learning of students with ASD are not available. Gamification in the disability sector should be encouraged to develop contextualized gamification tailored to the specific needs of learners with ASD to promote their engagement and academic success. To this end, university students and entrepreneurs who develop games for learners with ASD should receive micro-grants.

Set up a gamification lab for teachers and learners to brainstorm and try out a variety of game designs and provide sustainable solutions.

For Teachers and Parents

There is a lack of integration of courses on gamification into teacher and parent education programs. A specialization course on gamification for ASD should be introduced to enable educators to propose, design, and develop engaging and contextualized educational games for learners with ASD.

For Game Designers

The involvement of teachers, health professionals, and parents in the gamification process is crucial for the conceptualization and validation of game designs. They can form a collaborative team with the game designers and keep a reflective digital diary to add the social and educational challenges faced by ASD learners. These can be used to design role-play games with simple tasks such as brushing teeth and sticking buttons. A musical reward is provided to stimulate them when they give the correct answer.

Learners with ASD need to strengthen their vocational skills, for which scenario-based games on real work situations should be developed. Gamification experts should work with technology companies and vocational education and training institutes (VET) to understand what future employability skills are needed for learners with ASD.

Open-source games are a cost-effective option for gamification. This will help developers to improve existing games based on learners' needs and feedback. It will also speed up collaboration in adapting existing games for ASD learners and reduce time and costs.

A collaborative simulated game should be developed in which parents or teachers and learners with ASD can participate together. A customized AI-based real-time and offline game should be developed to track learners' progress in real time. These games would be useful for areas without internet access.

The design of the game should be simple, without sensory or cognitive overload. There must be the possibility to take a break when needed. It must include narrative elements and visual cues. The concept of failure should be eliminated. Games should offer unlimited attempts and rewards for each attempt.

Overall, the gamification industry offers great potential for the development of accessible, contextualized, innovative, and inclusive educational games for learners with ASD. By understanding individual needs, developers can design more effective and accessible games. However, further research is needed to refine these approaches and accelerate progress in gamified learning.

References

Aguiar-Castillo, L., Clavijo-Rodriguez, A., Hernández-López, L., De Saa-Pérez, P., & Pérez-Jiménez, R. (2021). Gamification and deep learning approaches in higher education. *Journal of Hospitality, Leisure, Sport & Tourism Education, 29*. https://doi.org/10.1016/j.jhlste.2020.100290

Aguiar-Castillo, L., Hernández-López, L., De Saá-Pérez, P., & Pérez-Jiménez, R. (2020). Gamification as a motivation strategy for higher education students in tourism face-to-face learning. *Journal of Hospitality, Leisure, Sport & Tourism Education, 27*. https://doi.org/10.1016/j.jhlste.2020.100267

Alkhawaldeh, M. A., & Khasawneh, M. A. S. (2024). Designing gamified assistive apps: A novel approach to motivating and supporting students with learning disabilities. *International Journal of Data and Network Science, 8*(1), 53–60. https://doi.org/10.5267/j.ijdns.2023.10.018

Almeida, C., Kalinowski, M., & Feijó, B. (2021). A systematic mapping of negative effects of gamification in education/learning systems. In *2021, 47th Euromicro Conference on Software Engineering and Advanced Applications (SEAA)*. IEEE. https://doi.org/10.1109/SEAA53835.2021.00011

Almeida, C., Kalinowski, M., Uchôa, A., & Feijó, B. (2023). Negative effects of gamification in education software: Systematic mapping and practitioner perceptions. *Information and Software Technology, 156*, 107142. https://doi.org/10.1016/j.infsof.2022.107142

American Psychiatric Association. (2013). *Diagnostic and statistical manual of mental disorders* (5th ed.). American Psychiatric Publishing. https://psycnet.apa.org/record/2013-14907-000

Angelelli, C. V., de Campos Ribeiro, G. M., Severino, M. R., Johnstone, E., Borzenkova, G., & da Silva, D. C. O. (2023). Developing critical thinking skills through gamification. *Thinking Skills and Creativity, 49*. https://doi.org/10.1016/j.tsc.2023.101354

Azadboni, T. T., Nasiri, S., Khenarinezhad, S., & Sadoughi, F. (2024). Effectiveness of serious games in social skills training for autistic individuals: A systematic review. *Neuroscience & Biobehavioral Reviews, 161*. https://doi.org/10.1016/j.neubiorev.2024.105634

Bai, S., Hew, K. F., & Huang, B. (2020). Does gamification improve student learning outcomes? Evidence from a meta-analysis and synthesis of qualitative data in educational contexts. *Educational Research Review, 30*. https://doi.org/10.1016/j.edurev.2020.100322

Barajas, A. O., Al Osman, H., & Shirmohammadi, S. (2017). A serious game for children with autism spectrum disorder as a tool for play therapy. In *2017 IEEE 5th International Conference on Serious Games and Applications for Health (SeGAH)*. IEEE. https://doi.org/10.1109/SeGAH.2017.7939266

Boonen, H., Maljaars, J., Lambrechts, G., Zink, I., Van Leeuwen, K., & Noens, I. (2014). Behavior problems among school-aged children with autism spectrum disorder: Associations with children's communication difficulties and parenting behaviors. *Research in Autism Spectrum Disorders, 8*(6), 716–725. https://doi.org/10.1016/j.rasd.2014.03.012

Boyd, L. E., Ringland, K. E., Haimson, O. L., Fernandez, H., Bistarkey, M., & Hayes, G. R. (2014). Evaluating a collaborative iPad game's impact on social relationships for children with autism spectrum disorder. *ACM Transactions on Accessible Computing, 7*(2). https://doi.org/10.1145/2656274

Camargo, M. C., Barros, R. M., Brancher, J. D., Barros, V., & Santana, M. (2019). Designing gamified interventions for autism spectrum disorder: A systematic review. In *Proceedings of the 1st Joint International Conference on Entertainment Computing and Serious Games (ICEC-JCSG)* (pp. 341–352). https://doi.org/10.1007/978-3-030-34644-7_28

Cañete, R., Martín-Mariscal, A., & Peralta, M. E. (2023). Visual stimulation and perception for children with autism: Exploring visual qualities for toy inclusion. In F. Chaari, F. Gherardini, V. Ivanov, & M. Haddar (Eds.), *Advances in design engineering III (INGEGRAF 2022)* (pp. 19–35). Springer. https://doi.org/10.1007/978-3-031-23144-5_2

Carneiro, T., Carvalho, A., Frota, S., & Filipe, M. G. (2024). Serious games for developing social skills in children and adolescents with autism spectrum disorder: A systematic review. *Healthcare, 12*(5), 508. https://doi.org/10.3390/healthcare12050508

Che Ku Mohd, C. K. N., Faaizah Shahbodin, G. P., Mohd Noor, H. A., Ananta, & Sedek, M. (2019). Using interactive games to engage children with autism on visual impairment. *International Journal of Recent Technology and Engineering (IJRTE), 8*(3), 5995–5999. https://doi.org/10.35940/ijrte.C5937.098319

Chen, J., & Liang, M. (2022). Play hard, study hard? The influence of gamification on students' study engagement. *Frontiers in Psychology, 13*. https://doi.org/10.3389/fpsyg.2022.994700

Chowdhury, M., Dixon, L. Q., Kuo, L.-J., Donaldson, J. P., Eslami, Z., Viruru, R., & Luo, W. (2024). Digital game-based language learning for vocabulary development. *Computers and Education Open, 6*. https://doi.org/10.1016/j.caeo.2024.100160

Chung, S., & Son, J.-W. (2020). Visual perception in autism spectrum disorder: A review of neuroimaging studies. *Journal of the Korean Academy of Child and Adolescent Psychiatry, 31*(3), 105–120. https://doi.org/10.5765/jkacap.200018

Costello, R., & Donovan, J. (2019). How game designers can account for those with Autism Spectrum Disorder (ASD) when designing game experiences. *International Journal of End-User Computing and Development, 8*(2), 27. https://doi.org/10.4018/IJEUCD.20190701.oa1

Craig, F., Tenuta, F., De Giacomo, A., Trabacca, A., & Costabile, A. (2021). A systematic review of problematic video-game use in people with Autism Spectrum Disorders. *Research in Autism Spectrum Disorders, 82*. https://doi.org/10.1016/j.rasd.2021.101726

Cruz, E. S., Estrella, A. D., Fernandez, C. C. G., Peradilla, L. S., & Quitalig, P. L. B. (2011). *Effect of video games on the attention span of selected children with autism* (Bachelor's thesis, Manila Central University). College of Arts and Sciences - Psychology.

Dichev, C., & Dicheva, D. (2017). Gamifying education: What is known, what is believed, and what remains uncertain: A critical review. *International Journal of Educational Technology in Higher Education, 14*(9). https://doi.org/10.1186/s41239-017-0042-5

Dziorny, M. (2007). Digital game-based learning and dyslexia in higher education. In *Proceedings of the Society for Information Technology & Teacher Education International Conference* (pp. 1189–1197). Association for the Advancement of Computing in Education. https://www.academia.edu/72696760/Digital_Game_based_Learning_and_dyslexia_in_higher_education

El Shemy, I., Jaccheri, L., Giannakos, M., & Vulchanova, M. (2025). Participatory design of augmented reality games for word learning in autistic children: The parental perspective. *Entertainment Computing, 52*, 100756. https://doi.org/10.1016/j.entcom.2024.100756

Elcik, Z. (2021). *Why is gamification an effective tool for autistic students?* https://researchautism.org/blog/why-is-gamification-an-effective-tool-for-autistic-students/

Elshahawy, M., Bakhaty, M., Ahmed, G., Aboelnaga, K., & Sharaf, N. (2022). Towards developing computational thinking skills through gamified learning platforms for students with autism. In M. E. Auer, A. Pester, & D. May (Eds.), *Learning with technologies and technologies in learning* (Vol. 456). Springer. https://doi.org/10.1007/978-3-031-04286-7_10

Ghasemi, A. M., Pourroostaei, A. S., Mohseni, E. A., & Fathabadi, R. (2021). Effectiveness of gamification-based education in the educational motivation of students with mental disabilities. *Journal of Teaching and Education, 15*(3), 429–438. https://doi.org/10.22061/jte.2019.4980.2147

Gobbo, M. R. d. M., de Barbosa, C. R. S. C., Morandini, M., Mafort, F., & Mioni, J. L. V. (2021). ACA game for individuals with Autism Spectrum Disorder. *Entertainment Computing, 38*. https://doi.org/10.1016/j.entcom.2021.100409

Hashim, H. U., Yunus, M. M., & Norman, H. (2022). AReal-Vocab: An augmented reality English vocabulary mobile application to cater to mild autism children in response towards sustainable education for children with disabilities. *Sustainability, 14*(8), 4831. https://doi.org/10.3390/su14084831

Hassan, A., Pinkwart, N., & Shafi, M. (2021). Serious games to improve social and emotional intelligence in children with autism. *Entertainment Computing, 38*. https://doi.org/10.1016/j.entcom.2021.100417

Hassani, F., Shahrbanian, S., Shahidi, S. H., & Sheikh, M. (2020). Playing games can improve physical performance in children with autism. *International Journal of Developmental Disabilities, 68*(2), 219–226. https://doi.org/10.1080/20473869.2020.1752995

Hastings, S. E., Hastings, R. P., Swales, M. A., & Hughes, J. C. (2021). Emotional and behavioral problems of children with autism spectrum disorder attending mainstream schools. *International Journal of Developmental Disabilities, 68*(5), 633–640. https://doi.org/10.1080/20473869.2020.1869414

Hayes, A. M., & Bulat, J. (2017). *Disabilities inclusive education systems and policies guide for low- and middle-income countries*. RTI Press. https://files.eric.ed.gov/fulltext/ED581498.pdf

Jadán-Guerrero, J., Avilés-Castillo, F., Buele, J., & Palacios-Navarro, G. (2023). Gamification in inclusive education for children with disabilities: Global trends and approaches—a bibliometric review. In *Computational Science and Its Applications – ICCSA 2023 Workshops* (Lecture Notes in Computer Science) (Vol. 14104, pp. 461–477). Springer. https://doi.org/10.1007/978-3-031-13587-3_32

Kalogiannakis, M., Papadakis, S., & Zourmpakis, A. I. (2021). Gamification in science education: A systematic review of the literature. *Education Sciences, 11*(1), 22. https://doi.org/10.3390/educsci11010022

Khabbaz, A., Fateh, M., Pouyan, A., & Rezvani, M. (2023). Designing a serious game for children with autism using reinforcement learning and fuzzy logic. *Journal of AI and Data Mining, 11*(3), 375–390. https://doi.org/10.22044/jadm.2023.12638.2417

Khaitova, N. F. (2021). History of gamification and its role in the educational process. *International Journal of Multicultural and Multireligious Understanding, 8*(5), 212–216. https://doi.org/10.18415/ijmmu.v8i5.2640

Khaleghi, A., Aghaei, Z., & Behnamghader, M. (2022). Developing two game-based interventions for dyslexia therapeutic interventions using gamification and serious games approaches. *Entertainment Computing, 42*. https://doi.org/10.1016/j.entcom.2022.100482

Kim, B., Lee, D., Min, A., Paik, S., Frey, G., Bellini, S., et al. (2020). PuzzleWalk: A theory-driven iterative design inquiry of a mobile game for promoting physical activity in adults with autism spectrum disorder. *PLoS ONE, 15*(9). https://doi.org/10.1371/journal.pone.0237966

Klock, A. C. T., Santana, B. S., & Hamari, J. (2023). Ethical challenges in gamified education research and development: An umbrella review and potential directions. In A. Toda, A. I. Cristea, & S. Isotani (Eds.), *Gamification design for educational contexts: Theoretical and practical contributions*. Springer International Publishing.

Kousar, S., Mehmood, N. Q., & Ahmed, S. (2019). Serious games for children with autism spectrum disorder (ASD): A comparative study. *University of Sindh Journal of Information and Communication Technology, 3*(3) https://sujo.usindh.edu.pk/index.php/USJICT/article/view/608

Kröger, J. L., Raschke, P., Campbell, J. P., & Ullrich, S. (2023). Surveilling the gamers: Privacy impacts of the video game industry. *Entertainment Computing, 44*, 100537. https://doi.org/10.1016/j.entcom.2022.100537

Kuo, H. J., Yeomans, M., Ruiz, D., & Lin, C. C. (2024). Video games and disability: A risk and benefit analysis. *Frontiers in Rehabilitation Sciences, 5*. https://doi.org/10.3389/fresc.2024.1343057

Lee, J., & Gutierrez, J. (2023). Computer-assisted gamification as an approach to support movement skills development in children with autism spectrum disorder. *Journal of Physical Education, Recreation & Dance, 94*(3), 35–40. https://doi.org/10.1080/07303084.2022.2156937

Legaki, N.-Z., Xi, N., Hamari, J., Karpouzis, K., & Assimakopoulos, V. (2020). The effect of challenge-based gamification on learning: An experiment in the context of statistics education. *International Journal of Human-Computer Studies, 144*. https://doi.org/10.1016/j.ijhcs.2020.102496

Linehan, C., Kirman, B., Lawson, S., & Chan, G. (2011). Practical, appropriate, empirically-validated guidelines for designing educational games. In *ACM Annual Conference on Human Factors in Computing Systems, May 7–12* (pp. 1979–1988). Vancouver. https://dl.acm.org/doi/10.1145/1978942.1979229

Liu, T., Oubibi, M., Zhou, Y., & Fute, A. (2023). Research on online teachers' training based on the gamification design: A survey analysis of primary and secondary school teachers. *Heliyon, 9*(4), e15053. https://doi.org/10.1016/j.heliyon.2023.e15053

López-Bouzas, N., del Moral-Pérez, M. E., & Castañeda-Fernández, J. (2024). Improved socio-emotional skills in students with autism spectrum disorder (ASD) following an intervention supported by an augmented gamified environment. *International Journal of Child-Computer Interaction, 42*. https://doi.org/10.1016/j.ijcci.2024.100683

Mahmoudi, E., Yoo, P. Y., Chandra, A., Cardoso, R., Denner Dos Santos, C., Majnemer, A., & Shikako, K. (2024). Gamification in mobile apps for children with disabilities: Scoping review. *JMIR Serious Games, 12*. https://doi.org/10.2196/49029

Malinverni, L., Mora-Guiard, J., Padillo, V., Valero, L., Hervás, A., & Pares, N. (2017). An inclusive design approach for developing video games for children with Autism Spectrum Disorder. *Computers in Human Behavior, 71*, 535–549. https://doi.org/10.1016/j.chb.2016.01.018

Marco, E. J., Hinkley, L. B., Hill, S. S., & Nagarajan, S. S. (2011). Sensory processing in autism: A review of neurophysiologic findings. *Pediatric Research, 69*(5 Pt 2), 48R–54R. https://doi.org/10.1203/PDR.0b013e3182130c54

Martín-Gutiérrez, A., Leal-Vega, L., Alcoceba-Herrero, I., Herrera-Medina, J., Arenillas-Lara, J. F., & Coco-Martín, M. B. (2022). Educational opportunities of virtual game-based initiatives for students with disabilities. In O. Bernardes, V. Amorim, & A. C. Moreira (Eds.), *Handbook of research on the influence and effectiveness of gamification in education* (p. 22). IGI Global. https://doi.org/10.4018/978-1-6684-4287-6.ch021

Mercado, J., Espinosa-Curiel, I., Escobedo, L., & Tentori, M. (2019). Developing and evaluating a BCI video game for neurofeedback training: the case of autism. *Multimedia Tools and Applications, 78*, 13675–13712. https://doi.org/10.1007/s11042-018-6916-2

Metwally, A. H. S., Yousef, A. M. F., & Yining, W. (2020). Micro design approach for gamifying students' assignments. In *In 2020 IEEE 20th International conference on advanced learning technologies (ICALT)* (pp. 349–351). IEEE. https://www.scitepress.org/Papers/2020/98187/98187.pdf

Mohammed, M., Fatemah, A., & Hassan, L. (2024). Effects of gamification on motivations of elementary school students: An action research field experiment. *Simulation & Gaming, 55*(4) https://doi.org/10.1177/10468781241237389

Mota, J. S., Canedo, E. D., Torres, K. S., & Leão, H. A. T. (2020). AssociAR: Gamified process for the teaching of children with autism through the association of images and words. In *2020 IEEE Frontiers in Education Conference (FIE)* (pp. 1–8). IEEE. https://doi.org/10.1109/FIE44824.2020.9274271

Murray, A., Mannion, A., Chen, J. L., et al. (2022). Gaming disorder in adults with autism spectrum disorder. *Journal of Autism and Developmental Disorders, 52*(6), 2762–2769. https://doi.org/10.1007/s10803-021-05138-x

Navan, A., & Khaleghi, A. (2020). Using gamification to improve the education quality of children with autism. *Revista Científica, 37*(1), 90–106. https://www.redalyc.org/pdf/5043/504373007008.pdf

Núñez-Naranjo, A., Sinailin-Peralta, J., & Morales-Urrutia, E. (2024). Gamification: From motivation and challenges to improving academic performance in learning mathematics. In C. Montenegro, Á. Rocha, & J. M. Cueva Lovelle (Eds.), *Management, tourism and smart technologies. ICMTT 2023* (Vol. 773). Springer. https://doi.org/10.1007/978-3-031-44131-8_11

Oliveira, W., Hamari, J., Joaquim, S., Toda, A. M., Palomino, P. T., Vassileva, J., & Isotani, S. (2022). The effects of personalized gamification on students' flow experience, motivation, and enjoyment. *Smart Learning Environments, 9*(1), 1–26. https://doi.org/10.1186/s40561-022-00194-x

Paulus, F. W., Sander, C. S., Nitze, M., Kramatschek-Pfahler, A., Voran, A., & Gontard, A. (2020). Gaming disorder and computer-mediated communication in children and adolescents with autism spectrum disorder. *Zeitschrift für Kinder- und Jugendpsychiatrie und Psychotherapie, 48*(2), 113–122. https://doi.org/10.1024/1422-4917/a000674

Penev, Y., Dunlap, K., Husic, A., Hou, C., Washington, P., Leblanc, E., Kline, A., Kent, J., Ng-Thow-Hing, A., Liu, B., Harjadi, C., Tsou, M., Desai, M., & Wall, D. P. (2021). A mobile game platform for improving social communication in children with autism: A feasibility study. *Applied Clinical Informatics, 12*(5), 1030–1040. https://doi.org/10.1055/s-0041-1736626

Pradiante, V. (2022). The contribution of game-based learning: Children with autism spectrum disorder and dyscalculia. *Proceedings of the 16th European Conference on Games Based Learning, 16*(1). https://doi.org/10.34190/ecgbl.16.1.620

Putz, L.-M., Hofbauer, F., & Treiblmaier, H. (2020). Can gamification help to improve education? Findings from a longitudinal study. *Computers in Human Behavior, 110*. https://doi.org/10.1016/j.chb.2020.106392

Ratinho, E., & Martins, C. (2023). The role of gamified learning strategies in student's motivation in high school and higher education: A systematic review. *Heliyon, 9*(8). https://doi.org/10.1016/j.heliyon.2023.e19033

Rezayi, S., Tehrani-Doost, M., & Shahmoradi, L. (2023). Features and effects of computer-based games on cognitive impairments in children with autism spectrum disorder: An evidence-based systematic literature review. *BMC Psychiatry, 23*. https://doi.org/10.1186/s12888-022-04504-2

Ribeiro Silva, L., Maciel Toda, A., Chalco Challco, G., Elias, N., Bittencourt, I., & Isotani, S. (2024). Effects of a collaborative gamification on learning and engagement of children with autism. *Universal Access in the Information Society*. https://doi.org/10.1007/s10209-024-01119-w

Rodriguez-Calzada, L., Paredes-Velasco, M., & Urquiza-Fuentes, J. (2024). The educational impact of a comprehensive serious game within the university setting: Improving learning and fostering motivation. *Heliyon, 10*(16). https://doi.org/10.1016/j.heliyon.2024.e35608

Sailer, M., Hense, J. U., Mayr, S. K., & Mandl, H. (2017). How gamification motivates: An experimental study of the effects of specific game design elements on psychological need satisfaction. *Computers in Human Behavior, 69*, 371–380. https://doi.org/10.1016/j.chb.2016.12.033

Sánchez-Martín, J., Cañada-Cañada, F., & Dávila-Acedo, M. A. (2017). Just a game? Gamifying a general science class at university: Collaborative and competitive work implications. *Thinking Skills and Creativity, 26*, 51–59. https://doi.org/10.1016/j.tsc.2017.05.003

Silva-Calpa, G. F. M., Raposo, A. B., & Suplino, M. (2018). CoASD: a tabletop game to support the collaborative work of users with autism spectrum disorder. In *2018 IEEE 6th International Conference on Serious Games and Applications for Health (SeGAH)* (pp. 1–8). IEEE. https://doi.org/10.1109/SeGAH.2018.8401358

Smiderle, R., Rigo, S. J., Marques, L. B., Coelho, J. A., & Jaques, P. A. (2020). The impact of gamification on students' learning, engagement and behavior based on their personality traits. *Smart Learning Environments, 7*. https://slejournal.springeropen.com/articles/10.1186/s40561-019-0098-x.

Smith, K., & Abrams, S. S. (2019). Gamification and accessibility. *International Journal of Information and Learning Technology, 36*(2). https://doi.org/10.1108/IJILT-03-2019

Smith, N. (2018). *Integrating gamification into mathematics instruction: A qualitative exploratory case study on the perceptions of teachers at the fourth and fifth-grade level* (Doctoral dissertation, William Howard Taft University). https://files.eric.ed.gov/fulltext/ED608250.pdf

Soltiyeva, A., Oliveira, W., Madina, A., Adilkhan, S., Urmanov, M., & Hamari, J. (2023). My Lovely Granny's Farm: An immersive virtual reality training system for children with autism spectrum disorder. *Education and Information Technologies, 28*, 16887–16907. https://doi.org/10.1007/s10639-023-11862-x

Stančin, K., Hoić-Božić, N., & Skočić Mihić, S. (2020). Using digital game-based learning for students with intellectual disabilities – A systematic literature review. *Informatics in Education, 19*(2), 323–341. https://doi.org/10.15388/infedu.2020.15

Suparjoh, S., Shahbodin, F., & Che Ku Mohd, C. K. N. (2020). Technology-assisted intervention for children with autism spectrum disorder using augmented reality. *International Journal of Recent Technology and Engineering (IJRTE), 8*(5) https://www.ijrte.org/wp-content/uploads/papers/v8i5/C6512098319.pdf

Tezcan, K. N., & Sadık, R. (2018). An analysis of the effect of educational game training on some physical parameters and social skills of children with autism spectrum disorders. *Asian Journal of Education and Training, 4*(4), 319–325. https://doi.org/10.20448/journal.522.2018.44.319.325

The New York Times. (2024, August 26). *Overlooked no more: Mabel Addis, who pioneered storytelling in video gaming*. https://www.nytimes.com/2024/08/24/obituaries/mabel-addis-overlooked.html#:~:text=In%20the%201960s%2C%20Mabel%20Addis,economic%20theory%20to%20sixth%20graders

Thorpe, A. S., & Roper, S. (2019). The ethics of gamification in a marketing context. *Journal of Business Ethics, 155*, 597–609. https://doi.org/10.1007/s10551-017-3501-y

Tlili, A., Denden, M., Duan, A., Padilla-Zea, N., Huang, R., Sun, T., & Burgos, D. (2022). Game-based learning for learners with disabilities—What is next? A systematic literature review from the activity theory perspective. *Frontiers in Psychology, 12*. https://doi.org/10.3389/fpsyg.2021.814691

Toda, A. M., Valle, P. H. D., & Isotani, S. (2018). The dark side of gamification: An overview of negative effects of gamification in education. In A. Cristea, I. Bittencourt, & F. Lima (Eds.), *Higher education for all: From challenges to novel technology-enhanced solutions. HEFA 2017* (Vol. 832). Springer. https://doi.org/10.1007/978-3-319-97934-2_9

Trang, S., & Weiger, W. H. (2021). The perils of gamification: Does engaging with gamified services increase users' willingness to disclose personal information? *Computers in Human Behavior, 116*, 106644. https://doi.org/10.1016/j.chb.2020.106644
UNESCO. (2024). *Global Education Monitoring Report: Learners with disabilities and technology- Advocacy brief.* https://unesdoc.unesco.org/ark:/48223/pf0000389161
UNFPA. (2022). *Are persons with disabilities included in the effort to leave no one behind?* https://asiapacific.unfpa.org/en/publications/are-persons-disabilities-included-effort-leave-no-one-behind
UNICEF. (2022). *UNICEF fact sheet- Children with disabilities.* https://www.unicef.org/sites/default/files/2022-10/GIP02115_UNICEF_Children-with-Disabilities-Factsheet-final%20-%20accessible.pdf
United Nations. (2024). *Disability and Development Report 2024: Accelerating the realization of the Sustainable Development Goals by, for and with persons with disabilities.* https://reliefweb.int/attachments/6608f12e-573f-4d2b-a732-e51677e52df4/ee4caf1158756ff-f6474ad07e8bb9f06.pdf
Valencia, K., Rusu, C., Quiñones, D., & Jamet, E. (2019). The impact of technology on people with autism spectrum disorder: A systematic literature review. *Sensors, 19*(20). 10.3390/s19204485
Van Roy, R., & Zaman, B. (2019). Unraveling the ambivalent motivational power of gamification: A basic psychological needs perspective. *International Journal of Human-Computer Studies, 127*, 38–50. https://doi.org/10.1016/j.ijhcs.2018.04.009
Wagle, S., Ghosh, A., Karthic, P., Ghosh, A., Pervaiz, T., Kapoor, R., Patil, K., & Gupta, N. (2021). Development and testing of a game-based digital intervention for working memory training in autism spectrum disorder. *Scientific Reports, **11***. https://doi.org/10.1038/s41598-021-93258-w
Wainer, J., Robins, B., Amirabdollahian, F., & Dautenhahn, K. (2014). Using the Humanoid robot KASPAR to autonomously play triadic games and facilitate collaborative play among children with autism. *EEE Transactions on Autonomous Mental Development, 6*, 183–199. https://doi.org/10.1109/TAMD.2014.2303116
Walsh, O., Linehan, C., & Ryan, C. (2024). Is there evidence that playing games promotes social skills training for autistic children and youth? *Autism*. https://doi.org/10.1177/13623613241277309
Wan, H., & Li, N. (2023). Intervention effect of interactive games and behavioral skill training on preschool autistic children. *CNS Spectrums, 28*(S2), S82. https://doi.org/10.1017/S109285292300456X
Wang, C., Chen, G., Yang, Z., & Song, Q. (2023). Development of a gamified intervention for children with autism to enhance emotional understanding abilities. In *Proceedings of the 6th International Conference on Digital Technology in Education (ICDTE '22)* (pp. 47–51). ACM. https://doi.org/10.1145/3568739.3568749
Wang, X., & Xing, W. (2021). Supporting youth with autism learning social competence: A comparison of game- and nongame-based activities in a 3D virtual world. *Journal of Educational Computing Research, 60*(1). https://doi.org/10.1177/07356331211022003
World Health Organization. (2023). *Autism.* https://www.who.int/news-room/fact-sheets/detail/autism-spectrum-disorders
Yildiz, İ., Topçu, E., & Kaymakcı, S. (2021). The effect of gamification on motivation in the education of pre-service social studies teachers. *Thinking Skills and Creativity, 42*. https://doi.org/10.1016/j.tsc.2021.100907
Zainuddin, Z., Chu, S. K. W., Shujahat, M., & Perera, C. J. (2020). The impact of gamification on learning and instruction: A systematic review of empirical evidence. *Educational Research Review, 30*. https://doi.org/10.1016/j.edurev.2020.100326
Zakari, H. M., Ma, M., & Simmons, D. (2014). A review of serious games for children with autism spectrum disorders (ASD). In G. Goos (Ed.), *Serious Games Development and Applications (SGDA 2014), Lecture Notes in Computer Science, 8778* (pp. 93–106). Springer. https://doi.org/10.1007/978-3-319-11623-5_8

Zeng, J., Sun, D., Looi, C.-K., & Fan, A. C. W. (2024). Exploring the impact of gamification on students' academic performance: A comprehensive meta-analysis of studies from the year 2008 to 2023. *British Journal of Educational Technology.* https://doi.org/10.1111/bjet.1347

Zhan, Z., He, L., Tong, Y., Liang, X., Guo, S., & Lan, X. (2022). The effectiveness of gamification in programming education: Evidence from a meta-analysis. *Computers and Education: Artificial Intelligence, 3*. https://doi.org/10.1016/j.caeai.2022.100096

Zhang, S., & Hasim, Z. (2023). Gamification in EFL/ESL instruction: A systematic review of empirical research. *Frontiers in Psychology, 13*, 1030790. https://doi.org/10.3389/fpsyg.2022.1030790

Zhang, W., Ghanbaripour, A., & Watanabe, T. (2024). Exploring the landscape of gamification in higher education: A systematic mapping study. In *Proceedings of The 15th Asian Conference on Education* (pp. 1–18). IAFOR. https://papers.iafor.org/wp-content/uploads/papers/ace2023/ACE2023_75643.pdf

Zhou, R., Xie, X., Wang, J., Ma, B., & Hao, X. (2023). Why do children with autism spectrum disorder have abnormal visual perception? *Front. Psychiatry, 14*, 1087122. https://doi.org/10.3389/fpsyt.2023.1087122

Zlotnik, S., Weiss, P. L., Ben Refael, Y., Rosen, R., Gal, E., & Hochhauser, M. (2024). Gamification attributes to enhance socio-vocational readiness among people with autism spectrum disorder and intellectual developmental disabilities: A conceptual paper. *International Journal of Human-Computer Interaction*, 1–13. https://doi.org/10.1080/10447318.2024.2381928

Chapter 10
The Approach to Inclusion in Literary Education in Spain: A Case Study

María Santamarina Sancho and Pilar Núñez-Delgado

Abstract This study explores the intersection between inclusive education and the teaching of literature, highlighting the role of gamification as an innovative pedagogical strategy. Through a qualitative analysis of primary school teachers' perceptions and practices, the study reveals a discrepancy between the recognition of the importance of inclusive education and the limited implementation of inclusive strategies in the literature classroom. The findings emphasize the need for greater integration of gamification techniques into teaching methods to increase student engagement and promote an inclusive classroom environment. The study underscores the importance of strengthening teacher training programs to equip educators with the necessary tools to effectively incorporate gamification into the literature classroom and ultimately promote a more participatory and socially engaged educational framework.

Keywords Inclusive education · Case study · Gamification · Literary instruction · Teacher training

Literary Education Within the Educational System: A Conceptual Overview

Literature has always been an integral part of the education of children and young people, as it represents a cultural heritage to which every individual has a right and for the preservation and appreciation of which society bears a collective responsibility. The prevailing scientific and critical paradigms of each historical period have

M. Santamarina Sancho (✉)· P. Núñez-Delgado
Faculty of Education, University of Granada, Granada, Spain
e-mail: mssancho@ugr.es; ndelgado@ugr.es

I. Boghian, G. Mareş (eds.), *Gamification and Inclusion*, Inclusive Learning and Educational Equity 12, https://doi.org/10.1007/978-3-031-98390-0_10

long shaped the pedagogical approach to literature in schools (Cañón, 2002). As Todorov (2017 [2007]) astutely notes, what is learned in school is not what literary works convey, but what critics discuss about them. Recent approaches such as semiotics and reception aesthetics (Iser, 1987) emphasize the active role of readers in the construction of literary meaning and encourage reflection on factors such as the characteristics of children and young adults as recipients, the elements that shape a reader, the literary canon in schools, and the most effective methods for teaching literature.

This critical influence can also be seen in the fact that of the many facets that a literary work encompasses (linguistic, aesthetic, social, cultural…), not all of them have had the same importance in the mediation of literature over time. Until the 1970s, the principles of the so-called rhetorical model prevailed, which focused on literature as a linguistic and historical product. During this period, innovative proposals emerged, including the literary workshops of Rincón and Sánchez-Enciso (1985), which aimed to promote students' enjoyment and appreciation of literature through participatory activities that presented literature as a dynamic experience, going beyond a model that considered students as passive readers and associated literature with long lists of authors, works and stylistic devices.

The curriculum reform introduced in 1990 by the Spanish LOGSE (General Organic Law of the Education System) was crucial to this change. It advocated an approach to the teaching of literature that took into account the experiences of children and young people as readers, as well as the broader social and educational context of the twentieth century. Subsequent work in this area led to the coining of the term "literacy education" (Colomer, 1991, 1996, 1999; Lomas, 2002; Mendoza, 2010)—a central element of our project—and to an expansion of research on the subject. In contrast to the traditional teaching of literature, which relies on an unchanging canon, the analysis of fragments and a diachronic perspective, literary education (Colomer, 1996, p.132) calls for a re-examination of the purpose of teaching literature in school, including a critical consideration of the content and the reading canon itself. In this regard, the inclusion of criteria relating to pedagogical inclusion in the reading canon is essential.

Educational Inclusion and Literary Education

Literary competence can be defined as a set of skills and knowledge that enable individuals to understand and appreciate literary texts—a competence that encompasses not only savoir but also savoir-faire (Perrenoud, 2009). In this context, Mendoza (2002, p. 9) emphasizes that the development of such competence is a lengthy process "that begins in early childhood and culminates in the systematization of skills and metacognitive references." Accordingly, our study addresses the stages of early childhood, primary and secondary education and takes into account—alongside Colomer's concept of literary education—the factors mentioned by Quet (2009) such as the ability to think critically, a sense of artistic curiosity, the ability to connect texts to each other and to other forms of expression, an awareness of social and political history, attention to form and content, and the ability to interpret texts beyond their explicit meaning.

Rienda (2014), on the other hand, suggests from a pedagogical perspective that the teaching of literature should include precisely those dimensions that define literature itself: linguistic, aesthetic, cultural, but also social, epistemological (literature as a means of understanding the world and oneself) and axiological. Here we find the third key element of our proposal: value education through literature, as expressed in the preamble of the Spanish LOE (2006), which assigns a prominent role to civic education within educational activities (add reference with page number or rephrase and remove inverted commas). As Haug (2017) argues, educational inclusion can be understood as both a methodological and an organizational imperative that works across different levels of the education system to achieve societal goals such as social justice and the full participation of all people.

Literary education has to face numerous challenges resulting from the social changes in which we are constantly involved. More and more literature is addressing the erosion of long-standing values in Western societies, values that are weakened by an efficiency-driven culture that questions the relevance of the humanities and results in educational systems becoming mechanisms for the reproduction of established norms, producing individuals who lack the ability to think independently or to question the world in which they live (Bourdieu & Passeron, 2001). Therefore, the promotion of critical thinking through reading and literature is often seen as essential (Martínez & Martos, 2019; Koek et al., 2019) to counteract the risk of becoming passive consumers.

If we understand values as those ideas or beliefs that uphold or establish the habits we value most (Bilbeny, 2018), we can speak of universal values—freedom, equality, dignity, prosperity, and progress—whose particularity in Europe is that Europeans are committed to them because they are aware of their fragility and the potential danger of transforming these values into their opposite (Bilbeny, 2018). Perhaps because of this heightened awareness of the current risks, numerous international and national bodies are expressing concern about unequal access to these rights and urging schools to play a proactive role in addressing this inequality. In this context, inclusive education is becoming even more important.

Research Objectives and Methodology

To understand the pedagogical realities related to inclusion, it is important to consider one of the main actors: the teaching staff. Therefore, this study focuses on the perspectives of a group of primary school teachers in relation to the question of whether they consider criteria related to pedagogical inclusion when selecting literary works for the classroom, and if so, what practices they adopt to take this concept into account in their teaching activities.

The methodological framework for this study is qualitative and uses a semi-structured clinical interview as the primary data collection tool, carefully adapted (Núñez & Santamarina, 2022) to gain an in-depth understanding of teachers' perspectives. The sample includes four current teachers—two men and two women—with similar professional backgrounds.

The value of determining this "knowledge base" (Shulman, 2005) lies in understanding how teachers transform content into didactic representations and apply these representations in the classroom. This foundation serves as a basis for strengthening the link between research and educational innovation and for fine-tuning the elements of the teacher education curriculum that need to be updated or improved. It is worth noting that research on inclusive education is sparse in the literature, which emphasizes the importance of this study alongside the previously described topics.

Research Questions and Research Objectives

The research questions guiding the design and conduct of this study are as follows:

1. What theoretical and practical knowledge do primary school teachers have regarding the concept of inclusion in the classroom?
2. What underlying ideas are reflected in these reported practices?
3. Do teachers apply criteria related to educational inclusion when selecting literary works for students?
4. Is there a connection between teachers' training and their concepts and practices?

These questions determine both the general and the specific aims of this investigation.

The general aim is to examine the reasoning of a group of primary school teachers in expressing their ideas and knowledge about inclusion and to determine whether they apply criteria related to this concept when teaching literature, for example when selecting reading material.

The specific aims are as follows:

1. To understand teachers' arguments regarding how inclusion is and should be practiced in the classroom.
2. To determine whether there is a discrepancy between reported practices and the outcomes of didactic processes related to school inclusion.
3. To determine whether teachers use criteria related to inclusion when selecting reading for the classroom.

Population and Sample

The participants were four primary school teachers (teaching children aged 6 to 12) from public schools in Andalusia, Spain, including two men and two women. The selection criteria included:

- Teach in public schools to minimize differences in professional training and experience.
- They have a teaching qualification for primary education and currently teach Spanish at this level.

Data Collection Instrument

The instrument used for data collection was a clinical, semi-structured interview in the Piagetian style. This type of interview was deemed best suited to our aims due to its flexibility (it is not a questionnaire with closed questions, but a guided conversation; Kvale, 2011), its ability to explore participants' responses in depth, and its adaptability to capture emergent themes and nuances (Moore et al., 2011).

The interview guide is divided into two main sections (Santamarina et al., 2024): The first covers the teachers' personal-professional background to create a relaxed atmosphere and initiate the interaction in a more conversational way; the second contains basic questions about teaching literature in the classroom and addressing school inclusion. It is important to remember that the interview protocol serves as a guide to introduce topics. However, given the open-ended structure of the interview, unplanned themes emerged during the process that the interviewer was able to explore to gain a more detailed understanding of the teachers' ideas through emergent, initially unexpected categories.

Research Procedure

As already mentioned, the phases of this study follow the clinical method. After the audio recording of the interviews, the content was transcribed and categorized for analysis. Initial data processing involved content analysis (categorization of meaning), followed by grounded theory to refine the insights gained. Some new categories emerged from the initial interview structure and subsequent analytic processes, which enabled the extraction of overarching metacategories and final categories, which are presented in Table 10.1 along with the corresponding codes.

To identify additional relationships within the information that may be less obvious when reviewing individual transcripts, and to enhance the interpretation of results by identifying correlations, frequencies and similarity coefficients between cases, we used QDA Miner software as a complementary tool.

In order to identify further potential relationships within the information that are not readily apparent when reading all transcripts, and to refine the interpretation of the results by identifying correlations, frequencies, similarity coefficients between cases, etc., we used QDA Miner software as a supplementary tool.

The following table (Fig. 10.1) shows the results in percentages and absolute values of the coding of the interviews.

Table 10.1 Metacategories, categories, and analysis codes. Source: Created by the authors

Metacategories	Categories	Codes
II. Concept of Literary Education	Definition of Literary Education	DEF
	Difference between Literary Education and Teaching Literature	DEL
	Contributions of Literature to Education	ALE
	Role of the School in Students' Literary Education	PEL
	Requirement for Literary Reading	OBL
	Content and Guidelines on Reading and Literary Education in the Curriculum	COC
III. Planning Literary Education in the Centre	Activities to Promote Reading	APL
	Reading Plan	PL
	Criteria for Selecting Readings	CSL
	Involvement of Families in the Reading Plan	PFL
	Role of the School Library	PBC
	Coordination Among Teachers at Each Stage	CEP
	Coordination Across Stages	CEE
	Participation of Other Entities	POI
IV. Practices of Literary Education in the Classroom	Weekly Time Dedicated to Reading	TSL
	Encouragement of Reading for Pleasure	FPL
	Types of Literary Education Activities	TAL
	Connection of Literature with Other Subjects/Areas	CLM
	Connection of Literature with Other Cultural Manifestations	CLC
	Literary Texts Used	UTL
	Use of Personal Reading Experiences	UEP
	ICT and Literary Education	TIC
	Collaboration with Families	CFA
	Favorite Activity of Teachers	AFP
	Favorite Activity of Students	AFA
	Literary Education and Inclusion in the Classroom	ELI

If we focus exclusively on the ELI category (literacy education and inclusion in the classroom), it is only addressed in two of the interviews. In the following section, we will conduct a more detailed analysis of the teachers' discourse on this topic.

In Table 10.2, we can see the similarity index that was used to confirm the validity of the categorization and the selected themes by calculating the Jaccard index [J (A, B) = $|A \cap B| / |A \cup B|$] (Custodio, 2019), which expresses the relationship between the size of the intersection of both data sets (interviews and themes) and the size of the union, with values ranging from 0 to 1. Table 10.2 shows the indices obtained.

These initial data are already revealing, as all interviewees show a high degree of similarity (over 0.5 in all interviews), which confirms the validity of the instrument used to obtain the desired information and the coherence between the cases.

	Cuenta	% Códigos	Casos	% CASOS	No de Palabras	% palabras
Concepto de educación literaria						
DEF	4	2,1%	4	100,0%	719	1,7%
DEL	4	2,1%	4	100,0%	339	0,8%
ALE	4	2,1%	4	100,0%	679	1,6%
PEL	6	3,1%	4	100,0%	604	1,4%
OBL	5	2,6%	4	100,0%	1173	2,7%
COC	6	3,1%	4	100,0%	673	1,6%
Planificación de la educación literaria en el centro						
APL	12	6,2%	4	100,0%	1802	4,2%
PL	19	9,8%	4	100,0%	1145	2,7%
CSL	8	4,1%	2	50,0%	734	1,7%
PFL	5	2,6%	3	75,0%	411	1,0%
PBC	6	3,1%	3	75,0%	666	1,6%
CEP	9	4,6%	4	100,0%	1193	2,8%
CEE	9	4,6%	4	100,0%	1261	2,9%
POI	8	4,1%	4	100,0%	1137	2,7%
Prácticas de educación literaria en el aula						
TSL	11	5,7%	4	100,0%	1158	2,7%
FPL	1	0,5%	1	25,0%	108	0,3%
TAL	16	8,2%	4	100,0%	2155	5,0%
CLM	5	2,6%	4	100,0%	1134	2,7%
CLC	3	1,5%	2	50,0%	443	1,0%
UTL	17	8,8%	2	50,0%	1708	4,0%
UEP	18	9,3%	4	100,0%	1320	3,1%
TIC	4	2,1%	4	100,0%	495	1,2%
CFA	4	2,1%	3	75,0%	577	1,3%
AFP	5	2,6%	4	100,0%	392	0,9%
AFA	3	1,5%	3	75,0%	502	1,2%
ELI	2	1,0%	2	50,0%	404	0,9%

Fig. 10.1 Coding of the interviews. Source: QDA Miner

Table 10.2 Similarity values between cases. Source: QDA Miner

	Case 1	Case 2	Case 3	Case 4
Case 1	1.00	0.908	0.593	0.507
Case 2	0.908	1.00	0.602	0.587
Case 3	0.593	0.602	1.00	0.879
Case 4	0.507	0.587	0.879	1.00

Analysis of Results and Conclusions

The categorization of the interview data and the software used guided our analysis from two perspectives. First, we examined the interviews collectively to identify common themes in the concepts and practices of the four subjects. Second, we analyzed each discourse individually to uncover subtle differences (Fig. 10.2).

According to the results, the most frequently categorized code was PL (Spanish Reading Plan). All four teachers frequently referred to their schools' reading plans, which are compulsory in Andalusia. However, differences in responses were found as none of the teachers talked about coordinated reading lists for the different grade levels; each decided independently. Although all the categories present in the interviews are of interest, we focus here on ELI (Literary Education and Inclusion in the Classroom), as this is the main objective of this study.

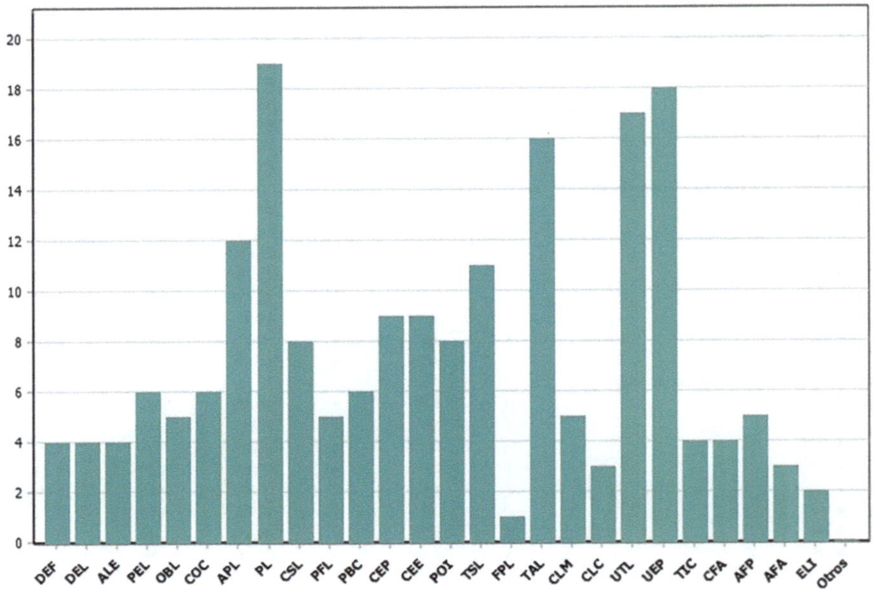

Fig. 10.2 Most categorised codes in the interviews. Source: QDA Miner

One teacher (case 3) commented "Well, in primary education, of course, the reading plan is already set, so you can't add much more. [...] I would like to include or select literary works that deal with educational inclusion, but there just isn't enough time..." Another teacher expressed a similar sentiment, "I for one do not believe I am trained enough to address inclusion in the classroom or through literature. How can you tell if these books cover these topics well or not?" The two teachers' comments—and the absence of this theme in the interviews with the other two—highlight a gap, as Sánchez Lara (2022) notes, in which the literary experience in school often reflects material and symbolic inequalities that manifest themselves in the form of epistemic invisibility, the exclusion of sociocultural diversity, and the undervaluing of biographical factors that shape meaning-making. In this context, scholars such as Booth and Ainscow (2011) argue for greater participation to reduce exclusion, for restructuring curriculum discourse by validating students' experiences, and for breaking down barriers by upholding the universality of knowledge.

When re-examining the discourse of the teachers interviewed, we also found that no specific classroom tasks related to literacy education and inclusion were mentioned; teachers referred to a lack of adequate academic training. Therefore, continuous professional development is crucial: if teachers report insufficient initial training in inclusive education, it is crucial for them to acquire or update knowledge that will enable them to deliver high-quality inclusive education. On this topic, teacher two commented "Well, it's difficult... with everything we have to do outside of school hours, it's hard to find time for training. [...] We could schedule one hour a week, maybe in the morning, for professional development at school; that might work."

In examining literary practices in the classroom, we wanted to find out what criteria play a role in the teachers' choice of reading. Two teachers, the youngest in the group and with the shortest professional careers, found that while school inclusion is indeed important, most school readings rarely address this issue. For LTU (Literary Texts Used), the third most common category, teachers agreed that many of the required readings in the reading plan were not directly related to educational inclusion. Given the increasing popularity of young adult literature for leisure, we advocate selecting literary works that also address the topic of inclusion (Del Pino et al., 2019).

We emphasize that reading, or rather literary education, is a socio-cultural process shaped by ideological and political mediations (Chartier, 2005). Recognizing that reading literature in school can either promote or inhibit inclusion in certain contexts, this article aims to provide a descriptive analysis of inclusive and exclusionary practices that emerge in literary reading experiences, with the aim of highlighting potential didactic-political pathways to inclusion.

Classroom Inclusion Through Gamification and Literary Education: Teaching Resources

As we have seen in the results described above, the use of gamification in Spanish classrooms as a technique to promote inclusion among students is far from mature, but there is no doubt that teachers consider this issue to be extremely important. The fact that it is also used in the teaching of literature can undoubtedly promote the educational process in these and other educational areas.

The importance of teachers in this sense is crucial, as they are responsible for using the most appropriate strategies and means to achieve this. In this regard, Rodríguez Jiménez et al. (2019) state that the role change that teachers must adopt is based on mediating in the different situations that arise in the classroom in order to achieve the same objectives in a context of equity and quality of education. The same authors show that students today devote a large part of their free time to video games or other leisure activities. If we start from this relationship of young people of different ages with leisure activities, gamification, we can assume that the use of these tools in the classroom can have a positive effect on students' motivation and, therefore, on their learning (Rodríguez Jiménez et al., 2019).

The sense of satisfaction that students get from playing increases concentration and facilitates learning. This is the case when a series of circumstances are taken into account (Aguilera et al., 2014):

- The student must have the necessary skills to carry out the proposed task.
- The level of the task to be solved must be within the possible performance level of the student.

- The feedback given by the game must be immediate, significant, and consistent with the effort.

The playful dynamic has broken into education and favors the diversity of the classroom as a whole (Vidal-Esteve et al., 2018). In the case of people with intellectual disabilities, for example, the aim is for them to be more autonomous and feel included in their social environment (Rodríguez Jiménez et al., 2019). According to these authors, gamification enables this through development of:

- Communication skills
- Social interaction
- The expression of emotions
- The symbolic function
- The ability to solve problems
- Participation in their own learning
- Creativity and the playful aspect

In our case, these are some fun and inclusive activities to use in the classroom to promote literacy:

- Shared Reading: Students sit in a circle and take turns reading fragments from a chosen book. This activity encourages active participation and the development of reading and listening skills.
- Collaborative Stories: The class is divided into groups and each group creates a part of a story. At the end, all parts are put together to form a complete story. This dynamic encourages creativity and teamwork.
- Dramatization of literary texts: Students choose a scene from a literary work and perform it in front of their classmates. This activity contributes to a better understanding of the text and promotes oral and physical expression.
- Word games: Use games such as Scrabble or Word Bingo to expand your vocabulary and improve your spelling in a fun way.
- Poetry workshop: Encourage students to write and share their own poems, exploring different styles and themes. This will allow them to express their feelings and thoughts creatively.
- Storytelling for equality: Organize storytelling sessions that address issues of equality and diversity and promote inclusive values from an early age.
- Box of magic words: Implement this literacy project that uses creativity and play to spark students' imaginations and encourage their interest in reading.
- Literary meetings: Organize meetings with authors or literary gatherings where students can share and discuss literary works to enhance their understanding and appreciation of literature.
- Cooperative games: Include games that require students to work together to build a sense of community and promote social skills.
- Multisensory projects: Develop activities that involve different senses (sight, hearing, touch) to explore literary texts and facilitate access to learning for all students.

These activities not only enrich literature lessons, but also ensure the participation of all students by respecting and valuing diversity in the classroom.

Another possible scenario for the gamification of literature lessons in inclusive education is the digitalization of learning. In the proposal presented by Rovira-Collado et al. (2016), for example, a possibility of gamification through "literary constellations" is presented, in which networks of works and trends are created. In short, literary constellations are a concept used in criticism and literary theory to describe a set of works, authors, themes, or styles that are interconnected and form a kind of network or system of mutual references. The term is inspired by star constellations, where different stars appear to be connected from our perspective.

In short, gamification of literature lessons not only improves students' motivation and interest in the subject, but is also an excellent tool for promoting inclusion in schools.

Conclusions

The educational process encompasses many aspects that influence teaching and learning outcomes. However, the current school paradigm, based on the principle of the democratic classroom, aims to promote the inclusion and optimal development of all learners within their peer group. Therefore, inclusive education is a challenge that promotes different innovative proposals and lines of research aimed at changing reality in favor of social engagement (García Tudela, 2019). Society demands fundamental principles—freedom, justice, and peace—that must be reflected on from early childhood, not only in an isolated and sporadic way, but also longitudinally and across disciplines. The ultimate goal is to shape people who are committed to respecting and combating all forms of intolerance throughout their lives (Arnáiz, 2019).

To achieve the various goals and objectives of the curriculum at the different school levels, the use of different methods is recommended. There are different classifications of possible teaching and learning methods, many of which have common elements. As García Tudela (2019) shows, the most widely used methods include the lecture-based approach, problem-based or project-based learning, cooperative learning, learning contracts, simulations, and play. Over time, play has always been seen as a fundamental activity for learning in childhood, although its social importance tends to diminish with age. This is reflected in the fact that while play-based methods predominate in early childhood education, they tend to disappear from the primary school years onwards.

Studies such as that by García Tudela (2019) show that gamified didactic units contribute to achieving a successful inclusion process, with intercultural coexistence in school playing a central role. Similarly, the study by Arnáiz (2019) concludes that gamification is an effective method that can help teachers to arouse students' interest and promote their inclusion in the classroom.

This study highlights that while teachers generally view gamification positively as a means of engaging students and promoting inclusion in the classroom, the practical implementation and relevant teacher training remains inadequate. In this context, several studies underline the clear need to improve both the theoretical and practical content on this topic in formal higher education (Moreno Fuentes, 2019; Castañeda-Vázquez et al., 2019).

References

Aguilera, A., Fúquene, C., & Ríos, W. (2014). Aprende jugando: El Uso de Técnicas de Gamificación en Entornos de Aprendizaje. *IM-Pertinente, 2*(1), 125–143.

Arnáiz, S. (2019). La inclusión en el aula de inglés a través del uso de la gamificación. *D!dactia, 15*, 1–11.

Bilbeny, N. (2018). ¿Hay unos valores europeos específicos? *La vanguardia*, 2-9-2018.

Booth, T., & Ainscow, M. (2011). *Guía para la Educación Inclusiva. Desarrollando el aprendizaje y la participación en los centros escolares*. OEI.

Bourdieu, P., & Passeron, J. C. (2001). *La reproducción. Elementos para una Teoría del Sistema de Enseñanza*. Editorial Popular.

Cañón, M. (2002). Disputa o convivencia: Literatura y educación. Sapiens. *Revista universitaria de investigación, 3* (1), 0.

Castañeda-Vázquez, C., Espejo-Garcés, T., Zurita-Ortega, F., & Fernández-Revelles, A. (2019). La formación de los futuros docentes a través de la gamificación, tic y evaluación continua. *SPORT TK-Revista EuroAmericana de Ciencias del Deporte, 8*(2), 55–63. https://doi.org/10.6018/sportk.391751

Chartier, R. (2005). *El presente del pasado: escritura de la historia, historia de lo escrito*. Universidad Iberoamericana.

Colomer, T. (1991). De la enseñanza de la literatura a la educación literaria. *Comunicación, Lenguaje y Educación, 9*, 21–31.

Colomer, T. (1996). La evolución de la enseñanza literaria. *Aspectos didácticos de Lengua y Literatura, 8*, 127–171.

Colomer, T. (1999). *Introducción a la literatura infantil y juvenil*. Síntesis.

Custodio, C. A. (2019). Endogeneidad y autoorganización como propiedades dinámicas de los clústeres productivos. *Revista Iberoamericana de Ciencias Sociales y Humanidades, 8*(15), 78–103. https://doi.org/10.23913/ricsh.v8i15.162

Del Pino, A., Barriga, E., & González, R. (2019). Hacia una escuela inclusiva: perspectiva de género y literatura. Polyphōnía. *Revista de Educación Inclusiva, 3*(1), 66–76.

García Tudela, P. A. (2019). Gamificación e inclusión: rutas de aprendizaje en Educación Primaria. XIX Congreso Internacioal de Investigación Educativa: Investigación Comprometida para la Transformación Social. https://www.researchgate.net/profile/Pedro-Garcia-Tudela-2/publication/334170720_Gamificacion_e_inclusion_rutas_de_aprendizaje_en_Educacion_Primaria/links/5d1b668c458515c11c0b14b1/Gamificacion-e-inclusion-rutas-de-aprendizaje-en-Educacion-Primaria.pdf

Haug, P. (2017). Understanding inclusive education: Ideals and reality. *Scandinavian Journal of Disability Research, 19*(3), 206–217. https://doi.org/10.1080/15017419.2016.1224778

Iser, W. (1987). *El acto de leer*. Taurus.

Koek, M., Janssen, T., Hakemulder, F., & Rijlaarsdam, G. (2019). Literature education as a school for thinking: Students' learning experiences in secondary literature education. *L1 Educational Studies in Language and Literature, 19*, 1–33.

Kvale, S. (2011). *Las entrevistas de investigación cualitativa*. Morata.

Lomas, C. (2002). La educación literaria en la enseñanza obligatoria. *Kikirikí, 64*, 43–50.
Martínez, A., & Martos, A. (2019). La lectura en los actuales contextos de educación social: claves desde la formación literaria. *Pedagogia Social, 33*, 19–29.
Mendoza, A. (2002). La renovación del canon escolar: la integración de la literatura infantil y juvenil en la formación literaria. In M. C. Hoyos Ragel et al. (Eds.), *El reto de la lectura en el siglo XXI* (pp. 21–38). Grupo Editorial Universitario.
Mendoza, A. (2010). La competencia literaria entre las competencias. *Lenguaje y Textos, 32*, 21–33.
Moore, P., Gómez, G., Kurtz, S., & Vargas, A. (2011). La comunicación médico paciente: ¿Cuáles son las habilidades efectivas? *Revista médica de Chile, 138*, 1047–1054.
Moreno Fuentes, E. (2019). El Breakout EDU como herramienta clave para la gamificación en la formación inicial de maestros/as. *Edutec, 67*, 66–79. https://doi.org/10.21556/edutec.2019.67.1247
Núñez, M.ª P. & Santamarina, M. (2022). Canon de lecturas, prácticas de educación literaria y valores de la ciudadanía europea. *Tavira. Revista Electrónica de Formación de Profesorado en Comunicación Lingüística y Literaria, 27*, 1–10. https://doi.org/10.25267/Tavira.2022.i27.1102
Perrenoud, P. (2009). Enfoque por competencias ¿una respuesta al fracaso escolar? *Revista Interuniversitaria de Pedagogía Social, 16*, 45–64.
Quet, F. (2009). Introduction. *Enseignement de la littérature: L'approche par compétences a-t-elle un sens?* s/n.
Rienda, J. (2014). Límites conceptuales de la competencia literaria. *Signa, 23*, 753–777.
Rincón, F., & Sánchez-Enciso, J. (1985). *Los talleres literarios*. Montesinos.
Rodríguez Jiménez, C., Ramos, M., Santos, M.ª J. & Fernández Campoy, J. M. (2019). El uso de la gamificación para el fomento de la educación inclusiva. *International Journal of New Education*, 3. https://doi.org/10.24310/IJNE2.1.2019.6557
Rovira-Collado, J., Serna, R., & Bernabé, C. (2016). Nuevas estrategias digitales para la Educación Literaria: gamificación y narrativas transmedia en constelaciones literarias. In R. Roig Vila (Ed.), *Tecnología, innovación e investigación en los procesos de enseñanza-aprendizaje* (pp. 2968–2976). Octaedro.
Sánchez Lara, R. (2022). Notas sobre la lectura literaria escolar como experiencia estética: algunos alcances pedagógicos. *Revista Contextos, 252*, 106–115. https://dialnet.unirioja.es/descarga/articulo/9110265.pdf
Santamarina, M., Núñez, P. & Gómez, L. (2024). Estudio de caso múltiple sobre la coordinación del profesorado de Educación Infantil y de Educación Primaria en el tratamiento de la competencia lecto-literaria. *Revista complutense de educación, 35* (4), 751–762. https://doi.org/10.5209/rced.89016
Shulman, L. S. (2005). Conocimiento y Enseñanza: Fundamentos de la Nueva Reforma. *Profesorado, Revista De Currículum Y Formación Del Profesorado, 9*(2), 1–30. https://revistaseug.ugr.es/index.php/profesorado/article/view/19743
Todorov, T. (2017 [2007]). *La literatura en peligro*. Galaxia Gutemberg.
Vidal-Esteve, I. et al. (2018). Revisión y análisis de investigación publicada sobre intervención gamificada en discapacidad intelectual. *Etic(a)net.Revista científica electrónica de Educación y Comunicación en la Sociedad del Conocimiento,18*, 274–297. https://doi.org/10.30827/eticanet.v2i18.11892

Chapter 11
Using Gamification to Enhance Learning, Reduce Stress, and Promote Inclusion in Academic Online Education

Ioana Boghian, Gabriel Mareş, Venera-Mihaela Cojocariu, and Carmen-Violeta Popescu

Abstract This article presents the results of a questionnaire-based study conducted at the "Vasile Alecsandri" University of Bacău, Romania. The aim of the study was to identify students' perceptions of online education and the potential of using games in education to improve learning, reduce the stress associated with online education, and promote inclusion in the context of and after the COVID-19 pandemic. The objectives of the study are to identify the following: students' perceptions of the challenges of online education; the effectiveness of online education in building and developing 21st-century competencies and skills; the effectiveness of the use of games and gamified didactic methods in improving learning, reducing the stress associated with online education, and promote an inclusive educational environment; suggestions for the implementation of gamification in online academic education for an inclusive classroom. The application of the questionnaire resulted in 212 responses from students of all five faculties of "Vasile Alecsandri" University of Bacău. The respondents are also enrolled in initial teacher education programs that will enable them to pursue a career as a teacher after graduation, and some of them already have teaching experience. The results show that, on the one hand, online education generates a certain level of stress among students and lowers their learning motivation. On the other hand, the use of gamification in online education

I. Boghian · V.-M. Cojocariu
Teacher Training Department, Vasile Alecsandri University of Bacău, Bacău, Romania
e-mail: boghian.ioana@ub.ro; venera@ub.ro

G. Mareş (✉)
Physiotherapy and Occupational Therapy Department, Vasile Alecsandri University of Bacău, Bacău, Romania
e-mail: mares.gabriel@ub.ro

C.-V. Popescu
Vasile Alecsandri University of Bacău, Bacău, Romania
e-mail: cmuraru@ub.ro

I. Boghian, G. Mareş (eds.), *Gamification and Inclusion*, Inclusive Learning and Educational Equity 12, https://doi.org/10.1007/978-3-031-98390-0_11

improves learning efficiency and academic performance, promotes the acquisition of general and domain-specific twenty-first century skills and competencies, and helps build an inclusive educational environment.

Keywords Gamification · Academic online education · Learner motivation · Learner stress · 21st-century competences and skills · Inclusion

Introduction

The introductory section of our chapter addresses the relationship between online academic education, gamification, learner motivation, learner stress, 21st-century competencies and skills, and inclusive education, drawing on existing educational research to highlight their interactions in the context of today's increasingly digital society and education (Alsswey & Malak, 2024; Hong et al., 2024; Jaramillo-Mediavilla et al., 2024; Sharma, 2024; Boghian et al. 2023; Ratinho & Martins, 2023; Adam & van den Berg, 2022; Alsadoon et al., 2022; Chen & Liang, 2022; Mohammed & Ozdamli, 2021; Parra-González et al., 2021; Klock et al., 2020; Bouchrika et al., 2019; Molinillo et al., 2018; Topîrceanu, 2017; Martí-Parreñoa et al., 2016; Su & Cheng, 2015).

To find the most suitable and efficient strategies for implementing academic online education, we need to look closer at students' perception of online education and the potential of using games in education to enhance learning, reduce the stress associated with online education, and foster an inclusive virtual classroom environment. Gamification had come across as a solution to enhancing learner engagement and efficiency in traditional face-to-face educational settings, in times prior to the COVID-19 enforced online education (Díaz-Ramírez, 2020; Klock et al., 2020; Sailer & Homner, 2020; Zainuddin et al., 2020; Bouchrika et al., 2019; Gil-Doménech & Berbegal-Mirabent, 2019; Göksün & Gürsoy, 2019; Huizenga et al., 2019; Koivisto & Hamari, 2019; Neiterman & Zaza, 2019; Alsawaier, 2018; Makransky & Lilleholt, 2018; Severengiz et al., 2018; Çakıroğlu et al., 2017; Hamari, 2017; Topîrceanu, 2017; Kayımbaşıoğlu et al., 2016; Martí-Parreñoa et al., 2016; Su & Cheng, 2015). Before the COVID-19 pandemic, online education had been mainly regarded as an area suitable for explorations, innovations, and a solution to specific learner issues such as meeting educational needs for students living long distances away from an educational institution, students enrolled in post-graduate or professional conversion study programs who have to fit work, family and study responsibilities in their daily schedule, or students with special educational needs among whom, given their disabilities, some may not be able to be physically present in class (Mateus et al., 2024; Smiderle et al., 2020; Arif et al., 2019; Camilleri & Camilleri, 2019; Molinillo et al., 2018).

The COVID-19 crisis has redefined the purpose of online education and forced a rapid transition to digital teaching-learning-assessment platforms, tools and applications that have been used, researched, improved and developed in the wake of the pandemic to date and will certainly be scientifically studied in the near future and beyond (Hong et al., 2024; Lampropoulos & Sidiropoulos, 2024; Mateus et al., 2024; Temel & Cesur, 2024; Cheng & Ebrahimi, 2023; Gironella, 2023; Ratinho & Martins, 2023; Pelegro, 2022; Pozo-Sánchez, et al., 2022; Torrado Cespón & Díaz Lage, 2022; Rincon-Flores & Santos-Guevara, 2021; Sercanoğlu et al., 2021; van der Lubbe et al., 2021).

In our country, the Covid-19 pandemic was the moment that strongly influenced the awareness of gaps and deficits in digital skills among students, as well as online education challenges and struggles for students with special educational needs, and also teachers. According to Eurostat data, in 2023, only 9.2% of Romanian users aged between 16 and 74 reported having used online courses or online learning materials in the last three months before participating in the European survey; participation in online education had increased by just over one percentage point compared to 2022, when 7.8% of Romanians had reported this (Eurostat, 2024). According to the same Eurostat study, in 2019, around 14.3% of Romanian users in the mentioned age segment reported having used online courses and online learning materials. In 2020, the first year of the pandemic, the percentage dropped to 8%, and since then the peak was reached in 2021 with 10.3% (Eurostat, 2024).

In light of this, research on online education has boomed to shed light on aspects such as the effectiveness of online teaching and learning and its impact on academic performance, learner engagement and motivation, the ethics of assessment, teacher-student interaction, physical and emotional well-being, the protection of personal data, and the right to education for students belonging to disadvantaged groups. Education and technology professionals are equally interested in making the best use of available digital resources (Jaramillo-Mediavilla et al., 2024; Lee, 2023; Othman & Ching, 2024; Perez-Aranda et al., 2024; Sharma, 2024; Shen et al., 2024; Subiyantoro et al., 2024; Temel & Cesur, 2024; Baah et al., 2023; Boghian et al., 2023; Lee, 2023; Montenegro-Rueda et al., 2023; Nguyen-Viet et al., 2023; Rumangkit & Larasati, 2023; Chen & Liang, 2022; Ertan & Kocadere, 2022; Green et al., 2022; Salemink et al., 2022; Aghadiati Fajri et al., 2021).

The advantages and disadvantages of online academic education have been highlighted in many studies over the last 10 years. Among the most frequently emphasized advantages of online academic education for typical and atypical students were (Culduz, 2024; Boghian et al., 2023; Liu, 2023; Turgunova & Rustamova, 2023; Green et al., 2022; Al Rawashdeh et al., 2021); Camilleri & Camilleri, 2019; Gil-Doménech & Berbegal-Mirabent, 2019; Molinillo et al., 2018; Gautam & Tiwari, 2016; Gilbert, 2015; Cojocariu et al., 2014; Talebian et al., 2014):

- *Ensuring a student-centered learning approach*—online learning involves a granularity of learning content and this supports the accessibility of the curriculum. Students participate in the process with or without video/audio, can engage how and when they want, manage their own time, complete assignments during live meetings or online, and have more opportunities to learn in their own style.
- *Increasing access to education for all types of learners*—the possibility for teachers from long distances or from abroad to teach courses to students even in remote locations, enabling economically and geographically disadvantaged students to access college studies; the possibility for teachers to reach and teach

students with various special educational needs (SEN); the availability of digital applications that can automatically record or transcribe lessons to meet the needs of students with SEN, and thus contributing to an inclusive virtual classroom.

- *Stimulating motivation and the active-interactive nature of learning*—the online implementation of the teaching process becomes more attractive, closer to the psychological characteristics of the new generations of digital natives. Learning approaches real life processes and content, both of which can be brought into the virtual classroom much more easily.
- *Enhancing learning accountability*—students take much more responsibility for their own education as they realize that they have individual time to learn and can use it according to their needs and the context in which they are learning (especially considering that some students record courses and activities that are carried out online in order to be able to repeat the content taught).
- *Higher impact on building digital competence*—online academic learning promotes the use of information and communication technology and thus the acquisition of new skills that are indispensable in today's society. In addition to building digital competencies, the use of information and communication technology also promotes the development of problem-solving skills and the search for creative solutions to challenges that students may face during online learning, enhancing their adaptive and innovative skills.
- *Time saving*—both students and teachers gain valuable time by not having to commute to universities or other places of study, and this is extremely important especially in large urban areas; for students with special educational needs, the time-saving effect of online teaching is even more important.
- *Speed of access to information*—another dimension of time saving is related to the ability to quickly access online the resources needed to prepare papers, projects, studies, materials, assignments or other academic tasks; this advantage is reinforced by the synchronous and asynchronous availability of learning resources, with the latter option helping to reduce drop-out rates among both typical and atypical students.
- *Saving financial resources*—even in face-to-face classes, students need electronic devices (tablet, cell phone, laptop, etc.). In addition, face-to-face teaching involves costs for transportation, accommodation, meals, snacks and, of course, clothing, which should be appropriate for the time of year and the context in which the educational activities take place. Electronic devices are therefore sufficient for online teaching, but the other costs mentioned above are significantly lower. From the perspective of education providers, the costs of heating or cooling buildings, electricity, and other utilities are much lower than in the situation where students learn face-to-face.
- *More comfort for all categories of beneficiaries*—people with social adjustment difficulties or social anxiety feel much more comfortable in online learning environments. On the one hand, online classes offer them the opportunity to communicate with peers or teachers through an interface, avoiding the face-to-face social contact that is anxiety-inducing for them. On the other hand, students who are predominantly kinaesthetic have the opportunity to move around while learn-

ing without disturbing their colleagues. Similarly, we can say that online teaching better accommodates learners with auditory or visual learning styles.

For students with special educational needs, in addition to the benefits already mentioned, online learning also offers an individualized learning pace, accessible learning resources, minimal distractions, individualized support and guidance, flexible scheduling, and a safe social space (Florida Virtual School Exceptional Student Education Team, 2025; Cataudella et al., 2021; Petretto et al., 2021; Edelhauser & Lupu-Dima, 2020; Bjekic et al., 2014; Madaus et al., 2011).

The main disadvantages of online academic education identified in the literature for typical and atypical students include a higher risk of superficiality of learning; dependence on technology; lack of motivation and drive; fatigue; boredom; stress, anxiety, depression, loneliness, emotional alienation; physical and social alienation; the level of academic acquisition in terms of professional and generic competencies and skills required in today's labor market; and a higher likelihood of illegitimate activities: cheating, plagiarism; organizational technical problems: low internet speed and internet disconnection (Culduz, 2024; Boghian et al., 2023; Liu, 2023; Turgunova & Rustamova, 2023; Al Rawashdeh et al., 2021; Gautam & Tiwari, 2016; Gilbert, 2015; Cojocariu et al., 2014).

For students with special educational needs, in addition to the disadvantages already mentioned, online teaching can also have the following effects on learners: loss of, or poor time management; less social interaction and the need for interactive environments and feedback; less encouragement and less motivation; increased stress; difficulties with planning and self-regulation; perceived uncertainties about exam requirements; more time and financial pressures on parents as they have to provide all the resources they need and, if necessary, a shadow or support person (Öhrstedt et al., 2024; Fernández-Batanero et al., 2022; Klock et al., 2020; Corby et al., 2012; Madaus et al., 2011).

To mitigate the drawbacks of online academic education and online education in general, and promote inclusion of students with special educational needs, educational scholars and digital resource developers have proposed gamification as a panacea for online learners' lack of motivation and drive, fatigue, boredom, emotional alienation, physical and social disengagement, anxiety and stress, and uncertainty related to the level of academic acquisition of professional and generic competencies and skills that are in demand in today's labor market (Tjoa & Poecze, 2020; Jaramillo-Mediavilla et al., 2024; Shen et al., 2024; Pelegro, 2022; Manzano-León et al., 2022; Wernbacher et al., 2022; Harrington & Melors, 2021; Mahmud et al., 2020; Alabbasi, 2018; De Souza Sombrio et al., 2016).

There are studies that speak more in favor of the disadvantages and negative effects of gamification in online learning, such as learners' boredom and lack of attention, loss of self- confidence, feelings of stress and helplessness, frustration, anger, discomfort and reluctance, dissatisfaction, distraction, confusion, and the desire to give up (Phung, 2020), with the standardized aspect of digital learning platforms and poor design being among the most important factors for reduced learner motivation and thus engagement (Pedreira et al., 2015; Urh et al., 2015; Browne et al., 2014).

However, the trend of the main scientific research findings seems to be in favor of the positive effects of gamification in online education (Khaldi et al., 2023; Montenegro-Rueda et al., 2023). In the literature, gamification is proposed as a solution to reduce and, if possible, eliminate the disadvantages of online academic education. The most frequently emphasized benefits of using gamification in online education cited in the literature include those described below (Khaldi et al., 2023; Sailer & Homner, 2020; Boghian et al., 2019):

- Increasing learner motivation—given the potential for reward, gamification increases motivation to participate in education and is therefore associated with engagement, learning with pleasure and for pleasure. The use of gamification in education offers the benefit of actively engaging focused and motivated participation in learning and assessment activities. For most students, the discovery of new elements that they can share with their peers in the course of the game is a challenge that they engage with greater ease than in situations where the challenge, the task, is to complete a task in a traditional way.
- Enhancing learner focus in assessment tasks—in assessment, particularly formative assessment, the use of applications that require the answering of questions causes learners to become more focused and active on the content being taught, and even competitive in a positive way during assessment, as they are encouraged to respond as quickly and as correctly as possible to the task indicated by the application.
- Fostering immediate feedback—gamified learning and gamified learning applications provide the opportunity to receive immediate feedback and correct misunderstood or poorly understood elements of learning. Completing gamified learning tasks makes students more curious, engaged, interested, and eager to take on the challenges they expect to find in gamified tasks.
- Individualized learning designs—gamification provides the opportunity to achieve an individualized learning design where the unique elements of each learner can be considered and easily integrated into a learning design that is more appropriate for each learner.
- Reduction and even elimination of discriminatory factors that can affect learning performance—through gamification, elements related to a range of personal characteristics that sometimes constitute discriminatory factors are blurred or removed, and the differences in cognitive potential, ethnicity, religion, and economic status become irrelevant during the gamified approach to learning. In this way, gamification can reduce the learning differences between typical students and students with special educational needs.
- Facilitating the link between theory and practical, everyday aspects—gamification facilitates the link between theoretical components and a range of practical, everyday aspects involving the use of soft skills such as critical thinking, problem solving, teamwork, cooperation, assertive communication and many others.
- Improving learners' academic performance—due to the above benefits and the fact that gamification of online learning motivates learners to engage individually with learning and solving learning tasks, it can contribute to better academic performance, which translates into better grades and higher levels of subject and generic competencies.

Based on the arguments presented above, we can argue that gamification in online academic education can improve learners' motivation, reduce learners' stress and improve students' subject-specific, domain-specific and cross-domain competencies and skills in the twenty-first century.

Materials and Methods

Research Problem, Aim, and Objectives

Research problem—Identifying student perceptions of the effectiveness of gamification in online academic education.

The aim of the study was to identify students' perceptions of online education and the potential of using gamification to enhance learning, reduce stress associated with online education in the context of and after the COVID-19 pandemic, and promote inclusion in academic online education.

Research objectives:

O1: to determine students' perceptions of the challenges of online education

O2: to reveal students' perceptions of the effectiveness of using gamification to enhance learning, reduce online learning stress, and promote inclusion in academic online education

O3: to highlight students' perceptions of the effectiveness of using gamification in online education to promote the building and development of domain-specific and general 21st-century competencies and skills, for typical and atypical students

O4: to make suggestions on how gamification can be used in online academic education to enhance learning, reduce stress, and promote inclusion

Research Methodology

The study was based on a self-report questionnaire administered to bachelor and master students enrolled at the five faculties of Vasile Alecsandri University of Bacău, Romania, between January 2021 and November 2024.

The 212 respondents fell into the following descriptive data categories Gender—83.5% women (n = 177), 16.5% men (n = 35); Age groups—36–41 years old—22.2% (47), 18–23 years old—21.7% (46), 30–35 years old—18.9% (40), 42–47 years old—15.1% (32), 24–29%—14.6% (31), 48–53 years old—5.2% (11), with the 31–35, 48–53 and 60–65 age groups each recording 1 (0.5%) respondent and the 54–59 age group 2 (0.9%) respondents; field of study—social sciences (communication sciences, economics, psychology and behavioral sciences - educational sciences, etc.)—52.8% (112).)—52.8 (112), humanities and arts (filology, etc.)—19.3% (41), engineering—15.6% (33), mathematics and natural sciences—6.6% (14), sport and exercise sciences as well as biology and biomedical sciences—each with 2.8% (6 each, 12 in total); teaching experience—yes—57.5% (122), no—42.5% (90), with the majority of those with teaching experience having taught for 5 years or less, in almost evenly distributed percentages, namely in urban and rural schools.

Research Tool

The research instrument consisted of a self-report questionnaire administered to bachelor and master students of different degree programs at Vasile Alecsandri University of Bacău regarding students' perceptions of online teaching and gamifying education to increase the efficiency of the academic educational process, reduce learners' stress, and foster an inclusive educational environment. The questionnaire was elaborated by two authors of this paper and was analyzed and revised by a team of experts in the field of educational sciences at Vasile Alecsandri University of Bacău. The questionnaire comprised multiple-choice and rating items and was divided into two main sections: one section was used to collect respondents' data (e.g., age group, study program, teaching experience, access to online learning devices and type of learning devices used, daily time spent on online learning, etc.) and one section on respondents' views on online education and gamification education in terms of the effectiveness of the online education process in promoting the acquisition of professional competencies and twenty-first century skills, reducing learner stress, and fostering an inclusive learning context.

Results and Discussions

To obtain results for O1 and to determine how students perceive the challenges of online education, we collected respondents' answers to a series of questions related to the availability and type of learning device, as well as the number of hours spent daily on online learning. The results of our questionnaire show that 90.6% (192) of the students surveyed have an online learning device that works, 5.7% (12) have such a device but have to share it with someone else, while 3.8% (8) have an online learning device that does not work well. In terms of the type of online learning device, the situation is as follows: 79.2% (168) use a laptop, 10.4% (22) a computer, 8.5% (18) a smartphone and 1.9% (4) a tablet. The majority of students involved in this research spend 3–5 h a day on online learning—40.1% (85), followed by 32.5% (69) who spend 1–3 h, 17.5% (36) of them spend 5–7 h on online learning, 8.0% (17) spend 7–10 h and 2.3% (5) spend more than 10 h a day on online learning.

When asked how students rate the level of stress caused by online learning, 37.3% (79) chose the middle option, namely that online learning causes some degree of stress. The following percentages indicate how much stress online learning causes: 27.8% (59)—to a very low degree; 22.2% (47)—to a low degree; 9.4% (20)—to a high degree; 3.3% (7)—to a very high degree.

To achieve our research objective O2 and find out how students perceive the effectiveness of using gamification to enhance learning, reduce online learning stress, and promote inclusion in academic online education, we analyzed their responses to three questions.

Regarding students' perception of whether gamification can improve learning and academic performance in online education, respondents' answers showed that the majority of students believe that the use of gamification in online education is more efficient compared to traditional, non-gamified face-to-face learning: 36.3% (77) chose this option; the next percentage is for the equally efficient response option—28.3% (60); the other options are 15.6% (33)—less efficient, with equal percentages for the two extreme response options, much less efficient and much more efficient, 9.9% (21) responses each.

Regarding students' perceptions of whether gamification of education through the use of educational games and the use of teaching methods with game elements (earning points, the idea of competition, solving problems with rewards, etc.) is a way to reduce the stress associated with online learning, students' responses revealed the following: The majority of respondents believe that the use of gamification in online academic education can reduce learner stress (36.8% (78)—to a great extent); the percentages for the other response options were: 31.1% (66)—to some extent; 15.6% (33)—to a very great extent; 11.8% (25)—to a small extent; 4.7% (10)—to a very small extent.

The students' responses to the question of whether they believe that the implementation of gamification in online teaching has a higher, more positive or lower impact on promoting inclusion of students with special educational needs than face-to-face teaching were as follows: The majority, 39.2% (83) believe that online teaching has a higher impact on promoting inclusion than face-to-face teaching; 23.1% (49) believe it has the same impact; 18.4% (39) believe that online teaching has a lower impact on promoting inclusion; 10.4% (22)—a much higher impact; and 9.0% (19)—a much lower impact.

According to the students who took part in this study, the use of gamification and gamified teaching methods therefore helps to reduce the stress caused by online teaching, improve learning outcomes and promote an inclusive environment.

To provide data for our third research objective, O3, and to shed light on students' perceptions of the effectiveness of using gamification in online teaching to promote the building and development of domain-specific and generic twenty-first century competencies and skills for typical and atypical students, we included some items in the applied questionnaire to collect data on their views of effective teaching methods and the skills and competencies that gamified teaching-learning methods promote.

Regarding the teaching methods used by instructors in the online courses and seminars that students find most effective and engaging, respondents rated debates and conversation as very effective 58% (123), closely followed by games of all kinds, teaching methods with game elements—55.2% (117); the next highest scores were for the effective option—34.4% (73) for debates and conversation, also closely followed by 34.4% (73) for games and teaching methods with game elements.

The majority of students therefore find debates and conversations, closely followed by gamified teaching to be the most effective and appealing teaching methods in online lessons.

Another element of the questionnaire aimed to determine students' perceptions of the effectiveness of using gamification and didactic methods with game elements in online teaching to build and develop 21st century skills and abilities.

The highest rated skills and abilities that students believe can be effectively built through gamified teaching in online lessons include IT skills—47.6% (101) for the "to a very high degree"' option and 30.7% (65) for the "to a high degree" option; creativity and innovative thinking—46.2% (98) for the "to a very high degree" option and 34.0% (72) for the "to a high degree" option; Flexibility and prioritization—36.8% (78) for the "to a very high degree" option and 34.0% (72) for the "to a high degree" option; Critical thinking—34.9% (74) for the "to a very high degree" option and 37.7% (80) for the "to a high degree" option; autonomy and decision-making—34.4% (73) for the "to a high degree" option and 39.6% (84) for the "to a high degree" option; effective oral and written communication skills—32.1% (68) for the "to a high degree" option and 39.6% (84) for the "to a high degree" option; working with deadlines—34.9% (74) for the "to a high degree" option and 32.1% (68) for the "to a high degree" option. The other competencies and skills that students rated as being effectively built through games and teaching methods with game elements in online education and which closely follow the percentages already presented are, in order of decreasing percentages for the "to a very high degree" and "to a high degree" options: domain-specific professional skills, analytical and research skills, complex problem-solving skills, stress resistance, teamwork, coping with emotional challenges, negotiation skills, managing human resources, leadership skills, entrepreneurial skills.

Another element of the questionnaire aimed to determine students' perceptions of the effectiveness of the use of educational games and teaching methods with game elements in online education in order to build and develop the dimensions of cognitive skills and attitudes as finalities of the educational act.

Among the highest rated cognitive, skill and attitude dimensions that students believe can be effectively built through educational games and teaching methods with game elements are, for the response options "to a very high degree" and "to a high degree": promotes learning new processes and procedures in line with professional training—40.6% (86) for the "to a very high degree" option, 33.5% (71) for the "high" option; promotes active student participation in the learning process—41.9% (89) for the "very high degree" option, 27.4% (58) for the "high degree" option; efficient transfer of specialized knowledge—35.8% (76) for the "very high degree" option, 36.8% (78) for the "to a high degree" option; understanding and acquisition of subject knowledge—39.6% (84) for the "to a high degree" option and 32.5% (69) for the "to a high degree" option; increasing learner motivation—35.8% (76) for the "to a high degree" option and 32.5% (69) for the "to a high degree" option; supporting and promoting collaboration and cooperation—38.7% (82) for the "to a very high degree" option and 34.4% (73) for the "to a high degree" option; providing a large amount of information—35.8% (76) for the "to a very high degree" option and 34.9% (74) for the "to a high degree" option; increasing self-esteem—30.7% (65) for the "to a very high degree" option and 32.5% (69) for the "to a high degree" option. The lowest scores for these options were for the effectiveness of educational games and teaching methods with game elements to reduce feelings of alienation associated with online education—20.3% (43) for the 'to a very high degree' option and 28.8% (61) for the 'to a high degree' option, followed by a close 31.6% (67) for the 'to some degree' option.

Our research objective O4 focused on providing suggestions on how gamification can be used in online academic education to enhance learning, reduce stress, and promote inclusion.

To this end, we also investigated students' opinions on whether they believe that gamification of education and the use of didactic games, didactic methods with game elements (collecting points, competitive spirit, problem solving with rewards, etc.) is a must in the context of online education, with the answer options being yes/no/don't know. The answers of the respondents are shown in Fig. 11.1.

The prevailing answers of "Yes" responses ($N = 94$, 44.3%) indicate confidence, knowledge, and a positive attitude towards the value and possibility of using gamification in online academic education to enhance learning, reduce stress, and promote inclusion, taken together. However, the "No" option ($N = 80$, 37.73%) is quite close to the previous choice. The results indicate a relative split in the respondents' opinion regarding the implementation of gamification in online academic education or a certain kind of diametrically opposed perspective in the sense of a rejection of the implementation and use of gamification in online academic education. If we add to these two perspectives the opinion of those who do not know ($N = 40$, 18.88%), we get an overall balanced perspective regarding this aspect, a result that is also highlighted by other researchers (Manzano-León et al., 2022; Wernbacher et al., 2022; Kalogiannakis et al., 2021; Harrington & Melors, 2021; Mahmud et al., 2020; Tjoa & Poecze, 2020; Alabbasi, 2018; De Souza Sombrio et al., 2016). The percentages in students' responses can also be explained by the fact that students may not be used to educational games and teaching methods with game elements applied in their lessons and therefore know less about the definition and aim of such pedagogical approaches. Furthermore, another study shows that the use of individual gamification elements in learning promotes extrinsic rather than intrinsic motivation of learners and that quantity of performance outweighs quality (Mekler et al., 2017).

Fig. 11.1 Results for students' view on whether gamification is a must in online education

Options	Counts	% of Total	Cumulative %
I don't know	38	17.9 %	17.9 %
No	80	37.7 %	55.7 %
Yes	94	44.3 %	100.0 %

In view of the fact that gamification, learning games and teaching methods with game elements have not occupied a relevant place in the local context in recent years, our first suggestion would be to incorporate such pedagogical approaches more frequently into the teaching-learning assessment process.

It follows that, for now, we must base our suggestions for implementing gamification in online academic education on specialized studies and practices that are already valued and offered as examples of best practices for teachers and curricula designers. These include the optimal use of all categories of role-playing games and simulations (Topîrceanu, 2017); the diversification of gaming applications by integrating different variants of "serious games, game-based learning, 3D simulations and virtual reality (VR)" (Ratinho & Martins, 2023, p. 2); the implementation of gaming platforms (for example, Kahoot and Quizizz) in the design and process of academic activities (Alsswey & Malak, 2024; Sercanoğlu et al., 2021; Göksün & Gürsoy, 2019; Ismail et al., 2019) with the integration of gamification elements in the teaching, consolidation, systematization, retention, and transfer process; the use of gamified e-learning quizzes that play a role in increasing learning motivation (Adam & van den Berg, 2022; Anunpattanaa et al., 2021); the development and application of teaching strategies that combine gamification with other techniques/methods or forms of organization (e.g., the SCAMPER technique, balloon competition, Mandala thinking, virtual escape rooms), both in the study of different academic disciplines and to promote student creativity, collaboration, and communication (Lee, 2023; Pozo-Sánchez et al., 2022); the development of authentic gamified online learning methods (Perez-Aranda et al., 2024); the integration of game-based formative assessment variants into academic processes (Zainuddin et al., 2020; Arif et al., 2019; Ismail et al., 2019; Severengiz et al., 2018); the use of games to assess students' academic acquisition (Pelegro, 2022). Overall, the studies agree that "the most common gamification elements used in e-learning that have a strong impact on students are points, leaderboards, badges and progress levels" (Salemink et al., 2022, p. 139).

In addition to the best practices mentioned above for students with special educational needs, there is also the component of differentiation of instruction that is specific to face-to-face instruction and should also be implemented in online instruction, for example, using concrete, simple language to formulate tasks, and give instructions; using visual/auditory aids as reminders and prompts; use lists, diagrams, and graphic organizers to structure information and tasks; simplify task instructions by defining stages; assign individual roles for solving team-work assignments; ensure an open, supportive communication environment in class (Costescu & Roşan, 2023).

In addition, a range of alternative, assistive high-tech hardware and software systems have been developed to meet the needs of students with SEN, for example, assistive listening devices, alternative keyboards, optical character recognition, Braille display, voice recognition software, screen magnification, screen reader, reminder systems, speech synthesis systems, dictation software, hearing aids, voice recognition software, and word prediction software (Pădure, 2023).

Conclusions

Regarding online education or the use of digital technology in any form, the perception of our students is influenced by the little experience they, including their teachers, have in this field. The Covid-19 pandemic has forced the use of digital learning technologies and in certain situations this has not been very comfortable, either due to physical limitations (lack of the necessary infrastructure, lack of specific equipment, etc.), but above all due to the lack of teaching experience in this direction. As a result of this pandemic, students and teachers had to radically change their relationship with education/training and try to adapt to the new challenges as quickly and efficiently as possible. The limited previous experience of students and teachers with digital learning technologies and the rapid shift to online education forced by the pandemic crisis, where teachers and students were still involved in the educational process in the classroom one day and had to switch to online the very next day, have caused anxiety and sometimes reluctance to such an experience in some of them.

The students who responded to the questionnaire are still of the opinion that online teaching is of lower quality than face-to-face teaching. This aspect can be linked to the aspects mentioned above, but also to the need to improve the teaching strategies that teachers can use in such a system. In recent years, national education policies have been increasingly focused on supporting teachers in building and improving their digital skills, which in turn affects the way students interact with this type of learning and education.

On the one hand, online education creates a certain amount of stress for students, and lowers learner motivation. On the other hand, the use of gamification in online education increases learning efficiency, learner motivation, learner self-esteem, and other skills and competencies, which is a necessity in today's educational context, also reducing the stress associated with online learning, and promoting an inclusive environment.

Our findings are consistent with the findings of other recent studies on the effectiveness of using gamification in education to reduce learner stress (Aghadiati Fajri et al., 2021; Green et al., 2022), increase learner motivation and engagement (Alsswey & Malak, 2024; Alsadoon et al., 2022; Anunpattanaa et al., 2021; Alsawaier, 2018; Baah et al., 2023; Göksün & Gürsoy, 2019), support students' higher academic performance (Jaramillo-Mediavilla et al., 2024; Lampropoulos & Sidiropoulos, 2024; Kaya & Ercag, 2023; Rumangkit & Larasati, 2023; Park & Kim, 2021; Díaz-Ramírez, 2020; Çakıroğlu et al., 2017) and promote collaboration and cooperation among students (Othman & Ching, 2024).

Our findings are also consistent with the conclusions of other studies, which acknowledge the need to continue experimental research on the implementation of gamification in academic education, both in face-to-face and online contexts, to measure the impact of gamification on learner development and progress, and to find the most efficient gamification practices in education in terms of benefits for students, both typical and atypical (Montenegro-Rueda et al., 2023; Mekler et al.,

2017; Pedreira et al., 2015). Future research should also consider students' personalities when designing gamified educational approaches (Zhan et al., 2022; Smiderle et al., 2020) as well as the necessary presence of the teacher in the gamified online educational environment to ensure and increase the positive impact and efficiency of such activities (Torrado Cespón & Díaz Lage, 2022).

References

Adam, E., & van den Berg, R. (2022). The influence of gamified e-learning quizzes on students' motivation – a case of programming students at a South African higher education institution. *The Independent Journal of Teaching and Learning, 17*(2), 44–62.

Aghadiati Fajri, F. A., Haribowo, P., RY, K., Amalia, N., & Natasari, D. (2021). Gamification in e-learning: The mitigation role in technostress. *International Journal of Evaluation and Research in Education, 10*(2), 606–614. https://doi.org/10.11591/ijere.v10i2.21199

Al Rawashdeh, A. Z., Mohammed, E. Y., Al Arab, A. R., Alara, M., & Al-Rawashdeh, B. (2021). Advantages and disadvantages of using e-learning in university education: Analyzing students' perspectives. *The Electronic Journal of e-Learning, 19*(3), 107–117. https://doi.org/10.34190/ejel.19.3.2168

Alabbasi, D. (2018). Exploring teachers' perspectives towards using gamification techniques in online learning. *The Turkish Online Journal of Educational Technology, 17*(2), 34–45. https://files.eric.ed.gov/fulltext/EJ1176165.pdf. Accessed on 26 March 2025

Alsadoon, E., Alkhawajah, A., & Suhaim, A. S. (2022). Effects of a gamified learning environment on students' achievement, motivations, and satisfaction. *Heliyon, 8*, e10249. https://doi.org/10.1016/j.heliyon.2022.e10249

Alsawaier, R. S. (2018). The effect of gamification on motivation and engagement. *International Journal of Information and Learning Technology, 35*, 56–79. https://doi.org/10.1108/IJILT-02-2017-0009

Alsswey, A., & Malak, M. Z. (2024). Effect of using gamification of "Kahoot!" as a learning method on stress symptoms, anxiety symptoms, self-efficacy, and academic achievement among university students. *Learning and Motivation, 87*, 101993. https://doi.org/10.1016/j.lmot.2024.101993

Anunpattanaa, P., Akmal Khalid, M. N., Iida, H., & Inchamnan, W. (2021). Capturing potential impact of challenge-based gamification on gamified quizzing in the classroom. *Heliyon, 7*, e08637. https://doi.org/10.1016/j.heliyon.2021.e08637

Arif, F. K. M., Zubir, N. Z., Mohamad, M., & Yunus, M. M. (2019). Benefits and challenges of using game-based formative assessment among undergraduate students. *Humanities & Social Sciences Reviews, 7*(4), 203–213. https://doi.org/10.18510/hssr.2019.7426

Baah, C., Govender, I., & Subramaniam, P. R. (2023). Exploring the role of gamification in motivating students to learn. *Cogent Education, 10*(1), 2210045. https://doi.org/10.1080/2331186X.2023.2210045

Bjekic, D., Obradovic, S., Vucetic, M., & Bojovic, M. (2014). E-teacher in inclusive e-education for students with specific learning disabilities. *Procedia Social and Behavioral Sciences, 128*, 128–133. https://doi.org/10.1016/j.sbspro.2014.03.131

Boghian, I., Cojocariu, V.-M., & Popescu, C.-V. (2023). E-Learning in higher education – pros and cons. In E. Soare & C. Langa (Eds.), *Education Facing Contemporary World Issues - EDU WORLD 2022, vol 5. European Proceedings of Educational Sciences* (pp. 294–304). European Publisher. https://doi.org/10.15405/epes.23045.31

Boghian, I., Cojocariu, V.-M., Popescu, C.-V., & Mâţă, L. (2019). Game-based learning. Using board games in adult education. *Journal of Educational Sciences & Psychology, 9*(1), 51–57. Archive of new issues (Journals). Accessed on 21 November 2024.

Bouchrika, I., Harrati, N., Wanick, V., & Wills, G. (2019). Exploring the impact of gamification on student engagement and involvement with e-learning systems. *Interactive Learning Environments, 29*(8), 1244–1257. https://doi.org/10.1080/10494820.2019.1623267

Browne, K., Anand, C., & Gosse, E. (2014). Gamification and serious game approaches for adult literacy tablet software. *Entertainment Computing, 5*, 135–146. https://doi.org/10.1016/j.entcom.2014.04.003

Çakıroğlu, Ü., Başıbüyük, B., Güler, M., Atabay, M., & Memiş, B. Y. (2017). Gamifying an ICT course: Influences on engagement and academic performance. *Computers in Human Behavior, 69*, 98–107. https://doi.org/10.1016/j.chb.2016.12.018

Camilleri, M. A., & Camilleri, A. C. (2019). The students' readiness to engage with mobile learning apps. *Interactive Technology and Smart Education*. https://doi.org/10.1108/ITSE-06-2019-0027

Cataudella, S., Carta, S., Mascia, M. L., Masala, C., Petretto, D. R., & Penna, M. P. (2021). Psychological aspects of students with learning disabilities in e-environments: A mini review and future research directions. *Frontiers in Psychology, 11*, 611818.

Chen, J., & Liang, M. (2022). Play hard, study hard? The influence of gamification on students' study engagement. *Frontiers in Psychology, 13*, 994700. https://doi.org/10.3389/fpsyg.2022.994700

Cheng, C., & Ebrahimi, O. V. (2023). A meta-analytic review of gamified interventions in mental health enhancement. *Cumputers in Human Behavior, 141*, 107621. https://doi.org/10.1016/j.chb.2022.107621

Cojocariu, V.-M., Lazar, I., Nedeff, V., & Lazar, G. (2014). SWOT analysis of E-learning educational services from the perspective of their beneficiaries. *Procedia - Social and Behavioral Sciences, 116*, 1999–2003. https://doi.org/10.1016/j.sbspro.2014.01.510

Corby, D., Cousins, W., & Slevin, E. (2012). Inclusion of adults with intellectual disabilities in post-secondary and higher education: A review of the literature. In P. Jones, J. Storan, A. Hudson, & J. Braham (Eds.), *Lifelong learning: community development* (pp. 69–86). Berforts Information Press.

Costescu, C., & Roşan, A. (2023). Practici incluzive pentru studenţii cu tulburare din spectrul autismului şi cei cu deficit de atenţie şi hiperactivitate. In M. Rusu (Ed.), *Dizabilitate şi incluziune în mediul universitar* (pp. 225–248). Editura Academiei Române.

Culduz, M. (2024). Benefits and challenges of E-learning, online education, and distance learning. In L. Gray & S. Dunn (Eds.), *Incorporating the human element in online teaching and learning* (pp. 1–27). IGI Global Scientific Publishing. https://doi.org/10.4018/979-8-3693-4131-5.ch001

De Souza Sombrio, S. G., Schimmelpfeng, L. E., & Ulbricht, V. R. (2016). The production of a gamified learning object accessible to people with visual or hearing disabilities for teaching geometry. In *Proceedings of the 2016 XI Latin American conference on learning objects and technology, San Carlos, Costa Rica, 3–7 October* (pp. 1–10). IEEE.

Díaz-Ramírez, J. (2020). Gamification in engineering education – An empirical assessment on learning and game performance. *Helyion, 6*, e04972. https://doi.org/10.1016/j.heliyon.2020.e04972

Edelhauser, E., & Lupu-Dima, L. (2020). Is Romania prepared for e-learning during the COVID-19 pandemic? *Sustainability, 12*, 5438.

Ertan, K., & Kocadere, S. A. (2022). Gamification design to increase motivation in online learning environments: A systematic review. *Journal of Learning and Teaching in Digital Age, 7*(2), 151–159. https://dergipark.org.tr/en/pub/joltida. Accessed on 21 November 2024

Eurostat. (2024). *Increase in online education in the EU in 2023*. https://ec.europa.eu/eurostat/web/products-eurostat-news/w/ddn-20240124-2. Accessed on 24 November 2024

Fernández-Batanero, J. M., Montenegro-Rueda, M., & Fernández-Cerero, J. (2022). Access and participation of students with disabilities: The challenge for higher education. *International Journal of Environmental Research and Public Health, 19*(19), 19. https://doi.org/10.3390/ijerph191911918

Florida Virtual School Exceptional Student Education Team. (2025). *6 Ways Online Learning Helps Students with Disabilities*. https://flvs.net/b/blog/2024/10/02/6-ways-online-learning-helps-students-with-disabilities. Accessed on 26 March 2025

Gautam, S. S., & Tiwari, M. K. (2016). Components and benefits of e-learning system. *International Research Journal of Computer Science (IRJCS), 3*(1), 14–17. http://www.irjcs.com/volumes/Vol3/iss1/03.JAJCS10082.pdf. Accessed on 23 November 2024

Gilbert, B. (2015). *Online learning revealing the benefits and challenges. Education Masters.* Paper 303. St. John Fisher College. https://fisherpub.sjfc.edu/education_ETD_masters/303. Accessed on 23 November 2024

Gil-Doménech, D., & Berbegal-Mirabent, J. (2019). Stimulating students' engagement in mathematics courses in non-STEM academic programmes: A game-based learning. *Innovation in Education and Teaching International, 56*, 57–65. https://doi.org/10.1080/14703297.2017.1330159

Gironella, F. (2023). Gamification pedagogy: A motivational approach to student-centric course design in higher education. *Journal of University Teaching & Learning Practice, 20*(3), 04. https://doi.org/10.53761/1.20.3.04

Göksün, D. O., & Gürsoy, G. (2019). Comparing success and engagement in gamified learning experiences via Kahoot and Quizizz. *Computers & Education, 135*, 15–29. https://doi.org/10.1016/j.compedu.2019.02.015

Green, K., Torres, K., & DeWalt, A. (2022). Let's play: Using gamification in university classes as a means to increase motivation and engagement while lowering stress. In *The Barcelona Conference on Education 2022: Official Conference Proceedings*, (pp. 87–98) https://doi.org/10.22492/issn.2435-9467.2022.7

Hamari, J. (2017). Do badges increase user activity? A field experiment on the effects of gamification. *Computers in Human Behaviour, 71*, 469–478. https://doi.org/10.1016/j.chb.2015.03.036

Harrington, I., & Melors, M. J. (2021). Utilising online gamification to promote student success and retention in tertiary settings. *International Journal of Higher Education, 10*(7), 45–52. https://doi.org/10.5430/ijhe.v10n7p45

Hong, Y., Saab, N., & Admiraal, W. (2024). Approaches and game elements used to tailor digital gamification for learning: A systematic literature review. *Computers & Education, 212*, 105000. https://doi.org/10.1016/j.compedu.2024.105000

Huizenga, J., Admiraal, W., Ten Dam, G., & Voogt, J. (2019). Mobile game-based learning in secondary education: Students' immersion, game activities, team performance and learning outcomes. *Computers in Human Behavior, 99*, 137–143. https://doi.org/10.1016/j.chb.2019.05.020

Ismail, M. A. A., Ahmad, A., Mohammad, J. A. M., Fakri, N. M. R. M., Nor, M. Z. M., & Pa, M. N. M. (2019). Using Kahoot! as a formative assessment tool in medical education: A phenomenological study. *BMC Medical Education, 19*(1), 1–8. https://doi.org/10.1186/s12909-019-1658-z

Jaramillo-Mediavilla, L., Basantes-Andrade, A., Cabezas-González, M., & Casillas-Martín, S. (2024). Impact of gamification on motivation and academic performance: A systematic review. *Education Sciences, 14*, 639. https://doi.org/10.3390/educsci14060639

Kalogiannakis, M., Papadakis, S., & Zourmpakis, A.-I. (2021). Gamification in science education. A systematic review of the literature. *Education Sciences, 11*(1), 22. https://doi.org/10.3390/educsci11010022

Kaya, O. S., & Ercag, E. (2023). The impact of applying challenge-based gamification program on students' learning outcomes: Academic achievement, motivation and flow. *Education and Information Technologies, 28*, 10053–10078. https://doi.org/10.1007/s10639-023-11585-z

Kayımbaşıoğlu, D., Oktekin, B., & Haci, H. (2016). Integration of gamification technology in education. *Procedia Computer Science, 102*, 668–676.

Khaldi, A., Bouzidi, R., & Nader, F. (2023). Gamification of e-learning in higher education: A systematic literature review. *Smart Learning Environments, 10*, 10. https://doi.org/10.1186/s40561-023-00227-z

Klock, A. C. T., Gasparinic, I., Pimentab, M. S., & Hamaria, J. (2020). Tailored gamification: A review of literature. *International Journal of Human-Computer Studies, 144*, 102495. https://doi.org/10.1016/j.ijhcs.2020.102495

Koivisto, J., & Hamari, J. (2019). The rise of motivational information systems: A review of gamification research. *International Journal of Information Management, 45*, 191–210. https://doi.org/10.1016/j.ijinfomgt.2018.10.013

Lampropoulos, G., & Sidiropoulos, A. (2024). Impact of gamification on students' learning outcomes and academic performance: A longitudinal study comparing online, traditional, and gamified learning. *Education Sciences, 14*(4), 367. https://doi.org/10.3390/educsci14040367

Lee, K. W. (2023). Effectiveness of gamification and selection of appropriate teaching methods of creativity: Students' perspectives. *Heliyon, 9*, e20420. https://doi.org/10.1016/j.heliyon.2023.e20420

Liu, Y. (2023). Matches and mismatches between university teachers' and students' perceptions of E-learning: A qualitative study in China. *Heliyon, 9*(6), e17496. https://doi.org/10.1016/j.heliyon.2023.e17496

Madaus, J., Banerjee, M., McKeown, K., & Gelbar, N. (2011). Online and blended learning: The advantages and the challenges for students with learning disabilities and attention deficit/hyperactivity disorder. *Learning Disabilities: A Multidisciplinary Journal, 17*, 69–76.

Mahmud, S. N. D., Husnin, H., & Tuan Soh, T. M. (2020). Teaching presence in online gamified education for sustainability learning. *Sustainability, 12*(9), 3801.

Makransky, G., & Lilleholt, L. (2018). A structural equation modeling investigation of the emotional value of immersive virtual reality in education. *Educational Technology Research and Development, 66*(5), 1141–1164. https://doi.org/10.1007/s11423-018-9581-2

Manzano-León, A., Aguilar-Parra, J. M., Rodríguez-Moreno, J., et al. (2022). Gamification in initial teacher training to promote inclusive practices. *International Journal of Environmental Research and Public Health, 19*(13), 1–11.

Martí-Parreñoa, J., Seguí-Masa, D., & Seguí-Masb, E. (2016). Teachers' attitude towards and actual use of gamification. *Procedia - Social and Behavioral Sciences, 228*, 682–688. https://doi.org/10.1016/j.sbspro.2016.07.104

Mateus, C., Campis, R., Jabba, D., María Erazo, A., & Romero, V. (2024). *Gamification as a tool for inclusion*. IntechOpen. https://doi.org/10.5772/intechopen.113229.

Mekler, E. D., Bruhlmann, F., Tuch, A. N., & Opwis, K. (2017). Towards understanding the effects of individual gamification elements on intrinsic motivation and performance. *Computers in Human Behaviour, 71*, 525–534. https://doi.org/10.1016/j.chb.2015.08.048

Mohammed, Y. B., & Ozdamli, F. (2021). Motivational effects of gamification apps in education: A systematic literature review. *BRAIN. Broad Research in Artificial Intelligence and Neuroscience, 12*(2), 122–138. https://doi.org/10.18662/brain/12.2/196

Molinillo, S., Aguilar-Illescas, R., Anaya-Sánchez, R., & Vallespín-Arán, M. (2018). Exploring the impacts of interactions, social presence and emotional engagement on active collaborative learning in a social web-based environment. *Computers & Education, 123*, 41–52. https://doi.org/10.1016/j.compedu.2018.04.012

Montenegro-Rueda, M., Fernández-Cerero, J., Mena-Guacas, A. F., & Reyes-Rebollo, M. M. (2023). Impact of gamified teaching on university student learning. *Education Sciences, 13*(5), 470. https://doi.org/10.3390/educsci13050470

Neiterman, E., & Zaza, C. (2019). A mixed blessing? Students' and instructors' perspectives about off-task technology use in the academic classroom. *Canadian Journal for the Scholarship of Teaching and Learning*. https://doi.org/10.5206/cjsotl-rcacea.2019.1.8002

Nguyen-Viet, B., Nguyen-Viet, B., & Nguyen-Duy, C. (2023). Dataset on the effect of gamification elements on learning effectiveness among Vietnamese students. *Data in Brief, 51*, 109734. https://doi.org/10.1016/j.dib.2023.109734

Öhrstedt, M., Käck, A., Reierstam, H., & Ghilagaber, G. (2024). Studying online with special needs: A student perspective. *Journal of Research in Special Educational Needs, 24*, 771–785. Available from:. https://doi.org/10.1111/1471-3802.12670

Othman, M. K., & Ching, S. K. (2024). Gamifying science education: How board games enhances engagement, motivate and develop social interaction, and learning. *Education and Information Technologies*. https://doi.org/10.1007/s10639-024-12818-5

Pădure, M. (2023). Rolul Biroului pentru Studenţi cu Dizabilităţi. In M. Rusu (Ed.), *Dizabilitate şi incluziune în mediul universitar* (pp. 65–106). Editura Academiei Române.

Park, S., & Kim, S. (2021). Is sustainable online learning possible with gamification?—The effect of gamified online learning on student learning. *Sustainability, 13*, 4267. https://doi.org/10.3390/su13084267

Parra-González, M. E., López-Belmonte, J., Segura-Robles, A., & Moreno-Guerrero, A.-J. (2021). Gamification and flipped learning and their influence on aspects related to the teaching-learning process. *Heliyon, 7*, e06254. https://doi.org/10.1016/j.heliyon.2021.e06254

Pedreira, O., Garcia, F., Brisaboa, N., & Piattini, M. (2015). Gamification in software engineering–A systematic mapping. *Information and Software Technology, 57*, 157–168. https://doi.org/10.1016/j.infsof.2014.08.007

Pelegro, R. (2022). Gamification in online education. *SSRN Electronic Journal*. https://doi.org/10.2139/ssrn.4054977

Perez-Aranda, J., Medina-Claros, S., & Urrestarazu-Capellán, R. (2024). Effects of a collaborative and gamified online learning methodology on class and test emotions. *Education and Information Technologies, 29*, 1823–1855. https://doi.org/10.1007/s10639-023-11879-2

Petretto, D. R., Carta, S. M., Cataudella, S., Masala, I., Mascia, M. L., Penna, M. P., Piras, P., Pistis, I., & Masala, C. (2021). The use of distance learning and e-learning in students with learning disabilities: A review on the effects and some hint of analysis on the use during COVID-19 outbreak. *Clinical Practice & Epidemiology in Mental Health, 17*, 92–102. https://doi.org/10.2174/1745017902117010092. PMID: 34733348; PMCID: PMC8493828.

Phung, Q. D. (2020). *The negative effect of Gamification in E-learning in the eyes of University students* (Master thesis). Jonkoping University. https://www.diva-portal.org/smash/get/diva2:1463534/FULLTEXT01.pdf. Accessed on 24 November 2024.

Pozo-Sánchez, S., Lampropoulos, G., & López-Belmonte, J. (2022). Comparing gamification models in higher education using face-to-face and virtual escape rooms. *Journal of New Approaches in Educational Research, 11*(2), 307–322. https://doi.org/10.7821/naer.2022.7.1025

Ratinho, E., & Martins, C. (2023). The role of gamified learning strategies in student's motivation in high school and higher education: A systematic review. *Heliyon, 9*, e19033. https://doi.org/10.1016/j.heliyon.2023.e19033

Rincon-Flores, E. G., & Santos-Guevara, B. N. (2021). Gamification during Covid-19: Promoting active learning and motivation in higher education. *Australasian Journal of Educational Technology, 37*(5), 43–60.

Rumangkit, S., & Larasati, H. (2023). The role of gamification, perceived playfulness, learning engagement, and learning motivation on academic achievement in hybrid learning. Conference paper. *ICOBAR 2023-E3S Web of Conferences 426*, 02002. https://doi.org/10.1051/e3sconf/202342602002.

Sailer, M., & Homner, L. (2020). The gamification of learning: A meta-analysis. *Educational Psychology Review, 32*, 77–112. https://doi.org/10.1007/s10648-019-09498-w

Salemink, E., de Jong, S. R. C., Notebaert, L., MacLeod, C., & Van Bockstaele, B. (2022). Gamification of cognitive bias modification for interpretations in anxiety increases training engagement and enjoyment. *Journal of Behavior Therapy and Experimental Psychiatry, 76*, 101727. https://doi.org/10.1016/j.jbtep.2022.101727

Sercanoğlu, M., Bolat, Y. İ., & Göksu, İ. (2021). Kahoot! as a gamification tool in vocational education: More positive attitude, motivation and less anxiety in EFL. *Journal of Computer and Education Research, 9*(18), 682–701. https://doi.org/10.18009/jcer.9224882

Severengiz, M., Roeder, I., Schindler, K., & Seliger, G. (2018). Influence of gaming elements on summative assessment in engineering education for sustainable manufacturing. *Procedia Manufacturing, 21*, 429–437.

Sharma, V. (2024). *Gamification: A new era of inclusion in education*. Adwell.

Shen, Z., Lai, M., & Wang, F. (2024). Investigating the influence of gamification on motivation and learning outcomes in online language learning. *Frontiers in Psychology, 15*, 1295709. https://doi.org/10.3389/fpsyg.2024.1295709

Smiderle, R., Rigo, S. J., Marques, L. B., et al. (2020). The impact of gamification on students' learning, engagement and behavior based on their personality traits. *Smart Learning Environments, 7*, 3. https://doi.org/10.1186/s40561-019-0098-x

Su, C. H., & Cheng, C. H. (2015). A mobile gamification learning system for improving the learning motivation and achievements. *Journal of Computer Assisted Learning, 31*(3), 268–286. https://doi.org/10.1111/jcal.12088

Subiyantoro, S., Degeng, N. S., Kuswandi, D., & Ulfa, S. (2024). Developing gamified learning management systems to increase student engagement in online learning environments. *International Journal of Information and Education Technology, 14*(*1*), 26–33. https://doi.org/10.18178/ijiet.2024.14.1.2020

Talebian, S., Mohammadi, H. M., & Rezvanfar, A. (2014). Information and communication technology (Ict) in higher education: Advantages, disadvantages, conveniences and limitations of applying e-learning to agricultural students in Iran. *Procedia-Social and Behavioral Sciences, 152*, 300–305. https://doi.org/10.1016/j.sbspro.2014.09.199

Temel, T., & Cesur, K. (2024). The effect of gamification with Web 2.0 tools on EFL Learners' motivation and academic achievement in online learning environments. *Sage Open, April-June 2024*, 1–19. https://doi.org/10.1177/21582440241247928

Tjoa, A. M., & Poecze, F. (2020). Gamification as an enabler of quality distant education. In: *Proceedings of the 22nd international conference on information integration and web-based applications & services*, Chiang Mai, Thailand, 30 November–2 December, pp. 340–346. ACM.

Topîrceanu, A. (2017). Gamified learning: A role-playing approach to increase student in-class motivation. *Procedia Computer Science, 112*, 41–50. https://doi.org/10.1016/j.procs.2017.08.017

Torrado Cespón, M., & Díaz Lage, J. M. (2022). Gamification, online learning and motivation: A quantitative and qualitative analysis in higher education. *Contemporary Educational Technology, 14*(4), ep381. https://doi.org/10.30935/cedtech/12297

Turgunova, F., & Rustamova, S. A. (2023). Advantages and disadvantages of online education. Problem and solution. *Journal of Foreign Languages and Linguistics, 5*(5) https://phys-tech.jdpu.uz/index.php/fll/article/view/7917. Accessed on 23 November 2024

Urh, M., Vukovic, G., Jereb, E., & Pintar, R. (2015). The model for introduction of gamification into e-learning in higher education. *Procedia - Social and Behavioral Sciences*, 388–397. https://doi.org/10.1016/j.sbspro.2015.07.154

Van der Lubbe, L. M., Gerritsen, C., Klein, M. C. A., & Hindriks, K. V. (2021). Empowering vulnerable target groups with serious games and gamification. *Entertainment Computing, 38*, 100402. https://doi.org/10.1016/j.entcom.2020.100402

Wernbacher, T., Zauchner, S., Denk, N., et al. (2022). E-mint: a gamified app for empowering parents in their role as stem gatekeepers. *European Conference on Social Media, 9*(1), 202–210.

Zainuddin, Z., Shujahat, M., Haruna, H., & Chu, S. K. W. (2020). The role of gamified e-quizzes on student learning and engagement: An interactive gamification solution for a formative assessment system. *Computers & Education, 145*, 103729. https://doi.org/10.1016/j.compedu.2019.103729

Zhan, Z., He, L., Tong, Y., Liang, X., Guo, S., & Lan, X. (2022). The effectiveness of gamification in programming education: Evidence from a meta-analysis. *Computers and Education: Artificial Intelligence, 3*, 100096. https://doi.org/10.1016/j.caeai.2022.100096

MIX
Papier aus verantwortungsvollen Quellen
Paper from responsible sources
FSC® C105338

If you have any concerns about our products,
you can contact us on
ProductSafety@springernature.com

In case Publisher is established outside the EU,
the EU authorized representative is:
Springer Nature Customer Service Center GmbH
Europaplatz 3, 69115 Heidelberg, Germany

Printed by Libri Plureos GmbH
in Hamburg, Germany